W9-BYI-304

Praise for Gold!

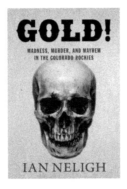

GOLD!

MADNESS, MURDER, AND MAYHEM
IN THE COLORADO ROCKIES

IAN NELIGH

"Gold isn't just a mineral or a way to get rich—for some Coloradans, it's an obsession. That's the premise of Ian Neligh's new book *Gold! Madness, Murder and Mayhem in the Colorado Rockies*, which tells the story of the gold rush and follows that vein all the way through today's prospectors. Written in a compelling journalistic style (Neligh edits the *Clear Creek Courant* in Idaho Springs), each chapter is devoted to a different fascinating gold hunter, alternating between the Wild West of the 1800s and the colorful characters who make up today's Colorado prospecting community." —*Colorado Life magazine*

"Ian Neligh recounts the story of the Colorado gold rush, bringing it forward to contemporary times, melding the old and the new. He tells about the men who still moil for gold in the Colorado Rockies." —*Denver Post*

"Journalist Ian Neligh traveled Colorado to learn more about the history and the present-day reality of gold mining. During his research, he uncovered a centuries-long story of obsession that often included murder, gun fights, deadly accidents, overnight fortunes and even cannibalism. Neligh is a practiced writer whose style mixes history and modern realities seamlessly. If you are a history buff or just enjoy a good true story, this book is for you." —*Colorado Country Life*

SPURRED WEST

ROGUES, TREASURE SEEKERS, BOUNTY HUNTERS & COLORFUL CHARACTERS PAST AND PRESENT

IAN NELIGH

WEST
MARGIN
PRESS®

Names: Neligh, Ian Paul, author.

Title: Spurred West : rogues, treasure seekers, bounty hunters, and colorful characters past and present / by Ian Neligh.

Description: [Berkeley] : West Margin Press, [2019] | Includes bibliographical references. | Summary:"A collection of stories and interviews of the events and characters who contributed to the formation of the Wild West, with regional focus on the Colorado Rockies"— Provided by publisher.

Identifiers: LCCN 2019022662 (print) | LCCN 2019022663 (ebook) | ISBN 9781513262420 (paperback) | ISBN 9781513262437 (hardback) | ISBN 9781513262444 (ebook)

Subjects: LCSH: Frontier and pioneer life—West (U.S.) | Brigands and robbers--West (U.S.) | Indians of North America—West (U.S.) | West (U.S.)—History. | Rocky Mountains—History.

Classification: LCC F591 .N415 2019 (print) | LCC F591 (ebook) | DDC 978—dc23

LC record available at https://lccn.loc.gov/2019022662

LC ebook record available at https://lccn.loc.gov/2019022663

Printed in USA

Proudly distributed by Ingram Publisher Services

Published by West Margin Press®

WEST
MARGIN
PRESS®

WestMarginPress.com

WEST MARGIN PRESS
Publishing Director: Jennifer Newens
Marketing Manager: Angela Zbornik
Editor: Olivia Ngai
Design & Production: Rachel Lopez Metzger
Design Intern: Michelle Montano

Contents

For Dave,
Many thanks

Introduction

It was an old gas station somewhere between Cody and Casper, Wyoming, filled with things that had sharp teeth. Through the distorted lens of childhood memory I recall it being dimly lit inside, packed full of taxidermied rattlesnakes, coyotes, and other predators pried from the dark corners of the West. Shelf after shelf contained some new and wondrous curiosity: snakeskin boots with fanged rattlesnake heads still attached, scorpions on cowboy hat bands, snarling dead animals—the store felt wild.

Driving through Wyoming from Colorado to Yellowstone National Park was a regular pilgrimage for my family, and the strange little store in the middle of nowhere was a guaranteed stop along the way. From the walls hung stuffed heads of the incomprehensibly strange Jackalope, that enduring Western myth (and joke) about a jackrabbit with horns. The store also had giant containers of water, beef stew, coffee, crackers, and a massive barrel full of pickled eggs—everything necessary for a day of rugged adventure in the wilderness. I don't know if I ever saw the store's owner, but if I did he must have been a bear of a man, with a thick beard, a booming laugh, and maybe a hint of something menacing in his eyes; the kind of man who would cheerfully resort to cannibalism rather than go on a vegan diet.

One year, for no discernible reason, we stopped visiting the strange little store in the middle of the Wyoming shortgrass prairie. But that didn't keep my imagination from traveling down those dim aisles packed with their monstrous cargo. The massive knives with bone handles behind the counter, jackets constructed of fur and bear claws; all these things only grew in my imagination with each passing year until I didn't know if it had been real or not. To me, it was a piece of the Wild West.

It wasn't until I was an adult returning on a trip home one year that I remembered to ask about the store, realizing with a start that it had once existed outside of my childhood fantasy. It was then my parents told me it had mysteriously burned to the ground many years ago and no longer existed. But it did remain firmly in my memories, and it became wilder with each passing year.

As a journalist working in the Rockies, I'd often seen the relics of the Old West, that time between the end of the Civil War and the late nineteenth century. Ghost towns, abandoned gold mines, and derelict forts still haunt the lonely places between the valleys and mountain passes. I've known people who discovered old six-shooters while out panning for gold, or a stash of vintage weapons hidden in a cave behind their house.

The Old West had a specific time and geographic location, and its remnants litter the landscape today like memorials to a time gone but not forgotten. The *Wild West*, on the other hand, was part real and part imaginary. It was where steely-eyed gunslingers traveled from town to town, bandits robbed stagecoaches, and cowboys rescued damsels in distress. It was a world created by those who hungered for tales of adventure, and by authors who were happy to provide them to their audiences. Some of it was real, but much was exaggerated. The real West was filled with farmers, ranchers, and miners, people whose lives were grown from the soil, scraped from the rock and pulled down from the mountains. Those stories were smaller and more difficult, and Americans didn't want those stories. They wanted heroes and villains.

Dime novels made legends of real-life characters like Wild Bill Hickok and Billy the Kid. Some even straddled the shifting line between the two Wests, like William "Buffalo Bill" Cody, who did his best to educate the world on his version of the real West while further perpetuating the myth of the other. As the gun smoke and dust eventually settled over the era, the Wild West lived on in books, movies, and the limitless borderlands of our thoughts. Time replaced the Old West with the new, but I wanted to know how much was real and what was still left, if there were still traces of the original hiding in the corners of the vanished frontier beyond just imagination. I spent a year searching for the answer, interviewing gunslingers, bounty hunters, bare-knuckle boxers, treasure hunters, brand inspectors, and more to compare them to their historic counterparts. I found the spirit of the Wild West lives on much as it did over a hundred years ago, but sometimes it evolved into something new. It is still wild, dangerous, and unpredictable. And sometimes, every once in a while, it has sharp teeth.

CHAPTER 1

FORGING THE WILD WEST

I t was pandemonium. Thousands of people began to pour into the City of Rochester, New York, on the morning of August 12, 1895. The staggering influx of passengers took the railway companies by surprise; it was the most business they'd seen in years. Families entered the city by the wagonload, and before nine in the morning the streets were filled to brimming.

Town leaders tried to anticipate the crowds and prepare Rochester's own trolley car system, but it utterly failed. It was soon discovered the passenger cars couldn't meet the staggering demand. By all accounts, the city's new arrivals were all heading in the same direction. Their destination was one of the city's parks where a stadium was constructed the day before.

"Forty thousand people passed through the canvas entrance; and at both performances it was necessary to close the gates and deny admission to several thousand people for the good and sufficient reason that there was absolutely no place to put them without inconveniencing the many thousands who had obtained seats," said one reporter witnessing the spectacle.

The anticipation from those lucky enough to secure a seat in the stadium must have been unbelievable. What they were about to see was famous on both sides of the Atlantic and had amazed audiences since 1883. A massive spotlight shone in the arena, and night became day. Soon they would see a show like none other. There would be cowboys, Native Americans, horseback soldiers from around the world, breathtaking historical reenactments, sometimes with those who took part in the actual battles. The evening would showcase the best trick shooting, riding, and other wonders brought to them by a cast of five hundred exceptionally talented people. For that one evening, the audience would get a thrilling glance into the Wild West.

A man with an unmistakable Van Dyke beard and shoulder-length hair and wearing a buckskin jacket galloped out into the arena. To the thousands of onlookers, he needed no introduction. He was a true celebrity of the time, his face gracing numerous action-packed dime novels. The man removed his cowboy hat, saluting the audience by holding it to one side in a flourish, and exclaimed, "Ladies and gentlemen, permit me to introduce to you a congress of the rough riders of the world."

Buffalo Bill and His Wild West Show

For William "Buffalo Bill" Cody's Wild West show, it was one of the best attended shows of the season. Awestruck crowds watched the thrilling retelling of the Pony Express, witnessed an attack on a stagecoach, followed a buffalo hunt, and viewed a siege on a lonely wagon train as it crossed the plains. Soon the air was thick with gun smoke and dust, but always the iconic figure of Cody was recognizable on horseback by the cheering crowds as he was never far from the action.

Despite hardships both of the economic and physical variety, Cody's Wild West show had persevered for the past twelve years and would for another eighteen, outlasting a host of feeble attempts by others to cash in on the Wild West craze. Cody was a natural and none could match his showmanship.

For Cody, the arena was his canvas. He painted a vivid portrayal of the vanishing American West using those who had lived it as his medium. It was not, however, an entirely accurate depiction, despite his attempts at realism. But for his audience, none of that really

Buffalo Bill's Wild West and Congress of Rough Riders of the World - Poster showing cowboys rounding up cattle and portrait of Col. W.F. Cody on horseback. c.1899. *(Courtesy of the Library of Congress)*

mattered. After all, Cody wasn't recreating the Old West but the Wild West. This was a frontier of cowboys, bulldoggers, trick shots, and bucking bronc riders.

"What a magnificent show it was from beginning to end; and how happily were blended the two elements of entertainment and instruction," one newspaper writer recalled. "Volumes of the most graphic descriptive literature could not convey to the mind a fractional part of the clearness and vivid incisiveness of the scenes depicted in the Wild West arena."

It was a West filled with exaggerated and violent reenactments, the often simplistic portrayals of Native Americans and their conflict with white settlers. And always it was about Buffalo Bill who came riding in to save the day. With some variation Cody brought this story from town to town, from Great Britain to Europe and back again. It was his interpretation of the frontier that became cemented in the imaginations of generations to come. It became the template for the myth of the Old West.

"For a few brief hours the vanishing west is visible to the citizens of Little Rock," one reporter in Arkansas said after the Wild West show rumbled through town. "In a few brief years the men and the deeds who wrested from the wilderness the splendid empire stretching from the

Mississippi to the Sierra Nevada Mountains, will have passed into tradition, but today they came into view, a splendid living panorama, and the central figure of all was the magnificent figure of W.F. Cody, still riding with the grace of a centaur, still shooting with the unerring aim which made his very name a terror to the Indians, but his thinning locks and the touch of silver which time is adding with a kindly hand are a reminder of the other changes which are fast effacing in the great domain, which he has seen spring from the wilderness, the old landmarks and the old faces which are vanishing into history."

Cody had taken his fame as an army scout and his reputation as a prolific buffalo hunter to unheard-of levels of celebrity, which included novels, plays, and ludicrous stories based on the exaggerated, or outright fictional, events of his life. Cody had managed to turn himself into a legend and, for a time, audiences just couldn't get enough.

"And last of all the center of this glittering spectacle, comes Buffalo Bill, that unique, picturesque personality, without a precedent, without a successor, the single product of an era," one writer gushed. "Who is Buffalo Bill? Col. W.F. Cody, late chief of the Government scouts of the United States. What is Buffalo Bill? The most popular, fascinating figure in America to-day, one of the most graceful and expert horsemen in the world."

Cody's performance for the City of Rochester in 1895 was a roaring success, but dark clouds loomed on the horizon for the performer. Just the year before, his credentials and the right even to call himself "Buffalo Bill" were called into question in newspapers of the time.

"Several newspapers throughout the country have recently been publishing statements, emanating from more or less unreliable sources, claiming that Buffalo Bill (Col. William F. Cody) was not the legal or moral holder of that title," said writer Frank A. Small for the *Courier Journal*.

The issue questioning the scout and entertainer came about exactly a year earlier when the well-known "poet scout" Captain Jack Crawford claimed a Wichita banker named Billy Mathewson was in fact the real Buffalo Bill. Crawford was a well-known scout himself, an author of popular Wild West stories, and had once joined Cody in his early attempts to regal audiences from the stage.

Crawford accused William Cody of imposing himself on the Eastern United States, adding because an author once wrote about Cody in a book that it ruined "a great many Americans youths by firing their young hearts, incidentally filling the Western penitentiaries with wicked Easterners, who aspired to come West and be 'Buffalo Bills' themselves."

"Asking Col. Cody what he had to say about it, the smile that overspread his countenance, the toss of his head, the shrug of the shoulders, the wave of the hand and the look of contempt as his athletic figure appeared to rise in height, brought to mind the words of Brutus to the fiery Cassis, as he said: 'It passes me by like the idle winds, which regard not,'" Small wrote.

Clearly it did bother Cody that someone was trying to take away his name and reputation earned on the frontier. After all, it was his very credibility in the West that helped pave the way to his success as a showman. Cody then went about showing the writer pages from a scrapbook which held letters of thanks and appreciation for his many deeds from admirers, including William T. Sherman, George Armstrong Custer, and many more.

"Smiling at my expressions of astonishment, Col. Cody returned the book to its usual resting place saying: 'I don't think it is necessary for me to speak, except this [Mathewson] says I worked for him. I never laid eyes on him, and, of course, never worked for him. He, like thousands of Western men, may be good and true and have contributed his share in his immediate locality in the making of history of the times, but this is the first intimation that I have had that any reputable person other than myself has ever claimed the title of Buffalo Bill," reported the *Courier Journal*.

Despite this, it is generally acknowledged the frontier was at one point full of "Buffalo Bills." That Mathewson had the nickname before Cody is probable. Cody's claim to the name only became official, not after winning a buffalo-shooting contest, as he claimed, but when he was introduced to the world by an author.

That author was the adventurer, legendary scoundrel, and obsessive liar who called himself Ned Buntline.

King of the Border Men

Truth for Ned Buntline, whose real name was Edward Zane Carroll Judson, was an entirely unnecessary and boring inconvenience. For the popular fiction writer, reality provided something of a distraction from the nuts and bolts of telling a really good story. A short man with a walrus mustache, Buntline had a trademark limp from a broken leg that hadn't healed right after jumping from a hotel window while he unsuccessfully tried to escape a lynch mob. The ungraceful plummet to the Earth only occurred after being shot by the brother of a man he killed who had accused him of stealing his wife. After breaking his leg, Buntline was caught and hanged from an awning post but, as fate would have it, was cut down by a passing stranger. Adventurer, marksmen, bail jumper, serial adulterer, Navy veteran—Buntline had lived a life as wild as any he could make up. In 1869 when he came to Fort McPherson, Nebraska, he was the highest paid writer in the United States, making $20,000 a year, which equates to $369,000 today.

There are different versions of how Buntline met Cody. What ultimately matters is that Buntline was in Nebraska looking for a story, and he found one. The writer followed Cody and, for a time, a detachment of the Fifth Calvary to Colorado's Fort Sedgwick. During the journey Cody spun his own stories of his frontier prowess. Buntline took what he learned and headed back east to write *Buffalo Bill the King of the Border Men; The Wildest and Truest Tale I've Ever Told*. Predictably, the story was entirely false. Buntline exaggerated or changed many of Cody's already thrilling real-life accounts into something almost unrecognizable. Buntline even turned Cody, who had an unhealthy appreciation for the consumption of spirits, into a champion of the Temperance movement. It was, of course, a roaring success and the first of several fictional stories he would go on to write about Cody.

Capitalizing on the achievement and Cody's sudden fame, the two began working together to provide theatrical presentations to a public hungry for tales of the West as told and acted by those who actually lived the stories. Real scouts including Cody and, albeit only briefly, his friend James Butler "Wild Bill" Hickok and John Baker "Texas Jack" Omohundro entertained crowds during part of the year and then returned to the frontier to continue their work as scouts for the remainder. Cody's continuing performances were inspired by some of his actual deeds in the West, such as his fight and eventual scalping of a Cheyenne sub chief named Yellow Hair in a fight to the death. It seems as if Cody sought out more and more thrilling events to participate in so he could regale his eastern audiences with fresh material.

In 1882 Cody and promoter-manager Nate Salsbury came up with the idea of a Wild West show over lunch one spring day in New York City. The idea was not just to tell the audience about the thrilling adventures, cowboys, Native Americans, and stunning horse- and marksmen of the West—but show them. Cody didn't want to put on a circus but rather something that was both educational and exciting, a show that gave its audience a glimpse into a vanishing world and kept as authentic as possible. In Omaha, Nebraska, in May of 1883 the earliest version of Cody's Wild West show, then called "The Wild West, Honorable W.F. Cody and Dr. W.F. Carver's Rocky Mountain and Prairie Exhibition," started with a raucous bang. For the next thirty years Cody exhaustively traveled North America and Europe loading and unloading a small army of performers, buffalo, and horses on and off trains, moving across the Atlantic and back again. Just before the turn of the century, the Wild West provided 341 performances in more than 130 cities, traveling 11,000 miles in the process.

Cody was said to have been a kind man and paid all performers, including Native Americans, the same rate, which was not the norm for the time. He brought the world his version of the Wild West, often including notable celebrities such as Annie Oakley, Bill Pickett, Sitting Bull, and Will Rogers. Oakley chose to join Cody's show and leave another because of the thoughtful way he treated the horses and other animals, unlike the managers of the other exposition she was involved with at the time.

Eventually, Cody's Wild West show went bankrupt in 1913 and Buffalo Bill Cody died while visiting his sister in Denver in 1917—but the Wild West itself would endure.

Bison, the Magnificent Animals

William Cody certainly capitalized on the Old West and what it provided before and after he became famous. He also knew it was quite literally disappearing. Certainly the people and places of the time were vanishing, but so too were the mighty animals he derived his famous nickname from. As the numbers of buffalo plummeted and almost reached extinction, Cody championed their preservation and he wasn't the only one.

In my year-long undertaking to travel the West to research its historical origins and to interview those living intentionally, or otherwise, in its long shadow, I had to take into account the large role the land and wildlife played, and I figured the Genesee buffalo herd was a good place to start. Like the fingerprints at a crime scene, the Old West has left its mark in subtle ways across the region, and there would be no better example of that than what I was about to see.

It is May in Colorado. By the time I reach my destination, it is raining. Large, heavy clumps of snow slough off from the trees, landing with loud thumps on the ground. Beneath the snow, thick mud cause my truck tires to spin and struggle to gain traction as I reach the forested parking lot. Soon Shannon Dennison pulls up in her car, and I get out in the rain and almost knee-deep slush to introduce myself. Dennison wears a black knit hat with TETON embroidered on it and a red Grand Teton jacket proudly displaying her background at the Wyoming national park. She is the Cultural Resources Administrator and Buffalo Bill Museum Director for the City and County of Denver's Mountain Parks. She agreed to meet with me and show me the iconic Genesee buffalo herd.

Maintained by Denver for more than one hundred years, the buffalo herd, technically called American Bison, roam by the road to the Rockies along Interstate 70 on the way to the state's ski resorts. The sight of the herd of about thirty bison rings as a melancholy reminder of the systematic eradication of the giant animal. Once seen in the millions, the American Bison almost went extinct because of European American settlers. During Buffalo Bill Cody's time, the bison were shot and killed to provide food for the crews building the railroads, for sport, and to remove an essential food source for Native American tribes so the government could more easily control them.

Denver's mountain park system was developed in 1912 with the purpose to make sure the city still had a link to the Old West. It must have been fairly obvious to the city's leaders that the time period was rapidly fading; its participants were almost gone and then even Cody's Wild West would soon be a memory.

An American Bison or "buffalo" herd, maintained by the City of Denver, wanders a snowy field in Genesee, Colorado. *(Photo by Ian Neligh)*

"Bison were a huge part of the American West, and so I think the two strongest motivations [for the park to take action] were conservation and also making sure that people had that tangible connection to the Old West and Denver's identity," Dennison says.

Matthew Brown, the bison caretaker for the Genesee herd, pulls up in his pickup and Dennison and I climb into the cab. Brown, in a worn Carhartt jacket and blue jeans, lives in a home with his family on the 580 acres that house the bison herd. He navigates the truck up a snow-clogged dirt road to a gate, hops out to open it, and drives through, then goes out and closes it behind us.

"We had five calves [born] yesterday and possibly more last night—but I haven't gotten a full count on them," Brown says, climbing back up into the truck. The herd is one of two the city maintains. The other, a smaller group, is located at Daniels Park about thirty-four miles away. When the city was gathering the original herd of bison, it was collected from a variety of locations, including from the bison herd then living near Yellowstone National

Park. DNA tests reveals the Genesee herd is directly connected to the rare original American Bison herds.

"They were almost gone, they were almost extinct," Brown says as we drive past the animals. "[Denver] wanted to help preserve a piece of the American Wild West and help save this species of animal."

Brown would be the first to admit that bison are a little "ornery." The much larger Yellowstone Buffalo herd, which roughly numbers about five thousand, sees visitors gored every year after getting too close. However, since Yellowstone was founded in 1872 only two people have ever been killed.

"We keep a close eye on these fences. That's always an issue we have with the public and the animals," Brown says. "The public just doesn't know to stay three feet away from the fence, because that fence will stretch three to five feet before it snaps."

While incidents at the Genesee herd are almost unheard of, people do occasionally get too close to the fence to grab a selfie, causing a few nonlethal close encounters.

"You keep 'em fed, keep 'em watered, and you keep 'em happy, and they'll stay in," Brown says. "These fences here are merely to keep people away from them, and if [the bison] wanted to leave they could open these fences up like a wet paper bag and they'd be in the next county by sunset."

Then after a second Brown adds, "They can push through almost anything—they can push over a truck like this without even thinking about it."

I think about this with growing apprehension as we drive by a few more of the bison regarding us idly from the side of the small road cutting through the property.

"People often think that they're much like cattle and the cow can move quickly if it wants to—but these animals will start to charge like that," Dennison says, snapping her fingers. "And they can really surprise you if you are not prepared."

Brown says despite being in captivity, the bison hold onto their wild nature to where they could be dropped off in the wild and would have no issue surviving on their own. For example, the herd will form into circles with the bulls protecting from the outside when there's a threat from a coyote. Interestingly, if one is cut and bleeding, the

Buffalo caretaker Matthew Brown stands next to the original railroad crates used in 1912 to move the bison from Yellowstone to Colorado. *(Photo by Ian Neligh)*

others will roll in the blood, likely to confuse potential predators about which one is actually wounded.

"You get to learn their body language, and when they start licking their lips they're starting to get irritated; when their tail starts to go up, they're mad—and then when that tail turns into a question mark, it's coming," Brown says. "When you're close to them and they start tracking with one eye . . . you either start looking for a truck, a tree, or start thinking about climbing the fence. You really don't realize how fast you can run until you have a nine-hundred-pound cow behind you. When she's close enough and you can hear her panting and snorting, it gets your heart rate going a little bit."

We end up in a storage barn on the property, which holds several of the original wooden crates used to ship the buffalo by train down from Yellowstone more than one hundred years ago. The crates were believed to be originally used by Buffalo Bill Cody's Wild West show when transporting their own bison herd around the country, and later reused for the Denver herd. The crates are crude, even cruel, and narrower than one might expect—but they were ultimately successful in recreating a buffalo herd on the Front Range.

"Denver wanted to preserve a piece of the Wild West and raise bison for people to come up from Denver to look at—and to help protect these magnificent animals," Brown says.

Beautiful and dangerous, they belong in the West and they're absolutely magnificent. But while most people try to give the region's largest living animal the space it needs to live in the new West, there are some who put on cowboy boots and try to ride their distant and equally dangerous cousins for sport.

CHAPTER 2
THE
BULLFIGHTER

Spending more time in the air than on the ground, the bull is a spinning two-thousand-pound nightmare of hooves and horns. The rider hangs onto the back with one hand to what is essentially a homicidal centrifuge. The state fairgrounds in Pueblo, Colorado, the packed and roaring stadium, the blaring music, fellow cowboys—everything is a blur of bucking insanity. Then it happens: the whiplashing rollercoaster ends and the rider is flung loose, legs kicking, to drift through space above the rodeo grounds and away from the bull, his inelegant feet going one way with arms pinwheeling in another. The dusty rodeo grounds come up fast to make his less-than-friendly acquaintance with a bone-jarring thud and a cloud of dust. Knocked a little senseless, the cowboy scrambles to his feet, boots working hard to make purchase in the fine dirt, as he tries to make sense of where he is and how he can get out of the arena. He knows that he's in danger. Through that disorientating fog comes the bull charging straight at him. They bred the bull for its aggression and murderous intent—and this is its chance for a little payback.

Thirty-two-year-old Wacey Munsell seemingly comes out of nowhere, stepping in front of the bull. Wearing clown makeup and baggy clothes, Munsell instantly attracts its attention, giving the cowboy time to run for the fence. Sometimes after a ride, a bull will walk back to the open

pen, knowing its job is done; but sometimes it's looking for blood. This one decides not to end the night on an easy note. The giant animal goes for Munsell, who moves to the side and toward the bull, putting it off its target. The bull wheels around and charges again, and Munsell avoids being gored by staying just a step or two ahead. He and another bullfighter try to steer the bull back to its pen using their bodies and the bull's massive momentum against itself. There's no Spanish bullfighting cape, nothing to hurt or further antagonize the bull; just its natural aggression and the deft movements of the bullfighters. It works 99 percent of the time, but this isn't one of those times. The bullfighters decide discretion is the better part of valor and run for the fence. The bull still has its eyes on Munsell and is just feet—then inches—behind him as he moves towards the fence. He reaches it and clambers up as fast as his boots will allow him. Denied, the bull turns in frustration and leaves the arena. Munsell climbs back down. While he saved the bull rider and himself, it's not a performance he is happy with.

"I don't like doing that because that just means the bull might have bested me in some way," Munsell later tells me. "And the second thing is the fence is never your friend. That fence doesn't give—and that bull's head is much harder than any bone in your body, so something is going to give between the bull's head and the fence, and it is generally you."

There's also a professional pride in not being chased out of the arena. After all, Munsell is one of the top ten bullfighters in the United States.

"I never want to get run up a fence. It is just something in me that doesn't want to be beat like that," Munsell says. "Even though I'm not competing—I'm competing against the animal and I just never want the bull to leave the arena the winner."

The Birth of the Rodeo Clown

Rodeo is an essential part of Munsell's life and his family's going back three generations. The bullfighter lives in Ulysses, Kansas, where he grew up watching his father, Doug Munsell, work as a rodeo clown.

"My mom and dad joke around that pretty much the day they had me, they strapped me in a car seat and we went rodeoing," Munsell says. "It was what we were good at."

He also recalls being involved in his father's rodeo clown comedy acts from a very early age. The first rodeo he remembers taking part in was when he was four years old in White Deer, Texas, where his father worked as a bullfighter. Munsell tells me that only in the last twenty or thirty years has there been a significant difference between a bullfighter and the more traditional "rodeo clown." Today a rodeo clown is primarily there to entertain the audience, whereas a bullfighter's job is strictly to save bull riding contestants—even though they're often both dressed like clowns.

In the early days of rodeo, the two jobs were one. The concept of a rodeo clown came about in the early 1900s when rodeo producers were looking for some way to fill the time between competitions and essentially "asked one guy to go out and tell jokes."

"Because back then rodeos lasted hours on end, so they needed something to go in there and fill the time, so they told some guy to . . . go be funny," Munsell says. Before long, the exciting and incredibly dangerous sport of bull riding was incorporated into rodeos.

"Some of them were kinda mean, so they would tell that guy, 'Go in there and distract that steer or that bull,'" Munsell says. "So the clown transitioned into a lifesaver, so forever the two were always intermixed—you were funny and you fought bulls. But here in the last twenty years they've expanded, and one guy does one and I do the other."

When Munsell's father was in the business, he was considered a rodeo clown—even though the most important aspect of his job was to save lives.

"A clown had to be funny and tell the jokes and do the comedy acts and also had to fight bulls. My dad had done a lot of that," Munsell says. "Most rodeo bulls are bred for their tenacity and aggression because it makes for a cooler show. It wouldn't be exciting if the bull didn't chase somebody, buck the guy off, and walk out the gate; that's not very exciting."

Munsell grew up around cattle and cowboys and often watched his father's acts from the fence, yelling advice. Despite the obvious danger, Munsell never got nervous about his father's numerous close calls. His father, after all, was a professional.

"I was probably less excited than a lot of people just because I'd been to so many at such a young age, so it was pretty second nature," Munsell says. "I didn't get too wrapped up if a bull got a hold of him or something. And I'd go up there and tell him, 'Oh man, you could've done this or that to avoid that.'"

Munsell was thirteen years old when his father decided to take him to the Rex Dunn's Bullfighting School, named for the famous bullfighter. The transition from standing on the sidelines to being chased by bulls happened almost immediately.

"He took me down there to see if I wanted to do that or not. So we went down there and were fighting full-blooded Mexican fighting bulls the first day," Munsell says. Admittedly, while the bulls weren't fully grown, they were fast, mean, and awfully aggressive.

"They didn't bump me around a lot down there and I enjoyed it, and that's probably when I decided that this is probably what's best for me," Munsell says.

In high school and college he went on to try his own hand at bull riding. "The adrenaline running through you is second to none," Munsell says, thinking back to that time. "On the back of a bull it is easy enough to ride one that is bucking straight away, but when one is spinning and turning back, that adds to the higher degree of difficulty. Man, it is maybe sort of like a controlled car wreck." But as much as he enjoyed it, he found it wasn't for him.

"I'd always known I'd be involved in rodeo in some facet. I just didn't know what," Munsell says. "I was capable of riding bulls fairly decent but I'd hit a rough patch and was, at that time, getting more bullfighting jobs in high school." And that's what he's done full time ever since.

Down to a Science

There are countless videos on the internet of Munsell being thrown by a bull, stomped on, trampled, kicked, and flung by a pair of horns high into the air. Like a rag doll, the bullfighter has been whipped all over the stadium and often in front of a cheering crowd. One video shows a frenzied bull's back legs landing on Munsell's back, slamming him flat to

Bullfighters hurry into position to help a rodeo contestant thrown from a bull during the Professional Bull Riders world finals in Las Vegas, Nevada in 2017.
(U.S. Customs and Border Protection photo by Bob Bushell)

the ground. You can't help but cringe when seeing it happen, knowing it's like someone dropping a motorcycle on him.

"Well, it certainly takes a special person to do the job," Munsell remarks about the danger. "You're purposely running in front of an animal that's out to kill you."

For Munsell, part of the thrill is about being able to control an animal that's fifteen times his size without touching it. But more importantly, he says it is about being in the right place at the right time to help the bull rider in danger.

"When you pull a guy out of a bad jam and he tells you thanks, that's super gratifying," Munsell says. "You see a lot of these kids and they don't get up and move as quick as they should, which makes my job a little harder than it should be."

Munsell makes it a point to tell the bull riding competitors to help him out and move as soon as they hit the dirt. The sooner they start moving away from the bull, the easier it becomes for him to control the animal safely away. "If you're getting up and moving, it makes my job a heck of a lot easier than if you're lying around pouting," Munsell says.

During the actual bull riding competition, the bullfighters are careful to keep their distance from the animal, about ten to fifteen feet away, to avoid negatively impacting someone's ride. "A spinning bull is always going to get you more points, so we never want to draw the attention of the bull to us while he's spinning," he says. At the same time the bullfighters have to be ready to launch themselves forward in the blink of an eye. Munsell admits, "It's a very fine line to keep your distance far enough away to let the bull buck and do its thing and not distract him, but a close enough distance where we can get in the middle of a situation as quick as we can."

Sprinting across an arena toward a charging bull, instead of away, seems a little counter-intuitive. Every fiber of his being that cares about his own safety must be screaming to turn and run the other way. "It is completely backwards," Munsell agrees.

The art and science of bullfighting has evolved over the past fifteen years. Bullfighters endlessly view videos of their performance, critiquing their game like NFL players.

"So you train yourself to look for certain things that the rider is doing that may indicate coming off the bull," he says. "I understand how cattle move—and good cow sense, I think, can make a good bullfighter great."

And of course while there are competitions for bull riders, there are also competitions for bullfighters. In that arena, Munsell has won two world championships and two national championships. He describes the contests as being a big, dangerous game of tag between him and the bull, with the bull being judged essentially on its aggression and tenacity—or basically its will to kill the bullfighter.

"I'm being judged on how close I can get to the animal and executing certain moves, and getting awarded for how close I'm getting and how well I pull off the maneuvers around that bull," Munsell says. The bullfighter cannot touch the bull and must use its own inertia against it.

"A lot of bulls are trained, and they know when they've done their job and they know when to leave," he says. But some bulls learn and remember moves used by bullfighters, and can use that to surprise the next one they find themselves up against.

A Dog-Eat-Dog Industry

For Munsell, fighting bulls is a full-time job that starts in January and runs most of the year. "It's year-round, [and] there's a lot more indoor venues than people would think. If you've got a nice barn, we can have a rodeo," Munsell says.

Things are changing in America. The Western and rural lifestyle is in a constant state of decline, but the number of rodeos held every year are actually increasing. Rodeos reached their peak in the early 1990s but decreased every year until 2006, when it reached its lowest number of 560 rodeos in the United States. But there's still an audience, and with prize money growing ever higher, that number has begun to creep up once again. Today there are six hundred professional rodeos held across the country and approved by the Professional Rodeo Cowboys Association. Membership in a popular organization like the Professional Bull Riders association has grown from twenty members in the early '90s to about one thousand today.

The competition for bullfighters is steep. Being one of the top ten bullfighters in the country helps Munsell get the jobs he needs to stay competitive in the business. "It sure enough is a dog-eat-dog industry," he says, adding there used to be a saying that bullfighters are a dime a dozen, but now it is more like a penny a dozen. "I'm very fortunate to have known a lot of really good bullfighters and they thought enough of me at a young age that I might be a good fill-in for them when they retired."

A bullfighter can make between $100 and $500 per rodeo. "You've got to treat this profession as a business and not be going for cheap money, because you don't make a very good living at it if you're going cheap," Munsell notes.

Healthy Respect for the Bull

Most people wouldn't step foot anywhere near a bull, and with good reason. But with a lifetime of being around bulls and bullfighting, Munsell no longer holds any fear when he steps into the arena.

"I know how to control those nerves better than most," he says. "People always ask me, 'Are you scared of those bulls?' No, not really—

I've been around them all my life. I have more of a respect for the animal than I do a fear [of them]." Smart bullfighters keep a healthy respect for the animal and what it is capable of. Because a bull is fifteen times his size, Munsell believes it will take only one kick or one well-placed blow to the head to take someone out permanently.

"It's not a fear. If I died fighting bulls, I'd probably die a happy guy because I went doing what I enjoyed," he says.

Munsell has on occasion been treated as a human-sized soccer ball and is regularly flung into the air. Injuries are just a part of the job, an accepted hazard. Bullfighters often break multiple bones and worse, but they understand what they've signed up for.

"I've been very fortunate as far as injuries go, knock on wood," he says. "And I just kind of attribute that to good fundamentals and doing things correctly. Good fundamentals get you a long way."

Even the best training can only prevent accidents some of the time. Just a month ago, Munsell was at a rodeo in Dodge City watching a cowboy dismount from a bull when things suddenly went wrong.

The rider flew off a bull's back just as the animal kicked up and turned, flipping the man in the air. Munsell raced to help the contestant and got hit on the head by one of the cowboy's spurs. This was a particularly awful injury because the spurs used by the riders are dulled so as not to pierce the skin of the animal. A sharp spur might just cut Munsell, but a dull one was assured to do more tearing than cutting—and in the process cause a nastier wound.

"I'm going through the gap, he's landing, and something just hits me in the head," Munsell remembers. "And I didn't think nothing of it because it wasn't a super hard hit or anything, so I just keep going and passed around that bull, and I can see red coming down my face, and I just take my hand and check up there and I'm bleeding like a goddang stuck hog."

After the bull was back in the pen, Munsell walked over to the athletics trainer who looked at him with a horrified expression on his face. Munsell's injury was a nasty, deep slice just above his eye and had to get stitched up.

"It's not scary at the time because you don't know what's just happened because it happened so fast," Munsell says. "When you sit down and think about it, you're like, 'Son of a gun, that coulda put my eye out…' That's the only thing that kind of scares me, is when it is something like that."

Another similar injury occurred at the Denver Stock Show eight years before. A bull bucked its rider off, and when Munsell raced in the animal ran him over. He fell as the rider was getting to his feet.

"I just thought I hit my head on something really hard and just kind of sat up and gathered myself, and a buddy of mine standing in the back of the chutes said, 'Hey, you need to get yourself checked out.' And I said, 'Man, am I bleeding? Because I can taste blood?' And he said, 'Yeah, go look.'" Munsell had landed face first on the rider's boot spur, which punctured through his cheek and knocked out a tooth.

"Same kind of thing, I just hate things happening in or around my head," Munsell says. "You can hit me anywhere else you want—just not my head."

Not being hurt often means getting off the ground and avoiding being stomped on by a bull, which can weigh more than a thousand pounds. Munsell wears safety gear comprising of a protective vest, and leg and knee protection designed to let striking hooves and horns slide off easily—but at some points it must feel a bit like a can of sardines being run over by a car.

A Bullfighter's Legacy

While the West and Western culture is Munsell's way of life, he says one day if he has children he'd like them to experience it—but he wouldn't push their involvement in rodeos. He knows being a bullfighter is a profession that has an expiration date on it.

"Every former bullfighter that I know has said the same thing: the bulls will let you know when you need to quit," Munsell tells me. "I don't want to get to that point."

His own father worked in the industry until he was forty-one. Munsell says he couldn't see himself working much past that age.

"Being in the position I'm in, being one of the top guys in the game, I don't want to do anything to prevent me not being seen in a positive way when I do retire," Munsell says. "There's a lot of great bullfighters that went out way too late, and they were very good when they were in their twenties and thirties—and could have had a better legacy if they had the foresight to retire sooner."

The oldest bullfighter he's aware of fought until he was fifty-five years old, something Munsell has no desire to do himself. He says he wants people to say he went out while he was at the top of his game. But that time is still years away. In the meantime, Munsell is back in the arena, in position and ready for whatever happens next.

CHAPTER 3

SHOOTISTS
OF THE **OLD**
(AND NEW)
WEST

The man is half bent over backward, precariously balancing on the heels of his cowboy boots, the fingers on his right hand itching for the handle of his single-action revolver. His left hand hovers in the air in front of him, fingers trembling with anticipation. In this position, he waits for maybe five seconds. Then the light in the center of a metal target twenty-one feet away turns orange, and he and the five other Cowboy Fast Draw competitors pull out their pistols and fire. He misses his shot. There's no doubt the man is as fast as an angry rattlesnake, especially when his holstered gun is horizontal with the target, but he can't get the points if he doesn't hit the target. There would be another chance. Again he assumes the half-bent position, thighs straining, left hand dangling in the air. His peers down the line take a somewhat more traditional vertical shooting position. The light turns orange and gunfire once again fills the air.

It is the Four Corners Territorial Fast Draw Championship in Pagosa Springs, Colorado, where the best in four states would see who is the fastest shootist of them all. They pull guns and fire in less than half a second, sending wax bullets into, or in some cases somewhat near, the target. All things considered, that was also the way it was when trying to shoot quickly back in the Old West. In a gunfight, speed was sometimes used at the fatal cost of accuracy. They often attribute the legendary Wyatt Earp as saying, "Fast is fine, but accuracy is final." Wild West lawman Bat Masterson agreed during an interview that speed was important during a gunfight, but nerve was even more so: "I knew a man named Charlie Harrison in the old days. He was the most brilliant performer with a pistol of any man I have ever seen and he could shoot straighter and faster than many of the great fighters, yet when he got into a scrap with a man named Jim Levy he missed him with all six shots at close range before Levy could reach for his weapon. Levy coolly dropped him with a single shot. Harrison was brave, but he had no nerve, you see."

Behind the target and a burlap-like curtain that stopped the errant wax bullets from harassing the town's tourists, I sit at a table with David "Mongo" Miller and his wife Shirley, also known as "Wench." "That's like you see in a saloon—not like you find on a jeep," David says of Shirley's alias. The retired couple, both dressed in period-authentic clothing, have long participated in the fast draw sport since its earliest days in 2004—and are some of the quickest around. David has finished tenth overall in the world six times.

Big Ugly, Annie Moose Killer, Ben Quicker, Mad Dog Martin, Mr. Big Shot, Nitro—everyone involved in the sport of Cowboy Fast Draw has an alias, not unlike the original Old West personalities like Sundance Kid, Billy the Kid, Wild Bill, Curly Bill, and Buffalo Bill. "You just kind of pick them at random," David admits, adding his own name Mongo was after the large, rather slow character played by Alex Karras in Mel Brooks's 1974 comedy classic *Blazing Saddles*. David served in the Marine Corps from 1969 to 1975 before selling dialysis machines, where he met Shirley, then a nurse. David sold computers for years before retiring in the early 2000s. Like many from his generation, he grew up watching television's classic black-and-white Westerns.

"We watched *Bonanza*, we watched *Gunsmoke*, we watched *Have Gun – Will Travel*, we watched all that stuff," David says. "That's what this is, it is all about the romance of the Old West. Being able to stand there dressed like Paladin or John Wayne and with a six-gun on your side and actually shoot in fast draw, even though we're not shooting at somebody—it is just still kind of about the romance of the Old West."

Gunfights in the Old West were rarely simple, clean, or for that matter particularly cinematic. In Thomas Dimsdale's 1921 book *The Vigilantes of Montana*, he records a fight in the winter of 1862 or 1863 between George Carrhart and George Ives, who were walking down the street of Bannack, Montana (now a ghost town), when an altercation broke out. The dispute became increasingly heated between the two men until Ives said he'd shoot Carrhart. Without further delay, Ives ran off to the local grocery to fetch his gun where it was waiting for him.

Carrhart ran to his cabin to get his firearm and then waited outside with the six-shooter held down by his side. When Ives burst out of the grocery store, he was armed and ready—but looking in the wrong direction. Carrhart waited for Ives to turn and face him. When Ives finally saw him, he swore, raised his six-shooter, and fired at Carrhart. The bullet missed, striking the side of a house next to where Carrhart was standing. Carrhart answered in kind by raising his own firearm and pulled the trigger, but his weapon misfired. Ives hastily shot a second time, but this bullet hit the ground in front of Carrhart.

Carrhart then took his second shot and aimed for Ives's face— but somehow the bullet missed. Possibly dismayed, Carrhart ran into a nearby house, stuck his six-gun out of the door, and fired again at Ives, who also shot back. The two blasted away at one another until Ives finally ran out of bullets. He turned to walk off when Carrhart came out of the house, with one shot left, and carefully aimed at Ives and fired. This time the bullet hit, striking Ives in the back and near one side. The bullet reportedly went straight through his body and hit the ground in front of Ives, kicking up dirt. Ives wasn't even close to dead. He turned and swore at Carrhart for shooting him in the back, then stormed off again to fetch another loaded six-gun. No doubt deciding he'd had enough, Carrhart fled from the scene. Supposedly the men ended their dispute soon after and lived together on Carrhart's ranch over the remainder of the winter.

Unusual stories like this show that two men even at close range sometimes had a difficult time hitting and killing the other. Misfires and misses were common. In my research I found an interesting story about two men who were playing cards when a gunfight broke out. One man got his gun out first, but because they were so close his opponent's pocket watch chain kept his six-shooter's hammer from falling and firing the bullet—which ultimately cost him his life.

The romance of the West is something largely concocted from nostalgia by people who didn't actually have to live through it. The Wild West wasn't full of men staring each other down the length of a dirty street, waiting for the clock to strike high noon before trying to gun each other down. Such fantasy is often the mortar of which most of the romance of the time is constructed. That's not to say that it didn't happen. There were men who unerringly hit what they were aiming at with predictably fatal results. One such man was given the nickname "Wild Bill" and may have been the greatest gunslinger who ever lived.

Tall Tales of Wild Bill Hickok

In all likelihood it was August 1865, several months after the Civil War, when *Harper's New Monthly Magazine* journalist George Ward Nichols found himself in Springfield, Missouri. Sitting in the shade of an awning, he was both fighting the need to take a nap and looking on at the residents of the area with thinly veiled superiority and contempt. "Men and women dressed in queer costumes; men with coats and trousers made of skin, but so thickly covered with dirt and grease as to have defied the identity of the animal when walking in the flesh," he said. He couldn't have known it at the time, but the story Nichols had come out to write would make history.

There is little doubt the exploits of then Army Scout James Butler "Wild Bill" Hickok were well known by the people in the region, for better or worse. Hickok, a gunslinger in the truest sense, arguably had the first recorded quick draw shootout of the West. All the same, dime novelists and Hickok himself exaggerated his story up until that time and going forward beyond his death to a ridiculous degree. Still, it cannot be discounted that Nichols was about to meet the deadliest gunslinger in American history.

A man roused the journalist from his judgmental stupor to introduce him to Hickok who had come riding down the street. "Let me at once describe the personal appearance of the famous Scout of the Plains," Nichols said. "'Wild Bill' who now advanced toward me, fixing his clear gray eyes on mine in a quick, interrogative way, as if to take my measure."

Before Nichols stood a slender, tall man, about six-foot-two, who wore bright yellow moccasins and a deerskin shirt. "His small, round waist was girthed by a belt which held two of Colt's Navy revolvers," Nichols said. It appears Hickok was more than happy to talk up his own legend and frontier prowess. Just a few days before, he had killed a man in a duel in the city's Park Central Square. Nichols heard an account of it from an Army captain who was enthusiastically working his way through a bottle of whiskey. Apparently there was bad blood between Hickok and a man named Dave Tutt, a former Confederate and gambler. According to the captain, Tutt had been looking to start trouble with Hickok for several days, and after a game of cards he had further provoked Wild Bill by taking Hickok's watch off the table and pocketing it for not paying his debts.

"I don't want ter make a row in this house. It's a decent house, and I don't want ter injure the keeper. You'd better put that watch back on the table," Hickok said in Nichols's account. Other reports of the incident had Hickok telling Tutt in no uncertain terms that if he took the watch he'd be a dead man. "But Dave grinned at Bill mighty ugly, and walked off with the watch, and kept it several days."

The captain then told Nichols one day that friends of Tutt's drew their guns on Hickok and dared him to fight, adding Tutt would wear the watch out in public tomorrow at noon in a personal affront to Hickok's honor—unless Hickok wanted to do something about it. The next day Hickok came out into the town square and found that a crowd had gathered, which included many of Tutt's friends. The two men came to within about fifty yards of each other with pistols already drawn. "At that moment you could have heard a pin drop in that square. Both Tutt and Bill fired, but one discharge followed the other so quick that it's hard to say which went off first," Nichols wrote.

Before even waiting to see if his bullet hit Tutt, Hickok turned on a crowd comprising of Tutt's friends and pointed his gun at them. According to the story, many had already drawn their own weapons or were starting to. "'Aren't yer satisfied, gentlemen?' Hickok asked the crowd. 'Put up your shootin-irons, or there'll be more dead men here.' And they put 'em up, and said it war a far fight," Nichols wrote.

As for Tutt, he had turned sideways in dueling fashion to make himself a smaller target—but Hickok's bullet hit him regardless and went into his side, striking him in the heart. Tutt stood still for a moment or two after being hit and, according to the inebriated captain, raised his gun as if to shoot again, then walked forward several steps before falling to the ground dead. When given the chance, Nichols didn't miss the opportunity to ask Hickok about the gunfight. "Do you not regret killing Tutt? You surely do not like to kill men?" Nichols asked him in a saloon.

"As ter killing men," Hickok replied, "I never thought much about it. Most of the men I have killed it was one or the other of us, and at such times you don't stop to think; and what's the use after it's all over? As for Tutt, I had rather not have killed him, for I want ter settle down quiet here now. But thar's been hard feeling between us a long while. I wanted ter keep out of that fight; but he tried to degrade me, and I couldn't stand that, you know, for I am a fighting man, you know."

Predictably Nichols's account, regardless of its accuracy or dubious colloquialisms, propelled Hickok to frontier stardom. At the time Hickok was already friends with "Buffalo Bill" Cody. In his fantastical autobiography, Cody said of his friend "Wild Bill" that the two had known each other since 1857. While he, or his biographers, claimed many things that are unlikely to have happened, the two did indeed serve together as scouts for the Army and later performed side by side in Wild West performances.

Hickok also made a good impression on General George Armstrong Custer. Custer described Hickok as a plainsman in every sense of the word, but unlike his peers: "Whether on foot or on horseback, he was one of the most perfect types of physical manhood I ever saw." Custer said Hickok was a man of courage, something he'd personally witnessed on many occasions. "His skill in the use of the rifle and pistol was unerring; while his deportment was exactly the opposite of what might be expected from a man of his surroundings. It was entirely free from all bluster or bravado. He seldom spoke of himself unless requested to do so. His conversation, strange to say, never bordered either on the vulgar or blasphemous. His influence among the frontiersmen was unbounded, his word was law . . . " But Custer added Hickok wasn't a man who went looking for trouble. Trouble, however, always seemed to find him. "'Wild Bill' is anything but a quarrelsome man; yet no one but himself can enumerate the many conflicts in which he had been engaged, and which I have a personal knowledge of at least a half a dozen men whom he has at various times killed, one of these being at the time a member of my command," Custer said. "Others have been severely wounded, yet he always escapes unhurt."

Just how many people Hickok killed either during the war, as a scout for the Army, or in the times between isn't exactly known. While being interviewed by journalist Henry Stanley, who was writing for the *Weekly Missouri Democrat* in 1867 and would later become famous for his own travels in Africa and coining the phrase "Doctor Livingstone, I presume," Hickok boasted killing a ridiculous number of men.

"He claimed to have killed 100 men and said he killed his first when he was 28 years old," Stanley said. "After a little deliberation, he replied, 'I would be willing to take my oath on the Bible tomorrow that I have killed over a hundred a long ways off.'" Whether Hickok was just inflating his already outrageous reputation or having a little fun with the former Confederate writer isn't known—but it was a time when men who already had nearly superhuman deeds under the belt often gleefully propelled themselves to superhero status for the eastern periodicals.

"No, by Heaven! I never killed one man without a good cause," Hickok replied when asked. "I was twenty-eight years old when I killed the first white man, and if ever a man deserved killing he did. He was a gambler and counterfeiter, and I was in a hotel in Leavenworth City then, as seeing some loose characters around, I ordered a room, and as I had some money about me, I thought I would go to it. I had lain some thirty minutes on the bed when I heard some men at the door. I pulled out my revolver and Bowie knife and held them ready, but half concealed, pretending to be asleep. The door was opened and five men entered the room. They whispered together, 'Let us kill the son of a bitch; I bet he has got money.'"

Hickok then claimed that he stabbed the man with his own knife and used his revolvers wounding another. He then rushed for help and came back with a soldier who captured the rest of the gang.

"We searched the cellar and found eleven bodies buried there—men who had been murdered by those villains," Hickok said. Stanley said Hickok then turned to him and the rest of the company listening to the tale and asked, "Would you have not done the same? That was the first man I killed and I was never sorry for that yet."

Colorful stories aside, there are some officially recorded deaths we know Hickok was responsible for, including David McCanles in 1861, who he shot from behind a curtain at a Pony Express Station in Nebraska. Depending on the source, McCanles was a bandit gang leader, a thief, a bully, or just a man looking to get money from the station which was owed to him. Regardless, McCanles came to that fateful day with help including two other men named James Gordon and James Woods. The story goes that after Wild Bill shot McCanles, James Gordon came into the station investigating the gunshots and was also shot by Hickok. Wild Bill stepped outside and then shot James Woods. Woods wasn't yet dead and the station manager's wife finished him off with a hoe. Wounded and trying to escape, Gordon later received the coup de grâce when some other station employees armed with a shotgun discovered him. The whole bloody affair was later deemed a matter of self-defense.

In October of that year Hickok joined the Union Army as a scout and likely saw more action. Then in 1865 he killed David Tutt over the pocket watch in Springfield, Missouri, and made history. Over the next several years he worked as a sheriff, Deputy U.S. Marshal, and City Marshal, killing five more men along the way. Among those five included John Kile, who, with Jeremiah Lonergan, both Seventh Calvary Troopers, got into a fight with Hickok in a saloon in Hays City. The story has it that in 1870 the troopers had Hickok on the floor and Lonergan kept him in place as Kile put his pistol in Hickok's ear and pulled the trigger. But the hammer fell on a dud, giving Hickok the chance to get ahold of his own pistol. In quick order he shot Kile in the leg, then put two bullets in Lonergan and killed him. Afterward, Hickok waited, armed at the town's cemetery, to see if any of the other troopers wanted to take an opportunity in the name of revenge. Apparently, none did.

The last man Hickok killed was fellow lawman Mike Williams in 1871. During an incident gambler Phil Coe allegedly took two shots at Hickok who responded by mortally wounding him. Hickok's deputy Williams burst out on the street to assist Hickok in the encounter and Hickok spun around and shot Williams dead. This was the end of his law enforcement career. Hickok worked for a time, unsuccessfully, at trying his own Wild West show and then later with his old friends Buffalo Bill Cody and Ned Buntline, but time and the call of the frontier lured him once again back West. Rudderless, as so many of the gunslingers were, Hickok drifted around from town to town trying to seek his fortune at the gambling tables. In 1872 he arrived in Georgetown, Colorado, a town known for its rich silver mines, and spent six weeks gambling without issue before heading off once again.

In Defense of a Bad Man to Fool With

By this point his reputation was quite fearsome; however, his time of shooting others was behind him. Hickok rightfully became paranoid and began sitting at card games so that he could face the door and see any potential attackers as they came for him. The discovery of gold near Deadwood, South Dakota, drew him to yet another boomtown. Finding the work of the gold fields not quite to his liking, he again ended up in town gambling. On August 2, 1876, Hickok, at age forty-eight, went to the Number 10 Saloon to play cards. The only available seat was the one with its back to the door. Legend has it that he took it and continued to play hand after hand in the seat, despite trying to get someone to switch with him. It was late afternoon when Jack McCall from Kentucky came into the saloon, pointed a gun at the back of Hickok's head, and fired. A special correspondent for the *Chicago Inter-Ocean* was in Deadwood and heard the shot, ran to the saloon, and rather ghoulishly reported the specific details of Hickok's demise.

"Yesterday afternoon about 4 o'clock the people of this city were started by the report of a pistol-shot in the saloon . . . Your correspondent at once hastened to the spot and found J.B. Hickok, commonly known as 'Wild Bill,' lying senseless upon the floor. He had been shot by a man known as Jack McCall. An examination showed that a pistol had been fired close to the back of the head, the bullet entering the base of the brain, a little to the right of the center, passing through in a straight line, making its exit through the right cheek between the upper and lower jaw-bones, loosening several of the molar teeth in its passage, and carrying a portion of the cerebellum through the wound."

Newspapers had incorrectly reported his death in the past, but this time it was real. James Butler "Wild Bill" Hickok was dead. During the murder trial, the reporter noted McCall assumed a nonchalance and bravado "which was foreign to his feelings, and betrayed by the spasmodic heavings of his heart." The paper said a witness at the card table during the shooting saw McCall place the barrel of his gun to the back of Hickok's head and say, "Take that," before pulling the trigger. At first McCall said the act was done in revenge for the death of his own brother. But this was just one of several stories McCall said in his own defense, which changed multiple times. McCall was somehow acquitted, then retried and ultimately hanged.

"It appears that Bill died in just the way and manner he did not wish to die—that is, with his boots on," said a writer for the *Kansas City Times*. "His life during the past five or six years has been one of constant watchfulness and expectation, as more than one reckless frontiersman had coolly contracted to take his life. But Bill was never off guard, and woe unto the wretched devil who failed to 'get the drop' on the long-haired William. More than one fool has had a bullet sent crushing through his brains from the ever-ready pistol of this cool and silent desperado . . . He has many warm friends in this city, as well as all over the West, who will regret to hear of his tragic end, the end he has so long been expecting."

In 1909 William Cody wrote a letter for the *New York Herald* defending his friend Hickok from being labeled one of the bad men of the frontier. Cody said Hickok was instead a "bad man to fool with."

"Never was there a man most misunderstood by the people of the present day who are impressed by the nickname, as it intimated a crazy thirst for human life," Cody said. "This is a wrong impression. Some consideration must be given to the peculiar conditions that existed in a section that was a more politically and socially volcanic, disorganized locality . . . " He reasoned that the frontier tended to draw those who were adventurous, vicious, and who were sometimes evading justice, which only grew worse after the Civil War. "There drifted in a host of men addicted to all kinds of excesses, and whose actions were almost, one might say, invited by the simple, unorganized and unprotected life then existing among the early settlers. Some idea of the atmosphere in which natives like Hickok and myself had been born and raised can be imagined from this description."

Looking in context, Cody believed Hickok was a necessary product of his time. Though an impressive gunslinger and not afraid of confrontation, as far as Cody was aware Hickok never provoked a fight.

Cody commemorated his friend: "'Wild Bill' now lies buried in the Deadwood Cemetery. His name will always live in a romantic history stranger than fiction."

The Sport of the Cowboy Fast Draw

While Hickok was dead, his story would become legend, myth, then movies and television. About 130 years after Hickok was buried in Deadwood, a fictionalized drama about the town, its salty residents, and the death of Hickok aired on television. David and Shirley Miller had been watching the show *Deadwood* one evening when Shirley turned to her husband and mentioned that she had never been to Deadwood. David decided the time was right that they make the trip from Colorado to the town. He glanced at the town's chamber of commerce website to see what events there were and spotted something about a "fast draw exhibition." Intrigued, they went to Deadwood and attended a shooting match. At this time, the Cowboy Fast Draw sport was only a few years old.

"I was sitting in the bleachers and I was like, 'This is not an exhibition—these guys are doing something,'" David remembers. Indeed, they were competing to see who had the fastest gun. David decided he was interested in trying his own hand at it. However, Shirley said she wanted nothing to do with it, having never touched a gun. She tells me she would often leave the room, or even the house, when David was cleaning his own firearms collection. Undeterred, David went to a Denver gun store and bought a Colt single-action revolver—also known as a Peace Maker, and the only firearm allowed in the quick draw competitions. "There's any number of manufacturers now that make a faithful reproduction of the Colt Peace Maker and that's what we have to use," David says, adding he went straight home and practiced in his basement with plastic bullets.

Just six weeks later the first-ever quick draw world championships came to Deadwood, and David went to compete against some of the fastest guns in the world. He ended up placing thirteenth out of sixty competitors. Shirley wasn't sure if she even wanted to be involved but at the last second decided to strap on a holster even though she'd never touched a firearm before then.

"I said those women made it look easy. I'll figure this out because—I love the costumes. Still do," Shirley says. "And I didn't even know how to load it, so my hand judge had to physically load my gun. Everything you could do wrong, I did, and I had so much fun ... I came in thirteenth in the world for the women that year—of course, there were only thirteen of us. And I've been hooked ever since."

As we talk, Shirley loads ammunition, putting primers in cases with wax bullets. Her fingers move with the type of secondhand nature that comes from having done a thing a thousand times before. David tells me the two of them took to the organization and, outside of the Marine Corps, he's never encountered a more tight-knit group of people. Over the years their own involvement in the sport grew to where they were both helping to set up other groups under the organization's banner.

"We started traveling around, helping people get started and helping matches run, and all of a sudden we got the reputation [of] 'Well, Mongo and Wench, they'll come down and help'—and we did," David says.

Fastest Guns in the World

With one shooter trying to be the fastest, David says there are often rivalries that naturally form from one competition to the next, that often last years and go from state to state.

"A lot of smack talk," Shirley agrees.

"Not bitter rivalries ... but there are definite rivalries. There are rivalries that have gone on for years," David says. "It's called fast draw, but the thing about it is that target down there is a big equalizer. I don't care how fast you are—if you can't hit that target you're not going to win a match."

David admits that there are a lot of competitors who are faster than he is. "But up until just recently, I was sitting fifth overall in the world in points because I have had a good season up to date—and I'm fast enough that you can't really lollygag. I'm not going to beat the fast shooters but I'm also known to have probably a 75 to 80 percent accuracy." And that's the issue. Someone can pull their gun and fire at just under the speed of light—but if they miss the target, then it's all for nothing.

Fast draw competitors fire their guns during the Four Corners Territorial Fast Draw Championship in Pagosa Springs, Colorado. *(Photo by Billie Diemand)*

"I think the secret is: don't overthink it," David says. "Get your head out of the way. Let your reactions take over. Once you practice a little bit and you get that natural movement down, let that take over and let that control you. Don't let your mind get in the way."

Often competitors are in such a hurry to draw their firearm at the competition, they miss the target—again, and again, and again. The winning shootist needs only to hit the target three out of five times.

"Sometimes you get up there with a guy and you're so intent, there's this rivalry thing...you might shoot eight to twelve shots before somebody finally wins three," David says. "Last year we had a group that went forty-seven shots—each opponent shot forty-seven times before we had a winner." At the distance of twenty-one feet, if the pistol's aim is even an eighth of an inch off, the bullet will miss the target.

Today David and Shirley dedicate most of their time to the sport, which essentially grew from the tales of Hickok's own gunslinging prowess. Cowboy Fast Draw competitors are not alone in their romance of the Wild West and appreciation of period-appropriate costumes.

There's the similarly themed World Fast Draw Association; and for those interested in live rounds, there's the Single Action Shooting Society or Cowboy Action Shooting, started in the 1980s, which also has competitors dress in Old West costumes. For enthusiasts who prefer their Wild West experience on horseback, there's the Cowboy Mounted Shooting, where competitors shoot at balloons using birdshot in timed events testing both horse and rider. Cowboy Fast Draw competitions have gained popularity even in Japan where, because of firearm restrictions, contestants use specially made revolvers constructed of hard plastic, capable of only shooting blanks or plastic BBs.

Anywhere you go, wherever it is, with whatever spin or angle is added, the enthusiasm for the West still endures.

CHAPTER 4

THE **MARCH**
POWWOW

Nearly two thousand Indigenous Americans representing about one hundred different tribes dance out onto the floor of the Denver Coliseum during the Grand Entry of the annual Denver March Powwow, each dressed in clothes significant to them and their tribe. Sitting in the stadium to watch the performers, I feel both profoundly humbled and amazed by the examples of intertribal dancing.

"There are approximately over five hundred tribes that are still here [in America]," an announcer says over the rhythmic beats of drums and music. "At one time there were tens of thousands of tribes. There are now only five-hundred-some recognized tribes—and each of them has a story to tell. The story of their creation and also the story of how we're to carry on...We choose to live spiritually. We choose to live through humor, to laugh and to carry on because there are generations to come. There are many more generations to come."

The men, women, and children dance past in a massive procession, their colorful regalia, feathers, and silver bells moving to the sounds of the drums and the dancer's intricate motions. For forty-five years Native American dancers have gathered in Denver, Colorado, for the March Powwow to celebrate their rich and diverse heritage and to compete in dancing contests.

While the history of Native Americans in the West predates the time of the Old West itself by more than fifteen thousand years, their individual histories played a significant role in the time period for its literature and creation of the myth of the West. In my research I didn't want to revisit the many accounts from that time period that were largely fictitious, racist, and used to justify war, rampant marginalization, and ultimately genocide against the region's indigenous people. From the Trail of Tears to the Sand Creek Massacre, the treatment of America's indigenous peoples is one of the most shameful parts of U.S. history. But Native Americans are also an integral part of the country's future. The March Powwow is arguably one of the largest gatherings of American Indians in the Front Range area, and I wanted the opportunity to see this example of the modern-day West firsthand. Instead of trying to interpret what I see, as someone with a white-European background, I decided instead to find the event's longtime executive director to understand more about the importance of the powwow and of one indigenous person's experience growing up in America.

Hand-in-Hand

I meet Grace Gillette at a Denver restaurant after the powwow and sit down over a couple glasses of ice tea. She has a terrific sense of humor. In her seventies, Gillette can trace her lineage back to the famous Arikara chief Son of Star. Her tribal name is SwaHuux, and she was born and raised on the Fort Berthold Indian Reservation in western North Dakota, which is home to the Mandan, Hidatsa, and Arikara Nation. Gillette has organized the powwow for the past thirty years.

"When they started doling out the reservations, they put us on the same reservation as the Mandan and the Hidatsa," Gillette tells me. "They put us on the same reservation . . . because of the three tribes that are there—Mandan, Hidatsa, and Arikara. The Mandan were practically wiped out by smallpox. It took a toll on the Hidatsa, and Arikara too. So in battling that disease it kind of pulled those three smaller tribes together, and so the government put them on the same reservation."

Gillette remembers when her family moved to the community of Mandaree when she was very young. "The school wasn't even finished,"

Gillette says, explaining how new Mandaree was at the time. "I was in the first first-grade class. There were thirteen of us. There was probably seven of them who couldn't speak English because it was a Hidatsa community and very rural, and so English wasn't spoken in the home."

Both of Gillette's parents were of the generation that was taken from their homes and forced to go to a boarding school where they were punished for speaking their native language. "So English was spoken in our home but when their friends came over, or relatives, they all spoke Arikara. But of course children weren't supposed to listen, so we were shooed out of the room," Gillette laughs. "As long as I can remember, my father was a lay minister. He was a congregational minister, and so growing up the Christian beliefs and the Arikara beliefs were just hand-in-hand. There was no conflict, there were no differences; they were just hand-in-hand."

Gillette said growing up she led what she calls a "blessed life" because she wasn't exposed to racism as a child.

"I knew no prejudice growing up, even in the surrounding towns. Unlike now where they're so prejudiced against the Natives they follow them around in stores—I never experienced that when I was growing up," she said. "It just wasn't something we thought about."

The world as Gillette knew it grew larger when in 1964 at age sixteen she got the chance to travel to Kentucky for a scholastic opportunity at the Berea Foundation School. She took a bus to the South in the middle of a time of deep civil unrest in the US, which included rampant segregation and discrimination. As a girl from the reservation, she was unprepared for what she would see. "That first bus stop into Kentucky I got out of the bus to use the restroom, and everything was marked 'blacks only,' 'whites only'—the bathrooms, the water fountains, the counters," Gillette remembers. She had never seen signs that designated based on race before on the reservation. "And I went in and said, 'I'm neither one, so where do I go?'"

She noticed both the white and black patrons at a diner wouldn't make eye contact with her or pretended that she wasn't there. Gillette ended up going to an elderly woman who seemed approachable and asked which bathroom she was allowed to use. "She said, 'Honey, if you're not black, then you are white.' So I went creeping into the white bathroom," Gillette says.

Young women dressed in both old style and contemporary
regalia stand on the sidelines during the Denver March Powwow.
(Photo by Eva Skye, with special thanks to the Denver March Powwow)

"She'd been leaving and when I came out she was sitting there, and she called me over and she said, 'Just what are you?' So that was my first introduction to discrimination."

Gillette says that in Kentucky when she arrived on campus, the students were disappointed that she wore only regular clothes and didn't come to school in traditional regalia of some sort. She soon made friends with both white and black students, but she recalls the locals harassing her for not being white or for associating with anyone other than whites. On one occasion people even threw beer bottles at her and her friends. She wanted to call the police, but her friends stopped her because they said that racism was normal for their community and they didn't want to draw any further attention to themselves.

"It was really kind of a culture shock for me," Gillette says.

Conversely, when Gillette came to Colorado in the '70s she found that Denver had a thriving Native American community. At the time there were about twenty organizations and weekly powwows. "There was so much going on in the community. There was a Native American bowling league, basketball leagues for men and women, there were softball leagues," she says. Gillette quickly became involved with those activities, including what would eventually become the Denver March Powwow.

"We're a very social people. We celebrate all life events. Probably the best example of a powwow dance back in the day is when the warriors would prepare to go out to hunt or to attack the enemy," Gillette explains. "When they came back in victory and just the men would dance . . . there they would sing, there was a special song to sing. Some tribes called it a calling song. When you hear this song, they're calling you to the circle, to the center of the camp." Once called to the circle, the tribe's leaders would explain why they were summoned and the singing and dancing would begin, while others would get into the center of the circle and reenact what they did through dance.

"To tell their story, they had a buffalo robe and they would paint what their history was, their brave deeds, and how many coups they counted, their game [hunted] and all of that," Gillette says. "And the women would stand at the outer edges and wear those [robes] to support their brother, husband . . . but they weren't allowed inside the arena because that was just the warrior dance."

She says that in time the women and the children wanted to dance too, so within her tribe they had to be led into the dancing arena by a warrior. "And prior to that, you have to have your Indian name and your eagle feather. So when a song is sung and you're out there, they can recognize you."

Gillette tells me about the enduring strength of Native Americans and the role of powwows. "As the wars went away, and all of that, they put us on reservations. We are a very resilient people. Our lifestyle changed as the world around us changed, and then [powwows] became social events like when there was a wedding or if someone came of age—they would have those kinds of ceremonies."

Voices of the Lakota

Gillette says it was likely in the early to mid-1950s when competition dancing started in the powwows, and it has continued to evolve ever since.

Today dancers are given numbers so that judges can watch their performances and give them points.

The powwow's dancing is divided into a host of categories—which is then further separated into different age ranges. For men and women, the styles of dancing include the Northern Traditional, which she tells me is the oldest of the dances, and the Southern Straight. The women's dancing styles also include the Jingle Dress and Fancy Shawl dances. For men, there are Grass Dancing and Fancy Dancing, both of which have origin stories.

Gillette explains the origin of the Grass Dance and the deeper meaning behind the movements. "From our region the origin legend for [the Grass] Dance style is there was a young man who couldn't run, dance, play, and ride horses like the other kids," she says. "So the family took him to the village healer and he suggested that this young man go fast and pray that the creator would show him the way to where he could do what he wanted. So as he sat on the plains and fasted . . . [the prairie] grass almost looked like ocean waves. And as he saw the prairie grass moving and swaying in the summer wind, it somehow took the form of a human being." After the young man finished fasting, he returned to his village and told the healer what he had seen. He was then told that was how he should dance.

"The original outfit for the grass dancer had the long prairie grass tucked around the waistline and around the legs, but now they use yarn, and some use ribbon," Gillette says to describe how the dance has moved to modern times.

As for the most contemporary of the dance styles, the men's Fancy Dance, Gillette says it likely had its beginnings in one of the most famous shows of the Old West.

"From the research I've done and the elders I've talked to, that kind of [dance] comes from the Buffalo Bill Wild West shows," Gillette reveals. "When he took the Indians touring, not only in America, but in Europe, where they thought the traditional dances and the grass dances were too sedate, they wanted something more exciting."

As famous and popular Buffalo Bill was then and is today, he gets mixed reactions from historians about the role he played in introducing Native Americans to the rest of the country and world. But Gillette believes his reputation is a positive one.

"He treated them with respect. He saw they were well taken care of and that they weren't looked at as an oddity," she says.

She recounts a Buffalo Bill–related experience she and some other members of the March Powwow had years ago, when they and others traveled to Manchester, England. Her group was waiting in the Salford Quays area waiting for their guide when one of their dancers, who was also a spiritual leader, said he could hear voices in Lakota. He asked if he could sing to them and Gillette said he could, and soon an appreciative crowd formed to listen.

"When we were doing that our guide arrived, and he was just astounded to see [the dancer] doing that," she says, adding the guide, who was normally talkative, had grown quiet for a time afterwards. He later thanked the dancer and told him about the history of the area where he had been singing.

"Apparently on that very spot where we were was where Buffalo Bill had an encampment, and there were all kinds of teepees and Natives there," Gillette says. In fact it was the exact site where in 1897 nearly one hundred Native Americans lived in their teepees while traveling with Cody's show. During their five-month stay in Salford, there was one recorded death of a Lakota warrior who died from a lung infection. To this day it's unknown where he was ultimately buried. For the Native Americans traveling with Cody, it was an opportunity to get away from an increasingly restrictive American government and a chance to continue to practice their traditions without hindrance. In some cases those who participated in the Battle of Little Big Horn, which resulted in the death of General George Armstrong Custer, were able to avoid the government while traveling with Cody's show. The significance of the location wasn't lost on Gillette and the others as they learned about the site.

"I thought that was pretty darn cool," she says. "It gave me the chills."

Committed to the Future

Over time a career in office management pulled her focus away from the March Powwow and in another direction, and Gillette found herself less involved with the event and its organization. Then one day while looking at a story on the cover of a Denver newspaper, she read that someone on the powwow's committee was misrepresenting the importance of the drums and songs used during the dance, calling them essentially meaningless.

"He said, 'Oh, it's nothing. Just a bunch of chanting, it doesn't mean anything.' And I thought, what the heck? So that really got my attention. This was not right," Gillette says. She adds that there is a great deal of meaning in the chanting and songs, which are sometimes very old. She tells me the songs are sometimes so old that it is impossible to know when it was first created.

"Our history is oral, so I don't think anybody can say that song was made in 1955 by so-and-so," she says. "There are just some songs that have been around forever, and I don't think any one person can be given a right of ownership."

Gillette says the person who spoke with the newspaper had "no knowledge" about the significance of the songs and drums. In fact, these were essential to the powwows.

"Each society had different positions and within those societies there was always a drum keeper—and the drums are treated like a human being," she says. "They are fed, they are given water, they are prayed with, they have a special place in the home of the drum keeper. It used to be not just anyone could go sit at the drum and sing. They had to be part of that drum keeper's family, and they only sang certain songs at [specific] times of the year or for certain occasions."

She adds that at the intertribal powwow a lot of the drum groups still respect those ways. People don't just sit down at a drum and start singing because it's not respectful.

"The answer this person gave who was a coordinator of the event . . . to say that they had 'no meaning, it was just a bunch of chanting'— to me, it just rubbed me the wrong way," she says. "One of our goals [at the powwow] is to present, is to bring cultural awareness to our people, to provide an event with educational value, and if one of the organizers doesn't know the educational value, then something's wrong."

She read that interview as a call to action, and it led to her becoming involved once again with the organizing of the powwow. She eventually worked her way up into the executive director position, a job she's happily embraced for three decades now.

"It's the best way for a Native child in Denver to stay in touch with their roots, even if it is once a year to go out there and take pride in who they are," Gillette says. "When they're in there, [they think] 'I'm just one of another instead of being one in a crowd'—and that's what I'd like to see more of."

Deep Pride

As I sit and watch the dancers, the drum keepers, every participant in the powwow, I see the deep pride Gillette speaks of. In a massive clockwise circle the dancers continue to come out onto the floor of the arena as the Denver March Powwow's drum circle sings "A Living Hoop." Soon the arena floor is full and the event's Grand Entry is complete. The powwow's dance competitions are about to begin. The story of the people of the American West continues. New generations are born to inherit the past, to forge a new future, and to preserve their heritage.

CHAPTER 5

CATTLE, BLOOD, AND THUNDER

Terry Florian walks along the suspended walkway, surveying the cattle below. The distant sounds of traffic and the bellowing of the cattle below are punctuated by the regular, easy staccato of his boots on the weathered boards of the raised platform. Always vigilant, he says he still has run-ins with modern-day cattle rustlers.

"We had some not-so-nice people that were stealing stuff here," Florian admits. The brand inspector supervisor carries a pair of well-worn manual shears and a narrow clipboard in both of his back pockets. The shears are used to get a closer look at a cattle brand to identify ownership, and the clipboard to keep track of his various charges. The tools of the trade haven't changed much in the last hundred years, nor has the type of person called to this unique career field. Just as they did more than one hundred years ago, brand inspectors still spend their days preventing the theft of livestock and, when able, returning them to their rightful owners. They're statutory peace officers with the power to arrest criminals, though they don't carry firearms anymore. Thefts happen somewhat frequently, but they rarely escalate to become a dangerous situation. Of course, there are exceptions.

The Producers Livestock Marketing Association, a Greeley cattle sale barn, is still largely quiet as we looked out over the pens below. A few cattle call out to each other as the sun burns away the overcast morning sky. A veteran of the business for thirty years, Florian is the latest in a long line of inspectors dating back to a time before Colorado was even a state. As we stand there and wait for a shipment of cattle to be dropped off, Florian recalls a rustling incident that took place almost twenty years ago involving some violent men who had stolen their neighbor's livestock.

"I called for the sheriff to go, then he figured out where I was going and said it was in my 'best interest to look the other way,'" Florian says. "They had shot at one of the sheriff's cars who went into their yard like three months earlier. That's why he said he wouldn't send any of his guys out there. I said, 'Well, I'm going anyway, with or without you.'"

Florian called one of his fellow cattle brand inspectors to tell him where he was going and then drove in his pickup truck to the property with the stolen calves. He told the men they were suspected of cattle rustling, which they accepted without issue. "They knew they were caught," Florian tells me, adding they already knew him and got along with him well enough. Brand inspectors eventually meet and get to know everyone in their district regardless of their potential for future cattle thievery. "They didn't see me as a threat, [but] I was scared," Florian says, chuckling at the memory. He doesn't seem like the type to scare easy.

"There were four or five of them guys and they're pretty good sized, and they're just kind of moving around your pickup wondering what the heck you're doing there," Florian says. "You tell them and they kind of hear what you've got going on, you know, 'what's the scoop?' We got it worked out."

But not entirely in the way he had hoped. The neighbors were ultimately too afraid to press charges against the men. "The people who owned them said, 'You know, that's a $300 calf and they could do $10,000 of damage to my place,' [and] because it was their neighbor, he said 'I don't care. They can have the calves,'" Florian says. The men ended up just paying for the stolen animals.

Brand inspectors have roamed the shrinking frontier, looking for lost and stolen cattle and horses since 1865. The job of cattle inspector was established for a very good reason. The history of rustlers is a terrible and bloody one, proving again and again the necessity for the specialized Western lawmen.

Bonanza

When gold was discovered in Colorado in 1859, those desperate to make their fortunes raced across the plains in a frantic scramble. Likely the thought of changing their economic destiny overnight caused many to risk life and limb. In the winter of 1860, the *Rocky Mountain News* did its best to warn the soon-to-be-arriving waves of hopeful prospectors and miners about the realities of living in the unforgiving mountainous climate. "Thousands will no doubt set out for Pike's Peak only intent upon getting there, without any provision for subsistence or comfort after their arrival, content to 'trust to luck' and let tomorrow provide for itself. To such we say, stay at home until you learn better sense, or you will stand a good chance of acquiring an education more rapidly than agreeable. We have barely sufficient provisions in this country to subsist those already here ... "

That gold rush drew an estimated one hundred thousand people to test their luck and resolve in the Rockies. It was dangerous, back-breaking work and gold was found only by a lucky few, but as the *Rocky Mountain News* predicted, the area just wasn't prepared for the influx of people seeking their fortunes. Indeed, there wasn't enough food to support the miners, merchants, and others trying to make a living in the shadow of gold's discovery. Local ranchers couldn't keep up with the demand for beef and a solution was desperately needed to feed the growing state. In time that riddle would be solved by legendary former-Texas-Ranger-turned-cattleman Charles Goodnight, who began driving cattle into the area as early in 1866.

Before long, there was a cattle boom in Colorado. This bonanza soon saw other Texas ranchers driving their cattle into the state, and other Western regions, as the local stockman scrambled to keep up with demand. While there were significant dips and valleys in the economic reality of raising livestock in the West, its long-term profitability was arguably more sustainable than the gold locked deep in the neighboring mountains.

With the creation of the Colorado Stock Growers Association in 1867 and other similar groups, books listing cattle brands were soon published to help curtail theft and determine the origin of the free-ranging cattle. Not unlike a mailing address, the brand could tell where and who a cow belonged to. Like the state's gold rush, the beef business became extremely lucrative to those who could stick it out, especially in the early 1880s. The all-time high price of beef, then almost $40 a head, brought in unheard-of levels of investment in the industry across Colorado, New Mexico, and Montana. Fortune was fickle and often an illusion, but those who could find opportunity grabbed at it and held on for dear life, because if you didn't—and many couldn't—you hit rock bottom with a bone-crushing thud. The line between legal and illicit was often just determined by who had the most friends in the right places or simply whether you were caught in the act. Almost from the beginning, beef proved to be an easy business to steal into, and cattle thefts soon became a rampant and violent problem that escalated into a war.

Cattle Thieves and Vigilantes

The prairies and mountains of this new frontier were soon fertilized by the blood of those stepped on in the sprint to reach the West's newfound levels of success, legally obtained or otherwise. Thieves with their newly obtained cattle raced to cross from one territory or state to the next to avoid the law. As wealthy as some cattle dealers were, like a Colonel Wheeler in Texas in 1875, they quickly found their livelihood and income disappearing in the wake, leaving reports of thefts, murders, and lynchings peppering the local periodicals like buckshot from a nervous coachmen's shotgun. In Wheeler's case, he went in pursuit of thieves who had stolen between four hundred and five hundred cattle from his ranch in Texas. Unfortunately, Wheeler and his men came across the thieves much sooner than expected and hadn't yet had time to build a proper posse. In the gunfight that followed, Wheeler was shot and killed.

The *Colorado Daily Chieftain* reported "considerable cattle and horse stealing" in Colorado in 1884 and the people's surging response with the law: "The cattle men have been doing detective work for some time past and during the past few days have succeeded in arresting and jailing thirteen men charged with stealing cattle ... Considerable excitement is said to prevail at Las Animas, and some fears of lynching are expressed, but we hope that law and order will prevail." Kansas was another popular destination for many thieves looking to unload their ill-gotten herds without raising too much suspicion. In 1890, law enforcement officers tried to track a gang of thieves, including cowboy L.W. Wallace, that was guiding cattle illegally from other states into Arkansas City, Kansas. Wallace was captured and later released on a legal technicality, and then immediately rearrested by officers in an attempt to make the charges stick a second time around. His case is not unusual. Catching a cattle rustler was difficult, but getting charges to end in a conviction seemed improbable.

However, months later the *Colorado Daily Chieftain* reported that a successful indictment was finally made against another group of Kansas cattle thieves. "The efforts made by the Colorado [Stock] Growers' association to protect their own best interests have of late met with unusual success," the paper stated, "and several reckless individuals who make a business of gathering up strays and selling them on their own account have had justice [dealt] out to them." The paper added the stock inspector secured the return of twenty-three head of cattle stolen from Colorado ranches and was back on the trail in Kansas looking for even more of the stolen animals. This success marked a change for the optimistic, that perhaps the tides have turned for justice to be on the side of the law.

But the truth was that while the area's fledgling courts successfully sent many cattle thieves to prison, they were oftentimes too slow— and some even deemed the process to be entirely unnecessary. Despite the best efforts of the budding laws and regulations requiring cattle be checked before being transported across state lines, rustling continued. Cattle thieving became so rampant that some decided to quit the business altogether. State Senator Durban of Wyoming told a Colorado paper that rustlers were ruining the cattle business of that state and that a war of extermination was likely soon to commence against the thieves. This brought some cattlemen to take the matter into their own hands in the most efficient, economical way they could determine. In Custer County, one paper reported that "Jerry Thompson, a notorious 'rustler,' and two companions, have been caught changing brands on cattle, and were all hanged to the same tree." In an article that same year, another newspaper boldly claimed that there was nothing short of a "WAR ON RUSTLERS: Cattlemen of the Northwest Preparing to Make Short Work of Outlaws."

The Wyoming problem was bad enough that some decided to take their cattle business to other states, such as Montana. Unfortunately, those who moved to Montana wouldn't find much of a reprieve from the problem there either. The *Silver Standard* reported that cattlemen were being relentlessly harassed by thieves in eastern part of the state. It seemed every year the rustlers became bolder and then began making organized raids on ranches without fear of the law. In fact, many considered law enforcement utterly powerless to stop them.

Such was the case in August of 1899 for James Averill, the postmaster in Sweetwater, Colorado, and his common-law wife. "Averill's ranch was a rendezvous for a large number of cattle thieves and rustlers," a reporter for the *Fort Morgan Times* said. "Averill and his female companion were among the most notorious of the 'Mavericks.'" Apparently, Averill and his wife stole unbranded calves and killed the dutifully following mother cows that were legally branded. The two had collected several hundred calves on their pasture. One day a neighbor saw "Mrs. Averill" round up one of his steers and shoot it. When men tried to inspect the pasture, Averill refused to allow them in. Fearing his notorious record of killing, the men decided to leave without pressing the issue further; but before long a group of about twenty "respectable and law-abiding people" came back to finish the job.

The newspaper said a "short hearing" was provided for the couple who insisted on their lives the calves were not stolen but instead purchased legally from Nebraska. "This was disproved without further parley," the reporter said. "Ropes were placed around their necks and thrown over the limbs of a spreading Cottonwood. They were drawn up by relentless hands, and in a few moments the bodies of the guilty couple swung lifeless, and the lynching party rode off as quietly as they came." The newspaper insisted no legal steps would need to be taken against the participants of the lynching as it was considered by them to be entirely justified and "marks the inauguration of a feeling among stockmen that the time has come when property must be protected." The reporter had also noted that out of sixteen indictments for cattle stealing in the county, none of the juries were able to convict due to fear of reprisals.

A growing frustration with the problem and the ever-present difficulty of securing successful convictions caused cases of vigilante law to break out. Some people turned to guns as the solution. "Cowboys" killed five thieves in two weeks in a show of strength, while cattleman and horse owners armed their employees with strict instructions to shoot any suspicious-looking persons near the ranches. "The outlaws are supposed to be not less than a hundred strong, and as they are well armed, it is thought there will be a pitched battle before long between the thieves and the cattlemen," South Dakota's *Herald Democrat* reported.

The war on cattle thieves was just heating up. In 1892, heavily armed cattlemen and those in their employment, numbering nearly two hundred, decided the courts to be no longer reliable and began hunting for cattle thieves south of Yellowstone National Park. Later that year near Buffalo, well-known Wyoming cattle thieves Mike Brown and George Hakes were both found killed by a gunshot in the back. Only a short time before, in that same vicinity, four other rustlers were found similarly murdered. "It seems that these thieves of whom there are about 50 alive, are being systematically hunted," said one reporter.

One can easily imagine this being a sinister time to live in certain parts of the West. There was a type of open warfare being waged between rustlers and stockmen, with suspected thieves being lynched without receiving fair trials and ranchers being put out of business by the rampant and aggressive thefts of their animals. Then there are also the innocent bystanders who come across dead people hanging from the branches of a tree or to happen upon a camp full of dead men.

Guns burned hot and casualties mounted on both sides. One account of cattle thieving in Bighorn Basin noted a vicious gunfight and its untimely end: "Upon its conclusion notably the cattle thieves and the officers lay dead on the open prairie, everybody completely riddled with bullets." At the same time and not far away, the bodies of rustlers Ora Walker and Asa Schuck were found shot in the back with sixty heads of cattle found in their possession.

Like the slow ponderous turn of a wagon wheel, things began to change in the Western states. Fewer cattle rustling incidents were reported and more stories passed around the violent confrontations between rustlers and those hot on their heels like angry hornets. As the 1800s drew to a close, court cases against rustlers ended with more successful convictions than in the past twenty years. In 1896 the law even found guilty Chas. O. Holliday, better known as "Kid" Holliday, the leader of one of the worst band of thieves in Colorado who had operated in the northeastern part of the state and in southwestern Nebraska. When officers and cattleman had found stolen calves in his corral in Kimball County, Colorado, Holliday cleverly escaped dressed in his wife's clothing and was on the run for two years before he was finally captured in Box Butte County, Nebraska.

Dead or captured, cattle thieves were dropping like flies and the papers printed headlines like "Gang Captured," "A Battle with Rustlers," "Cattle Rustler Run Down." The law followed and grew in effect as well. In 1899, on the cusp of the new century, one Colorado reporter boldly claimed that recent state legislation requiring cattle and horses to be checked for a certificate of inspection issued by a brand inspector before crossing the state line would entirely stop cattle rustling. It helped, but just as brand inspectors persisted in their roles, nothing could stop cattle rustling from entering the twentieth century and beyond.

Meet the Brand Inspectors

The Colorado State Brand Inspector's office, located just north of the town of Greeley in a large livestock sale barn, has sixty-eight brand inspectors, ranging in age from twenty to seventy years old. They sit behind cluttered desks in a narrow room working on laptop computers, with worn calendars, pictures of families, and large travel mugs in sight. The white walls display tired illustrations and paintings of cowboys lassoing cattle and riding horses, and there's even a trophy of a deer's head on a wall, serenely watching the inspectors as they work. These men and women serve the state's ten districts and inspect four million head of livestock, covering Colorado's 104,000 square miles a year. Over the last several years reports were filed with the brand inspectors regarding 1,760 lost or stolen cattle and 52 horses. In 2017 the state's brand inspectors traveled a staggering 1.1 million miles while performing their duties across Colorado and held onto 49,000 head of livestock while waiting for proof of ownership.

Outside the brand inspector office in the same building, an auctioneer speaks in a rapid-fire, largely incomprehensible language to declare the fate of some cattle. About six men sitting in the well-worn bleachers make cryptically subtle signs with their hands to the auctioneer, who notes their bids. I follow Brand Commissioner Christopher Whitney past them to the livestock pens and the waiting cattle beyond. Whitney oversees all brand inspector operations in the state of Colorado. A self-proclaimed recovering lawyer, he was originally appointed to the state's Brand Board, but when it looked like a new Brand Commissioner would be needed he decided to toss his hat into the ring. "In an exercise of poor judgment, I got selected," Whitney jokes. "This was about six and a half years ago."

Whitney grew up on a ranch in Ridgway, Colorado, and ended up practicing law across the country, including in Washington, D.C., before returning to Colorado. He says taking on the job of the state's head brand inspector seemed like a natural fit for him.

"We're an unusual organization. The predecessor to us was formed in the late 1860s by the industry for the industry and that remains the case in this sense: we are 100 percent paid for by the industry though inspection fees and assessments," Whitney says. "We don't get any state money. Although we are a state agency, we are 100 percent paid for by the customer."

This makes for an interesting relationship between the inspectors and the state's ranchers. Given the West's tumultuous cattle-thieving past, the livestock industry is now somewhat eager to be regulated, seeing the value in what the brand inspectors do. "And what we do is protect them from loss," Whitney says. "Our job is to protect the livestock industry from loss by theft or straying or illegal butchering."

As such, everything is carefully monitored. In Colorado, a change of livestock ownership requires an inspection from an inspector, sort of like a car registration when there's a need for a proof of ownership and a chain of title. Inspections also happen if someone travels within the state seventy-five miles with livestock in their trailer, or goes anywhere out of state, even if the state line is fifty feet away.

Whitney tells me this is not meant to be a bureaucratic hassle— it all ties back to ownership. "This is all about: do you have a legal right to have those animals in your possession? That's what it is all about. That is the baseline for what we do," he says. "And what that hopefully does is deter theft, obviously. It gives the market some confidence. If you are a lender and if you've lent against a herd, you'd like to know there's a structure out there that keeps an eye on that herd."

In Colorado, there are 32,700 registered brands. "A livestock brand in Colorado is personal property and is taken very seriously, so it passes by deed," Whitney says. "You have to have a deed to have a Colorado livestock brand. If you want to transfer it, if you want to give it to your wife, there has to be a formal transfer . . . so it is serious business." Oftentimes families inherit a brand from their parents and so on for generations. One lady at the Colorado Department of Agriculture tells me, with something bordering on reverence, how she expects to get her family's brand one day from her own father. Today inspectors keep track of all the brands digitally, but they are also stored in giant, oversized Rolodexes along one wall, a practice that dates to the late 1800s. Each card lists a brand along with the details of its ownership.

Due to the nature of the job, modern-day brand inspectors also act as statutory peace officers. They can make arrests and warranted and warrantless searches. Whitney says, "When a brand inspector wants to make an arrest or calls me and says, 'I think I'd like to make an arrest on something,' I generally ask them to coordinate with local law enforcement. And the reason I do is [because] I want a prosecution to stick. If you're doing something wrong, I don't want to just charge you—I want to convict you."

According to Whitney, one of the major issues for the agency is that as the state becomes ever more urban, there are fewer prosecutors who know livestock or understand it—or are even interested in pursuing a case involving livestock.

"They have heavy dockets, and the way to go up in the prosecutor's office is not to do cattle theft; it is to do a big murder somewhere or whatever," Whitney says. "So sometimes it's hard to get them to pay attention and prosecute a case." Whitney will often ask prosecutors if they're interested in a case involving the theft of $10,000, for which he generally receives an enthusiastic response in the affirmative. He then points out that the theft of seven cattle is easily worth that amount.

Colorado Brand Commissioner Christopher Whitney talks with brand
inspector Terry Florian while cattle are readied for auction.
(Christi Lightcap with the Colorado Department of Agriculture)

"The fact that they're on the hoof doesn't make them less valuable.
They're worth money," Whitney says.

As more people have moved to the city and the ranches are
generally consolidated by larger corporations, the issue of livestock
theft isn't in the forefront of most people's minds. However, the
problem is still very real for those who work in the industry.

Ritual Hanging

When I ask Whitney if cattle rustling still happens in Colorado,
he answers without hesitation. "Absolutely it happens, very much so,"
Whitney said. While the days of hanging a kicking cattle thief to
the nearest tree is a fading memory, stealing cattle is indeed a felony
and can easily land someone in prison. Whitney tells me that a couple
of years ago there were quite a few incidents of calves being stolen
because the market was so good and calves are essentially super
portable. "You can drive up to a fence, and so long as mama doesn't run

you down, you can pick up the calf, throw it in your pickup, and off you go," he says.

Brand inspector Florian estimates the inspectors get two or three cases of cattle rustling a month. Sometimes the missing cow is just a case of one wandering off to a neighbor's herd. If that's the case they'll remove the offending cow from the group and sell it off if the neighbor wants it sold, or send it back home. Often it's just a simple accident, though sometimes it's not. "We have quite a few baby calves stolen here," Florian says. "This is going to be kind of gross, but sometimes calves are stolen and eaten by seasonal workers. They can cook them and eat them in one meal, and they'll sell them too. They're not branded. They're not earmarked. We can see where they've dragged them under the fence. We knew who was doing it. Pretty much the whole time, but we'd find the gut piles and the hides."

Eventually one man responsible went to prison and another was deported. Just like in the 1800s, cattle could be stolen from Colorado and other Western states and shipped elsewhere. Whitney puts it like this: Wyoming, Utah, New Mexico, Arizona—all have excellent livestock enforcement. Some states, however, are not as proficient. If someone were interested in stealing an animal from Colorado, they generally wouldn't travel to one of those states with livestock enforcement programs in place. "You wouldn't go to one of our sale barns because we have brand inspectors at every sale, checking animals in," he reasons. "So you go to a state that doesn't pay quite as much attention."

In the 1800s, Kansas was, and likely still is, one state of particular interest to those looking to transport stolen cattle from Colorado. "So if you're going to steal one, that's where you go," Whitney says. "If you're going to steal one in Colorado, you don't bring it to a sale barn if you know anything about us because you know brand inspectors are there and they're going to look at them all."

The last major Colorado cattle rustling bust occurred in 2012 when a man named Monty Pilgrim was convicted by a jury of stealing cattle from five different ranchers. He was sentenced to ninety days in county jail, community service, repayment of $14,000, and three years of supervised probation. The judge, feeling lenient, said Pilgrim didn't need to go to prison to send a message that stealing cattle was wrong. But sometimes a cattle thief going to prison sends just the right type of message.

"I'm joking when I say this, but...we like at least one ritual hanging a year so that we can get the word out," Whitney says. "So we like to get a prosecutor to nail somebody on a fairly regular basis—otherwise you've got no deterrent, if people think they can just blow it off they will."

Certainly, working as a brand inspector today isn't quite the life-threatening ordeal it was 130 years ago, but that doesn't mean that it is without its risks.

"Well, in this day and age, who knows," Whitney says. "It could be dangerous walking out your front door. We don't overtly get in people's faces, so we're not carrying shotguns and we're not banging on doors; so most of it, I would say, is no more dangerous than most things. Unless you happen to bump into the wrong people, which there is no way to predict."

Whitney adds the brand inspectors generally know most of the people in their industry, so it is only the "bad guys" they have to worry about.

Cattle Brand: An Art Form

Effortlessly directing their horses in and around scared cattle, the pen riders control and organize the cattle being brought in for sale. I mistakenly thought the pen riders would be sunbaked old cowboys, not a group of young women who check their phones while waiting around for the next truckload of cattle to come in. Florian jokes with them, steps aside to let the cattle pass, and notes the brands as they move by. Over the years the job of the brand inspector hasn't changed all that much. The mission is still the same and brands are still used as livestock's return address. The only new development, which just came about recently, is the use of electronic tablets to record data instead of doing it by hand.

"You kinda have to get up with the times," Florian says. "For a long time we had a pager and you had to go buy you a roll of quarters, and if they paged you had to go find a payphone somewhere and call so you knew what was going on."

Brand inspectors can recognize a brand with the naked eye from across a field or a livestock pen. Florian does his best to point out a brand on the hip of a cow. He describes it as an L with a line hanging off the bottom. I nod my head because I believe that the symbol exists—not that I can actually spot it. He takes out a piece of paper and draws it.

I nod again, agreeing that it must exist somewhere on the animal and that maybe I see something that could possibly resemble the location he's pointing to. "See there, now you got yourself a job," he says knowingly to me. He tells me that 99 percent of people just can't identify brands.

"I give them all the credit in the world. It is an art form," Whitney says of those working under him. "If I had to make a living as a brand inspector, I'd be starved to death at the end of a week. They're good and they know what they're doing."

Whitney disregards the idea that radio frequency identification tags will be used on cattle any time soon instead of branding because of the technology's limitations. Cattle simply don't get in a straight line so they can be scanned one by one up close. Additionally, those types of tags move and fall out, and consumers probably wouldn't enjoy the prospect of finding one in their next burger.

In contrast, brands don't go away. Florian says, "The electronic ear tags, if somebody steals something, that's the first thing they take out—the ear tag, if they don't want nobody to know where it came from. If they're smart. Some of them aren't too smart. They stole baby calves from the calf lands out here and forgot to take their ear tags out. So we read the ear tags to see where they came from so we could send them back home."

Florian adds that if the cattle are worth enough, like calves from a dairy farm, ranchers will freeze brand the calves as soon as they are born. "Those little baby heifers a lot of times are worth four or five hundred dollars when they hit the ground, and they were losing them, so they just started popping a little tiny freeze brand on them when they were born— and end of story, they quit stealing them right then," Florian says. "And that's the best deterrent, a mark, something that anybody can see. Even at this point, the guys that are taking stuff are smart enough to know not to take branded stuff."

As for rebranding, it is illegal in the state to own a set of irons that allows doctoring of a brand so that it can be changed. Florian says it's easy to tell the difference and see a doctored brand anyway. "They look different. Most of the time if somebody alters one, there is a difference ... it's not going to look right."

"It's like trying to copy somebody else's signature," Whitney adds. Cattle is one of the state's largest industries and Colorado is the fourth largest exporter of beef in the country. "This is a huge beef-producing state," Whitney says. "So it's a big deal."

When Florian gets a report that someone is missing their cattle, he'll go into the area and start an investigation, looking to see if maybe they strayed off. He guesses a lot of ranchers often do some of their own investigating as well. "But we do what we can, and it helps a lot if they don't wait three months until they call us," Florian says.

But a rancher may not notice their cattle missing for a month because during the summer they often push their cattle onto rangeland maintained by the Bureau of Land Management, and while some have help to look after the herd, many don't and won't realize there's some missing until the fall.

"We work with stockman all the time and say, 'Look, when you see you're missing one, call the inspector and file a report'... because then we're on notice and we circulate that to the sale barns, to the sheriffs, county clerk, and recorder, other brand inspectors. If it is a suspected theft we'll pass it along to all the neighboring brand inspectors in the state; but unless the word gets out quickly, it's pretty tough," Florian says.

When there is an issue of cattle theft, the brand inspectors work with local law enforcement to make the arrest. Inspectors particularly enjoy working with the Colorado State Patrol because often the trooper has received specific training in making those types of arrests. Other law enforcement agencies including some local sheriff departments aren't always the easiest to work with.

"The sheriffs just aren't as willing to stick their neck out to help you like that," Florian says. Luckily, most people he deals with don't pose a threat. "[But] we've had these [people] tell you they're going to come and shoot you," he adds, snorting in derision. "Whatever, that's not going to happen. You just have to be very aware of what you're walking into all the time. You never know."

Situational awareness also applied to being around the animals. As dangerous as humans are, cattle have minds of their own as well. "The worst part of what we do is we spend most of our time with our heads down looking—and that's when you get run over, you got your head down not paying attention," he says. I look at him in surprise and ask if he's been run over by cattle. "Oh yes. More than a few," he laughs. Just another occupational hazard to him.

CHAPTER 6

THE MAN HUNTER

Tearing itself apart like two rabid dogs, in March 1863 the U.S. was entering the second year of its Civil War. The bloodshed was unparalleled in the nation's history—and just getting started. Raids, skirmishes, and battles erupted on land and sea. Earlier that year the Battle of Stones River claimed 23,515 lives; in just a month the Battle of Chancellorsville would take an additional 24,000 lives, and the Battle of Vicksburg for 32,273 more. Later that summer Gettysburg would claim a staggering 51,000 lives. The Battle of Chickamauga would follow with 34,624 killed. That same year, largely lost among the headlines of slaughter and horrific death tolls, the frontier's most prolific serial killers were hard at work in the Colorado territory.

In many respects the frontier didn't have an effective form of law enforcement. U.S. Marshals helped where they could, but the territory was huge, the towns small, and the potential for criminality massive. If they were able to catch a fugitive, vigilantes often saw to it the alleged criminal would never commit an illegal act again, whether they were guilty or not. If a town was able to afford law enforcement, it would hire one man to keep the peace. If the citizenry wanted justice bad enough, the town would come up with the money to hire someone qualified to track down the lawbreaker and bring them back—and sometimes just bringing back their head was good enough.

Fear, Mistrust, and Murder

After not hearing from his father Franklin Bruce for several days, Bruce's son went up to his sawmill close to Cañon City, Colorado, to look for him. He found Bruce face down in a meadow. There is conflicting information about how he was killed, but one historian noted that when Bruce was turned over they discovered he'd been shot in the heart and had "a cross" carved on his chest. Unknown murderers had killed him on March 16, 1863. Fremont County Sheriff Egbert Bradley and a deputy immediately began to search for the killers.

Two days later sixty miles away near Fountain Creek, Murdock McPherson and another man returned from visiting neighbors and were on their way back to their cabin for dinner. Outside the building, they came across the body of McPherson's business partner Henry Harkens. Harkens had been shot in the forehead and stabbed with a knife, and an ax was used to split open his head to his jawline. Both sides of his head were then smashed in so that his brain forcefully exited from his skull.

Sheriff Bradley and his deputy followed the trail of bodies from there to the Ute Pass, until they lost their quarry and reluctantly turned back. They hoped the murders would stop, but it was in vain.

On April 8, Jacob M. Binkley and Abram Nelson Shoup were traveling to Denver from Fairplay when they were ambushed in the night. Binkley was found the next day shot in the back while Shoup was stabbed several times in the chest; then he apparently got up and ran until he fell to the ground dead. Shoup's head was later found severely mutilated.

"Two more murders are added to the already startling list for the last month, and there seems no clue to the perpetrators," the *Rocky Mountain News* reported. "Something must be done, and a terrible example made of some of the miscreants who infest the county."

Fear, mistrust, and horror raced across the state. No one could make out the reasons for the murders or who might be committing them. Newspapers reported on mysterious folk spotted carrying guns and residents shooting at potential attackers. One man was arrested as a suspect; he turned out to be an escaped felon for unrelated crimes and was promptly lynched. Then about two weeks later, another grisly murder: just northwest of Fairplay, a man named Bill Carter was shot and killed near Alma. He was dragged off the road and his head was tomahawked. The beautiful Rocky Mountain spring days took on a sinister overcast as the killings continued with no suspect in sight.

Luck did favor one man to keep his life though. That night of Carter's death, Edward Metcalf was transporting a wagon full of lumber between Alma and Fairplay when he was ambushed at the same location. *The Weekly Commonwealth* reported, "A shot was fired at Mr. Metcalf who was sitting on the wagon, and the ball struck him in the side of the breast." As it happened, Metcalf had a printed copy of President Abraham Lincoln's Emancipation Proclamation in his jacket pocket to read later. It stopped the bullet and saved his life.

The newspaper went on to describe a second bullet: "Another shot was fired at Mr. Metcalf but missed him, the team becoming frightened started at full speed." Hearing the gunfire, a man named Allen grabbed his rifle and came out of a nearby house in time to see Metcalf race past him on the road. The murderers turned and fled but not before being spotted by both Metcalf and Allen. They were lucky. They'd just seen the Espinosa brothers and miraculously lived to tell about it.

Vicious Revenge

Law enforcement resources were limited in the Territory to begin with, but with the country embroiled in a vicious civil war, the land was wide open for people of all forces and intentions to roam. Many crimes may have been committed without the proper attention and resources the law would have given if the authorities weren't so distracted. It was in the long shadows cast by this dark period that seventeen-year-old Jose Vivian Espinosa and thirty-one-year-old Felipe Nerio Espinosa began killing and mutilating settlers. Some of the facts of their story have been unearthed like sun-bleached bones; however, the full extent of their crimes has been largely lost to the chaos of this bloody time. We do know that during their reign of terror, the brothers killed as many as thirty-two people in the Colorado Territory.

The brothers are considered among the first, if not the first, serial killers in the U.S. No one can say with absolute certainty why the

Espinosas killed settlers, but there are clues. For one, Colorado was recently made a territory of the ever-growing United States, and Americans were streaming into a land where Hispanic Americans had lived for generations after coming up into the area from Mexico. There are accounts of how the Espinosa family may have had land taken from them, sheep killed, or relatives assaulted. Still, they were prone to get into trouble and had a dangerous reputation in their community long before they brought it elsewhere.

Likely born in the New Mexico Territory, the Espinosa brothers lived in the San Luis Valley near the small village of San Rafael. Occasionally the brothers stole horses, or in one notable instance they took supplies from a wagon headed to a priest. The story goes they tied the driver to the wagon's tongue and made the horses stampede. The priest apparently saw the driver in his state of extreme distress and was able to come to his rescue. Notified of the incident, officials at Fort Garland sent soldiers out to capture the two brothers. Ultimately, the effort including an ill-conceived ruse ended poorly, with both brothers escaping and killing a soldier in the process. The soldiers ransacked the family's home looking for the stolen items and took pretty much everything that wasn't nailed down, setting fire to the rest. This event likely pushed the brothers into their bloody crusade of revenge. Later documents found showed the Espinosas had directed their vendetta at the seemingly endless stream of Anglo Americans moving into the territory in search of a new future.

The Espinosa brothers moved quickly and quietly, allowing them to escape lawmen like Sheriff Bradley despite their widespread notoriety. They operated like ghosts, impossible to track—until the deaths of Fred Lehman and Sol Seyga. Five miles from Fairplay, just a day after Bill Carter's death and Edward Metcalf's escape, Sol Seyga was found shot and killed while Lehman was hit with a bullet in the wrist. Lehman tried to escape and may have had a brief gunfight with the assassins before ultimately being gunned down. One account says that after the chase ended, his head was smashed in with a rock.

Lehman and Sevga's deaths prompted a civilian posse to be formed and led by John McCannon. At Four Mile Creek McCannon found evidence of camps left by the brothers. This was the first time anyone had come close to tracking the brothers. Not willing to let the opportunity slip through their hands, McCannon asked for volunteers that evening to continue the hunt. Under a full moon, seven members of the posse continued to search for the murderers.

Early the next day they came across the camp they'd searched for and quietly surrounded it. One volunteer named Joseph Lamb raised his rifle and took careful aim to shoot Jose Vivian Espinosa as he was working with his horse. The bullet punched straight through him, knocking him to the ground. Jose lay there, still holding his horse's reins, and still alive. Felipe Espinosa ran from the area and disappeared; he likely would have been shot by the posse if not mistaken for one of its similarly dressed members. Reins gripped in one hand, Jose pulled out his pistol with the other and shot at the posse. One man in the posse put down Jose's horse with a blast from his shotgun. A man named Charles Carter finally shot Jose directly in the face with his rifle, putting an immediate end to the outlaw.

As the posse went through the camp, Felipe suddenly surprised them with gunfire from a ledge. One bullet passed through Joseph Lamb's hat and clothes, miraculously without injuring him. Lamb returned fire with a shotgun, but it was too late. Felipe was gone again.

The May 21, 1863 edition of *The Weekly Commonwealth* newspaper reported: "The annals of crime, in history, furnish no parallel to the diabolical atrocity of these two outlaws, and too much praise cannot be awarded to the citizens of the mountains who have so persistently followed them up and taken so active a part in ridding the Territory of those demon foes to the citizens of the entire country—outlaws whose career of crime will form one of the most terrible epochs in the annals of Colorado, ever."

While maybe not the worst crime committed in the history of Colorado (that dubious distinction is probably awarded to the Sand Creek Massacre where as many as 170 Native Americans were killed without cause by soldiers), the crimes of the Espinosas are indeed up there.

Going through the campsite, the posse discovered a journal with a message from the Espinosas promising to exterminate Anglo Americans, that they had killed many and planned to kill even more. True to his word, Felipe returned home to enlist the help of his nephew Jose Vincente Espinosa, who, depending on the source, was either fourteen or sixteen years old at the time. Together they would carry on the crusade of murder.

They planned to continue their work in the mountains until it got too troublesome to avoid those searching for them, then go onto the plains to kill the settlers in their remote farmhouses.

Months later, Dolores Sanchez and a man by the name of Philbrook were en route to Fort Garland when they were attacked by the Espinosas. One of their oxen was killed but Sanchez and Philbrook ran their wagon until they were overtaken when the other ox was killed. Philbrook ran for his life with the two men close behind. Sanchez spotted two Mexicans standing by on the road and ran to them asking for help. They agreed to hide her, but Felipe had spotted the wagon and asked the Mexicans if they saw either the fleeing man or woman. One of the men, Pedro Garcia, said he had seen a man in the other direction but not the woman, who mistakenly stuck her head out to look and see what was going on. Felipe demanded they hand her over, but the men refused despite the risk of death. Afraid that Pedro would be killed for aiding her, Sanchez gave herself up to the Espinosas, stating they were God-fearing men and wouldn't hurt her. As Pedro Garcia rode away, he pleaded with them not to kill Sanchez. Felipe said if she were found dead, it was because the Espinosas had killed her.

They tied Sanchez up and went in search of Philbrook, who by that time was long gone, almost at Fort Garland. While the Espinosas looked for him, Sanchez untied herself and escaped. Philbrook, once at the fort, relayed their story. Frustrated, the fort's commander Colonel Samuel F. Tappan decided it was time for an immediate and final solution to the Espinosas and sent for Tom Tobin.

Thomas Tate Tobin

The Old West was full of tough men who could prove their value in a fight, but few were quite as qualified to hunt the killers as Tobin. Army scout, tracker, trapper, close friend to frontiersman Kit Carson, and acquaintance to showman Buffalo Bill Cody, Thomas Tate Tobin was clearly the right man for the job. Photos of Tobin from various points in his life show a man who could scare the paint off a barn. Tobin, who lived near Fort Garland, received the summons and

Tom Tobin became one of the West's most notorious bounty hunters when he agreed to track down the Espinosas. *(Public domain)*

arrived in time to hear a report from Sanchez, who eventually reached Fort Garland as well, and how she was assaulted by the Espinosas.

"Col. Tappan then told me he wanted me to go after them," Tobin said in a dictated statement in 1895. "I then told him I would go. He said if I would go capture them and bring their heads to him, he would see I was recompensed for it, for me to be careful and not make a mistake and bring other parties."

The colonel then asked Tobin how many soldiers he wanted to bring with him as his protection. As Tobin pondered the question, Tappan added if he did bring soldiers along it was advised to have an officer come along as well to keep them in check.

"They were all brave fighting men, if they should become dissatisfied, they would be as apt to kill me as Espinosa," Tobin said. He elected to go it alone. However, the colonel convinced him it was necessary for his safety to bring them along before setting out to track the killers down.

On September 7, Tobin headed out with fifteen soldiers and a lieutenant to put an end to the Espinosas once and for all. He also brought along a Mexican boy who kept track of Tobin's horse while he tracked their quarry. As it happened, they almost found the Espinosas that first day out, but ultimately the party lost them over a ridge. The next day Tobin came across the tracks of two oxen, which he was sure would point the way to the killers.

"I got down and examined the trail and found the two assassins were driving them. I tracked them around through the thick groves of pine and quaking asp, soon found they had let [one]...oxen go," Tobin said. "I knew then they had taken the other ox to their camp to butcher him. It was a great trouble to trail them. It was only by the broken twigs that I could follow them by."

James Crank who claimed he was one of the soldiers in Tobin's party revealed in a 1909 interview that the other soldiers in the party might also have been an issue. "Our boys had little faith in Tobin and his well-faded cow tracks as the sailors of Columbus had on that dismal voyage across the Atlantic Ocean four hundred years ago," Crank said. Regardless, Tobin forged on and planned to go ahead into an area where horses could not follow. Just a handful of men and the Mexican boy continued onward with the tracker, leaving the rest of the soldiers behind.

"Many places I would crawl under the fallen timber to keep the direction they were driving the ox, till I got out of the timber into a clear place where I could see their tracks again," Tobin said. Crank added the going was rigorous as they obeyed Tobin's instructions, making their way further into the dense foliage.

"On the little party went in a half bent position until they received a signal from Tobin that brought them to their knees," Crank said. "Having made considerable distance on their hands and knees they were signaled by Tobin to keep their lowest, which meant to slide along on their stomachs. After this Tobin had them keep low and remain perfectly quiet." Crank noted that Tobin took an extra cap for his rifle, placed it in one corner of his mouth, then poured out an extra charge of powder and made ready for the work at hand. Tobin spotted crows in the sky and told the soldiers he believed the Espinosas had killed the ox. One hundred yards farther and he saw magpies flying, which he watched until they identified the location of the camp to him. He told the soldiers not to fire until he gave them permission. They crept ever nearer until they spotted Felipe by a campfire.

"I took a step or two in front and saw the head of one of the assassins," Tobin said. "At this time I stepped on a stick and broke it, he heard it crack, he looked and saw me, he jumped and grabbed his gun. Before he turned around fairly I fired and hit him in the side; he bellowed like a bull and cried out, 'Jesus favor me.'" Felipe had been hit with a massive .54 caliber ball from a Hawken rifle, legendary in the West for being able to take down large game. Tobin told his party to get ready because if there were more in the camp they would soon show up.

"I tipped my powder horn in my rifle, dropped a bullet from my mouth into the muzzle of my gun while I was capping it," he said of the process to reload his single-shot rifle. The young Jose Espinosa soon appeared out of the bush and Tobin told the men to fire at him. All three men missed.

"I drew my gun up and fired at first sight and broke his back above his hips," Tobin said. "[Meanwhile, Felipe] Espinosa had started to crawl away. He did not go very far. He braced himself up [on] ... some fallen trees, with pistol in hand waving it over his face, using a word in Mexican that means *base brutes*. I had run down to where he was; I spoke to him and asked him if he knew me. I told him who I was; his reply was *base brutes*."

A soldier approached Felipe. Tobin warned him the outlaw was still quite dangerous, and almost on cue Felipe aimed and fired at the man, just missing.

"I then caught him by the hair, drew his head back over a fallen tree and cut it off. I sent the Mexican boy to cut off the head of the other fellow [Jose Espinosa]; he cut it off and brought it to me ... I rode up in front of the Commanding Officer's quarters and called for Col. Tappan. I rolled the assassins heads out of the sack at Col. Tappan's feet. I said, 'Here Col., I have accomplished what you wished. This head is Espinosa's. This other is his companion's head and there is no mistake made.'"

The commander then told Tobin he was aware of an award for the killers of $2,500. It took years for Tobin to see any of that money. Under one governor Tobin received $500 and under another $1,000, but he never received the entire amount owed to him.

"I did not know anything about a reward when I started but I only thought it the duty of all citizens to rid this country of all such characters as quick as possible," Tobin said.

While not the only bounty hunter in the history of the West, Tom Tobin did become one of the most famous for his successful, and expedient, tracking and killing of the Espinosas. With the murderers now dead, it plainly demonstrated that justice in the territory could be enforced, not only by officers of the law or soldiers, but by the citizens who lived and toiled within its borders. It also showed that sometimes the right person could successfully do what the law could not.

CHAPTER 7

THE TALE OF TWO
BOUNTY
HUNTERS

In the late 1990s, I briefly attended a reserve police academy class in Albuquerque, New Mexico. At the time, I was still in the military watching airplanes bake in the desert sun on an Air Force flight line, unsure of what I was going to do once I got out and walked the streets as a civilian again. For a brief moment the call of going into law enforcement blipped distantly on my radar before the siren song of becoming a college student and later an underpaid newspaper reporter won out. Reserve officers are usually unpaid law enforcement officers called to assist the regular cops during holidays, special events, or when a shift is undermanned, and for a moment I thought the training could help inform my decision.

While I wasn't able to attend the entire academy course because of my unpredictable military work schedule, I did take several classes taught by veteran patrol officers. I soon found they had a sense of humor darker than the interior of a black hole. Once before class, several officers chatted with the students about the decapitation of the top of a man's head during a traffic accident the night before. The body part landed upright in the bed of the pickup truck the man was operating. Wiping away a single tear of mirth, one cop added that the horrific injury was so clean, it looked just like the driver had cut a hole in the bottom of the vehicle and was playing peekaboo with the officers.

Violence and shootings in Albuquerque were common. In a bit of random violence, a woman in her car was shot in front of me in traffic one evening while I was on my way to a video rental store. I knew friends who were shot at while on duty manning the gates of Kirtland Air Force Base. It wasn't uncommon for people to come running out of the dark and seek shelter on the military base from some crime they'd accidentally witnessed, such as a man being stuffed into the trunk of a car.

I remember one police officer thinking about how to explain the job to the class full of students when finally he shook his head in bewilderment and said, "It really is the Wild West out there."

And in some respects, it still is. The sun-blasted desert communities can boil to levels of lawlessness often not encountered elsewhere. In 2016, New Mexico had the highest rate of property crime in the country and was only second to Alaska for its number of violent crimes—including murder. It's no wonder then that bounty hunters roam the state still to this day.

Thrill of the Chase

Sporting a cowboy hat and white goatee, unless in disguise, Clint Simmons looks like the kind of man who hunts others for a living. Resembling Robert Duvall's character Captain Augustus "Gus" McCrae in the iconic television Western *Lonesome Dove*, perhaps it is not a surprise that Simmons also has traces of the classic Western accent no longer prevalent in many Colorado communities. He was recently in New Mexico hunting fugitives when he was spotted and recognized— and things went downhill from there.

"We were posted up outside his house and I'm sure the guy saw me," Simmons recounts. Sure enough, the fugitive ran from the residence, clambered onto a high-end motorcycle, and took off. The two men briefly made eye contact and Simmons gave chase. His quarry raced along a road that Simmons personally knew was a dead-end from scouting out the area the day before. Simmons followed, angled his vehicle sideways to block the exit, and snatched up his shotgun loaded with bean bag rounds. Once the man on the run found the dead-end, he twisted the motorcycle around and thundered down the little street toward where Simmons was

Bounty hunter Clint Simmons has successfully hunted down fugitives in the West for more than a decade. *(Courtesy of Clint Simmons)*

standing. Before Simmons knew it, the man was practically on top of him. Using the barrel of the shotgun like a spear, Simmons jammed the rider in the chest, knocking him and his bike over.

"This guy then bolted up like a bullet and started running away," Simmons says to me. Then after a moment he adds, "I won't shoot someone who is running away, just can't do it." There's a code for people in his profession, even if it often fluctuates from person to person. It turns out Simmons's son who was working with him and not far behind tackled the man to the ground. As they struggled in the dirt, the man tried as hard as he could to get out a knife.

"We thought he had a gun to start with, but he didn't have the gun—just a whole bunch of knives," Simmons says. "Before we got the man handcuffed, the neighbors saw the whole thing go down and called 911." By the time the scene was under control the police had arrived. Simmons adds, "Occasionally we get surrounded by law enforcement . . . we go by the book always just to stay out of jail."

The day's events were just Simmons's most recent fugitive recovery operation in a long line dating back almost ten years. Arguably one of the best bounty hunters the West has to offer, Clint Simmons has captured "hundreds" of fugitives. At nearly sixty years old, he has no plans to stop.

Simmons hails from a ranch near the town of Cortez, located on the southwestern side of the state where he grew up in the 1960s doing what he calls "cowboy things." One summer his father brought back with him a ranch hand and Vietnam veteran named Bob who had a colorful war record. Simmons reflects, "I didn't realize what a recon commando was until later in life." His father then assigned Simmons and his brother to work with the veteran over what felt like the longest six months of his life.

"Bob was fresh out of Cambodia and he was a sketchy fellow— but he was into physical fitness and teaching that you had to take care of yourself," Simmons recalls. "We were right at that age where we were pretty much smartass little boys and we got a brand-new understanding from Bob." But the experience with the veteran left a positive impression on him for life. Simmons grew up, got married, had children, and eventually became a finish carpenter. Whether it was his Western heritage or the powerful influence of the Vietnam veteran, Simmons did the occasional bounty-hunting work on the side.

About ten years ago, his carpentry work slowed and came to a shuddering stop. At the same time, his father passed away. It was one of those moments where everything in his life was called into question and Simmons knew it was time for a change. His cousin had long worked as a bail bondsman and Simmons decided to learn the ropes from him. He got a few projects here and there and impressed others with his ability to track people down. As a result, the work he got in the business grew, and Simmons picked up more contracts from other bail bondsmen.

"Then I got my bail bonding license. You have to become a really good bounty hunter when you make bad bail decisions," Simmons jokes. Going from carpenter to one of the busiest bounty hunters in the state was not what he would call a difficult transition.

"It was like flipping a switch," he says.

Sly Bastard

There aren't many people who take on bounty hunting because of its rather unique, and often dangerous, reputation, but Simmons is not alone in pursuing his chosen career field.

Across the windy lot of the Colorado Springs strip mall, I follow thirty-eight-year-old Dustin Schindler to his red sedan. Leaning forward and squinting into the gale, I could just make out his black baseball hat, reddish brown beard, black shirt, khaki pants, and the badge clipped to his belt next to the Glock 19, a 9mm pistol. At a distance he reads like law enforcement—but he's not. There's a tattoo stenciled on the inside of each forearm of his family's last names. A Punisher metal pin, inspired by the vigilante comic book character, attaches to his hat brim. And if you look closely, the small letters on the badge reads FUGITIVE RECOVERY. He speaks fast, has a healthy regard for swearing, and is always laughing. Schindler carries a nervous, infectious energy I've never noticed in a police officer before—he's less German Shepard and more coyote. Unlike Simmons, Schindler's relatively new to the bounty hunting world, having only done the job for three years, but in that time he tracked down or helped apprehend nearly sixty people.

We reach his car as another gust of cold wind batters away at us. Schindler pops the trunk on his vehicle and opens it for me to see inside. Not recognizing what to look at, I take a step back, then forward again. Inside lies a police-like utility belt with a .45 caliber Kimber 1911 holstered in it, a stun gun, a boot pistol, an AR-15, a tactical shotgun, and a high-end digital camera. These are the tools of a bounty hunter—or, as Schindler prefers, "fugitive recovery" or "bail enforcement agent."

"You've got to be a little bit of a sly bastard in this industry," Schindler tells me. "That's where we separate ourselves from law enforcement . . . We use all sorts of dirty tricks in the book. We don't really care."

For a man with a trunk full of guns, Dustin Schindler is in great spirits. It is, after all, his birthday. Squeezed into a tight booth along the wall of a Panera Bread, Schindler tells me about the art of hunting humans as soccer moms, children, and business people wait in a long line next to our table.

"This industry is one of those where you can make a lot of money if you apply yourself—but you can also burn a lot of money," Schindler says. He doesn't get paid until the job is done, and often he ends up spending a lot of his money trying to track someone down. His gear and the small armory in his trunk were all paid for out of his own pocket.

"Our bulletproof vests, our plate vests, our guns—any of the equipment you need," he says, adding that literally all the money he makes goes back into his business, leaving him with virtually nothing.

"So it is not one of those things where you're going to become a millionaire," he admits. For Schindler, being a fugitive recovery agent is expensive, stressful, thankless, and without a doubt dangerous. He adds that unlike in the days of the Old West, people in his profession are often looked down on, especially by local law enforcement.

"So why do it?" I ask. Schindler shrugs. His path to bounty hunting came not from glory but from opportunity.

Schindler was born and raised in the city of Ferndale, Washington, a town with a population of about eleven thousand people. After finishing high school in 1998 and entering the Marines, he graduated basic training and the school of infantry training before being discharged for having knee issues.

"Got all the way to my unit and we're on a movement, and [it] just tore [my knee] apart," Schindler says. "And they're like, 'Okay, you're done.'" It was a serious blow, and without direction or prospects, he spent almost two years living out of his car.

"At eighteen your life is squashed in one little hit," Schindler says. "I slowly started putting myself together, and in May of 2001 I joined the National Guard." Then September 11 happened and everything changed. He went from not doing much to multiple deployments and a tour in Iraq in 2004. When he returned to the states, he and several of his military buddies discussed what they wanted to do once they got out. Several of his friends brainstormed about the possibility of becoming bounty hunters or bail enforcement agents. With the realities of needing to draw a paycheck, he soon abandoned that idea and ended up in a Washington factory making toilet paper before it eventually went out of business.

"The recession kind of really hit our area," Schindler says. He held a host of odd jobs just to get by, including security and maintenance. Finally, he took the classes to become a bounty hunter, something he kept thinking about over the years. In short order, he earned his fugitive recovery credentials and began work for a bail bonds company. In Washington the fugitive recovery industry is restricted and requires would-be bounty hunters to take classes on using pepper spray, handcuffing, and search and secure procedures, and to pass a background check. When Schindler followed his wife to Colorado Springs for a job opportunity, he found there were almost no restrictions in the state on those working in the industry. One only needed to be eighteen years old with no felony convictions.

"Anyone who doesn't have a felony can now become a fugitive recovery agent," Schindler tells me in disbelief. He adds that a license or any training isn't required in Colorado. Colorado is just one of eighteen states where would-be bounty hunters can get into the business regardless of training or education. "I was kind of shocked to hear this. What do you mean I don't need a license?" he says. "Well, that's kind of weird, you know?"

Sometimes, of course, the best training is the kind earned over the years, while on the job.

Tricks of the Trade

Meanwhile, across the hard-baked landscape of yucca and sagebrush-covered mesas of southeastern Colorado, Clint Simmons has already built a small empire tracking down fugitives. It's an area as well known for its Ponderosa pine–shrouded ancestral Puebloan ruins as it is for its growing crime rate. A local sheriff recently admitted in a newspaper that he didn't have the amount of manpower to deal with it. This is a tough land. In this environment Simmons grew busy, capturing what he describes as "hundreds" of fugitives over the years. Occasionally he would get several fugitives hiding out within three to four miles of each other.

"One day you just go and do a roundup," Simmons says to me. "Nobody wants to go back to jail. That's why they didn't go to court. Once they know they're going back to jail because they know they didn't go to court, it changes the way the animal acts." People become desperate and, not surprisingly, violent to avoid the steeper penalties associated with skipping bail.

Bounty hunters have always held a mystery of hardness and intrigue, and his exploits in the Southwest eventually drew the attention of reality television producers. Simmons was featured on two seasons of *Rocky Mountain Bounty Hunters* for the Animal Planet. One episode showed a fugitive trying to escape on a bicycle when Simmons comes around the corner of a building and wraps his arm around the man's neck before pulling him violently to the ground, where the man is then handcuffed. The show got canceled in 2015, which is just as well for Simmons who personally feels it was comprised too much of what producers back East thought they wanted to see and not enough of what actually went on in the bail recovery industry.

Simmons's television celebrity turned out to have its drawbacks in his professional life. On one occasion Simmons was in Billings, Montana, to take a man into custody when he was recognized. "I knocked on the door and the lady told me, 'Oh my God, Clint, you're on television. Come in here.' I was like, 'Wow, it seems like my cover has been blown,'" Simmons remembers.

Still, Simmons continued the work forging ahead past his television celebrity status. Five of his family members are now in the business and his son works as their primary recovery agent.

"It's very cool because he and I travel a lot together," Simmons says, adding they often act as each other's backup. "The first year my son started for us there were times when he was getting two or three fugitives a day. Yeah, he learned real well, he's slick."

Simmons had started one bail bonds business, which then expanded to five. For each business offering bail to someone who has tripped up on the long arm of the law, there is always a host of clients not interested in returning to court. As such, they need to be tracked down and made accountable. That's the part Simmons likes best.

Simmons can go in disguise when needed. Sometimes this includes dressing up as an old cowboy, a biker, or even a tourist. Dressing one way when he bonds people out of jail and then dressing another when he hunts them down is all part of the game. "It amazes me how a subtle change will completely lose you to someone. It's not as far as a fake mustache—it's a change of hat, a change of shirt, sunglasses, clear glasses," he says.

After almost a decade in a business, where most find it impossible to last more than a few years, Simmons can almost immediately recognize the people who will pose the biggest problems. Someone who is nice and seems upstanding and well meaning can easily be a chronic liar and a professional manipulator.

Simmons calls bounty hunting a crazy business. He and other successful bounty hunters must be one step ahead of a fugitive and there's a host of tools they can use to get that done. Simmons says his favorite tool is simply going to a fugitive's ex-girlfriend or ex-boyfriend to get information on where they might want to hide out. It works extremely well because their angry exes are usually delighted to rat them out to bounty hunters. He adds his children are also good at using social media to track people down. Even when on the run from the police, it seems people are still interested in updating their social media accounts to their detriment.

In the decade of looking for people who don't want to be found, Simmons says there were only two fugitives that he ultimately couldn't bring in—and one of them is dead. The other fled to Mexico, but it turned out the original arresting officer was making "bad arrests" so the charges were dropped anyway.

"No one has been able to get ahold of him in Mexico to tell him that his case has been dropped, so he's hiding out in Mexico not knowing," Simmons says. As for his current cases? "We've got ten or fifteen people out right now that we're actively searching for—but they will be caught."

The First Bounty

Success in this "crazy business" isn't easy. Dustin Schindler had to sell himself and his qualifications to the various bail bondsmen he came across in Colorado to get work. He got his first chance to find a fugitive in Colorado by tracking down a woman who skipped bail. The job the bondsman gave him was a test. If he did well, he'd get more jobs; if he couldn't find her, he'd be back to square one. Her name was Britney, someone he described as having a serious heroin addiction.

"The ones that aren't going to be easy honestly are our drug addicts . . . they don't stay in one spot," Schindler says. "They couch surf, they don't stay in one area, they don't stay with one set of friends."

Britney was in trouble with the law after driving under the influence. Schindler takes her arrest warrant and custody report out of a briefcase and slides it across the table to me. There's a black-and-white photo of the young woman, her booking number, and a signed release from the bondsman. Britney looks like someone's sister, a college student, or maybe your friendly neighborhood coffee barista—but she didn't look like the type of person to be hunted by bounty hunters.

Schindler points to some forms. "This is called a notice of forfeiture—this and the signed release from the bondsman really give us our power," he says. "This is where our power comes from. This is a release from the bondsman authorizing me to investigate, follow, apprehend, and transport the fugitive to the required facility."

Britney bonded out of jail for $10,000 and never showed up again in court. The bondsman was now on the hook to have her brought back to court within ninety days or else he'd be out the $10,000.

"You have a deadline. You always have a deadline, there's never a time when we go on a hunt where you're not thinking about a deadline or time," Schindler says. If the fugitive isn't returned in ninety days, then the bondsman must pay the court the money and then would have a year to bring the person in to get the money back. If the fugitive is brought in by a police officer or turns themselves in, the money paid to the court becomes forfeit.

"So at that point even though we've got a year, it's a very long year of pins and needles and you better be every second looking and trying to be ahead of the cops," Schindler says. "Because, no offense, we love the police, but at the same time they are a hindrance to our business. Because if they get them, I don't get paid."

He tells me that it took quite some time to track Britney down. One day he was driving around El Paso County on another case when he got a call from the owner of a storage unit who said she accidentally woke up Britney and her boyfriend. They had been sleeping in their car in one of the storage units. Now Schindler knew where to find her. All he had to do was bring her into custody.

"It was intense, to be honest with you," Schindler recalls. "When I got the phone call, you get excited, you know. Come on, this is your first chance to prove yourself in this state and you don't want to blow it, you don't want to screw it up or cause a liability."

He and his partner at the time hurried to the storage unit. They knew Britney's boyfriend was a former sheriff's deputy and was likely to own a firearm.

"We came guns drawn. We blocked both ends of the storage unit with vehicles," Schindler says. "She had locked herself in her boyfriend's truck. He was actually outside working on his trailer, he wasn't even in the vehicle." While Schindler kept an eye on the boyfriend, his partner told her she needed to unlock the truck and turn herself over to them.

"She didn't want to comply to the point where my partner actually had to bring out an ASP [baton] and tell her, 'You either comply or we're breaking the window,'" he says. "She actually, at that point, became very cooperative. We nicely put her in the back of one of our vehicles, and we took her to jail. That was it, said and done."

There is a fine line in the fugitive recovery business between doing something lawful and getting into a world of trouble. Schindler knew how important it was to be careful. "I always tell people this is not an industry for little boys. It is an industry for men, and if you don't understand how to be a professional, don't get involved—go ahead and do something else."

The people Schindler tries to find don't want to be found and will do what they can to keep from being returned to jail. Sometimes it gets violent. "He was hiding supposedly with a firearm," Schindler says of one man he had been looking for. "He refused commands to come out of the closet. My partner ended up tasing him."

Tasers are stun guns that send electrical pulses that shock a person's control of their muscles. They generally don't cause permanent damage but do manage to temporarily incapacitate a person's mobility—unless the voltage of the gun isn't high enough. The last thing Schindler expected after five long seconds of voltage running through the man was for the man to bounce right back up again, ready to fight.

"It literally, between me and him, became a boxing match. We were trading blows," Schindler says, not relishing the retelling of the story. "He wanted to fight, he wasn't going to go to jail, he was going to fight. And at that point I'm more than willing to oblige."

Finally the two tackled the man, got his arms behind his back, and handcuffed him. Schindler reveals that there is nothing worse in the book for people in his profession than hurting a fugitive. He and others are careful in only raising the level of force to meet the one they're experiencing. Plus, Schindler always remembers he has a wife and a child waiting at home.

"If I come home and it looks like I got my ass kicked, my wife knows why," Schindler says. "She might be curious. 'What happened this time?' I might tell her the story, 'Oh God, this freakin' moron was up on the roof and crashed through,' or 'We were in a foot chase and I hit my head on a freakin' fence pole,' because that kind of shit happens... it's part of the job. And she understands."

He's only been doing the work for a short time, but already he understands the challenges. Pulling a decent salary is one thing, but being able to track down fugitives running from justice is wildly different.

"There is an adrenaline rush and that is some of the drive. I wouldn't lie to you... [you get excited] because you know you're getting close and you know you're about to kick in a door and probably arrest a guy who has eluded cops," Schindler says. "You're proving yourself [that] you're hunting one of the most difficult creatures on planet Earth."

Schindler says he comes from a hunting family and it's an even more exhilarating experience hunting down and capturing another human to bring back to jail.

"I'm hunting a creature that no one gets to hunt," Schindler says. "There's only a few legal ways that you can get to do that." That said, Schindler admits he isn't sure if he would stay in the business for too many more years. Steady jobs can sometimes be hard to find, not to mention pay only comes in after the fugitive is found and finally returned to jail. For anyone raising a family, bounty hunting has its time limit.

Ain't for Everybody

The toiling nature of the business is why there are not many people like Clint Simmons who have been in it for as long as he has. Those who do it often just can't sustain the work for long.

What helps is lessening the danger if possible. Simmons and his employees make use of nonlethal force such as bean bag rounds to help subdue violent and noncompliant fugitives. Over the years they've learned the best way to avoid getting into a violent altercation with a fugitive is to employ the same tactics as Special Forces.

"Get in tight before anyone knows you're there and that works real good. Don't give them anytime," he tells me.

Nonlethal weapons are useful, but sometimes his people also carry concealed firearms, which have been drawn in emergencies. Not everything works the way it should and even a well-planned recovery can go, as he says, "straight to hell."

"Perfect plans, they become uncontrolled, and yes, it does happen. There's times when it is sketchy. Always say your prayers before you go," Simmons says. "This job ain't for everybody." Despite the risk, Simmons has no plans to stop working in the fugitive recovery industry. He is having the best time of his life.

"I crave it, I enjoy it, I like the travel, the adrenaline—I don't have as much wind as I used to have, but I've got younger people for that," he says.

Simmons adds he used to enjoy hunting deer and elk and honestly believed that hunting animals was the ultimate sport to partake in. Since his quarry is now human, he has come to find his interests have changed.

"If you've hunted a man, you're kind of bored with everything else," he says. "I don't have to wait until fall. I'm always out there trying to outsmart somebody who thinks they're smarter. And it is good for the mind, good for the heart." When speaking with Simmons, it's easy to see why the character of the Wild West still endures in some. There's a respect for a person's rugged individualism, self sufficiency, and recognition of the value of testing oneself to the limits—and not finding it wanting.

While some states do not allow bounty hunters or have made them irrelevant, Simmons doesn't believe that will ever be the case in the West. "It's the Wild West out there still," Simmons says. After a second, he adds that his job isn't just about catching the bad guys but also about making a positive difference.

"A lot of the people that I have arrested have become very good clients, don't ever run away again, take care of their business; some of them lose their addictions. We see success in some people sometimes," Simmons says. "We're constantly on the search for the bad guy but there are times when you see the good come out. I guess that's your reward—that and money."

In the hard-packed land of southwestern Colorado and northern New Mexico, where the farms and ranches are often distinguished by brush and barbed wire, Simmons is out there ever searching, looking for the next name on his list.

CHAPTER 8
WEATHER,
THE
"IRRESISTIBLE
VIOLENCE"

The West held many dangers for those not well educated to its many, often mercurial temperaments. The fact is, survival on the frontier for the explorers and settlers was brutal and uncompromising. Literally everything, from the harsh environment to the poisonous plant life to the ferocious wild animals, could easily oblige a newcomer with a quick and hasty departure from the world of the living. Water was scarce and unreliable, and death by starvation lurked as a real possibility. But of all the dangers of the West, the most lethal and unpredictable was the very weather itself.

One man to come up against the most extreme forces of nature and lived to tell the tale is explorer, mountain man, trapper, scout, and former slave James P. Beckwourth. Beckwourth had left home in St. Louis in 1816 at the young age of nineteen and went west toward the Rocky Mountains and Great Plains region. He lived with the Crow Nation for many years as a liaison with a fur-trapping company; he also claimed at one point to have been a chief of the Crow Nation. Around 1830 he was on his way to a Cheyenne village (what would later become Fort Laramie in Wyoming) with a party of Crow when the weather soon became lethal.

That first night Beckwourth and the Crow camped on the Sweet Water River. The next morning was "clear and cold," he told his biographer in the grandly titled book *The Life and Adventures of James P. Beckwourth, Mountaineer, Scout, Pioneer, and Chief of the Crow Nation of Indians*. His party wanted to make their way across a twenty-mile stretch of prairie to a mountain on the other side—a featureless stretch of ground without much in the way of trees or bushes. They hoped the other side offered desperately needed firewood and shelter to combat the extreme cold.

But the going was much rougher than expected. Beckwourth said, "When we had traversed this desert about midway, a storm came on, which is called by the mountaineers a Poo-der-ee. These storms have proved fatal to great numbers of trappers and Indians in and about the Rocky Mountains. They are composed of a violent descent of snow, hail, and rain attended with high and piercing wind, and frequently last three or four days."

The storm was so strong that the group couldn't see which way they needed to go to leave the desolate stretch of prairie. They became soaked from the ceaseless torrents of rain and hail and their wet clothing soon froze solid due to the plummeting temperatures.

"Still we kept moving, as we knew it would be certain death to pause on our weary course," Beckwourth said. "The winds swept with irresistible violence across the desert prairie, and we could see no shelter to protect us from the freezing blast."

Beckwourth and the others then came across a gully, which they crawled down in order to escape the weather. It kept them out of the wind but didn't do much to protect them from the snow and falling temperature. After some time he tried to move and found it required all his strength to free himself from the mass of snow that had accumulated on top of him. The weather was only getting worse; if they stayed, they would certainly die. He began searching around the gully for anything that could help them. Then about three hundred yards away he came across a gulch filled with driftwood. He made an opening in it and crawled inside the pile, then started a fire. Returning to his party, Beckwourth woke them and led the group back to huddle around the growing fire, hoping the warmth would be enough to keep them alive. Soon they discovered that two of their party hadn't joined them.

"I returned with two or three others to search for them, and we had to dig away the snow to arrive at them; but the vital spark had fled—

they were stiff in death," Beckwourth said. Beckwourth and the others stayed by that fire for the next two days before the storm finally moved on.

"It was a time of intense cold," Beckwourth said. "Our whole party were more or less frostbitten; my face and ears were severely frozen, and were sore for a long time."

Stories like Beckwourth's were not uncommon. Knowing how to survive what the West throws at you is half the battle. Where to find food, where to get shelter, and how to live in an environment that is notoriously unsympathetic was essential for those living in the time before indoor heating and drive-thru fast food.

It's probably not a difficult argument to make that modern-day Western residents have strayed somewhat from their hard-bitten predecessors. Frankly, it would be surprising if one in a hundred people randomly selected off the streets of Denver could make a fire with primitive tools—not to mention in the middle of a blizzard, in the dark, while battling severe frostbite like James Beckwourth. To find someone with that type of skillset, you'd have to look south of Denver and west of Colorado Springs to a remote stretch of forest outside of the historic mining town of Cripple Creek.

Mountain Man

Jason Marsteiner is in his mid-forties, lean, with a brown beard, wearing a flannel shirt and a well-worn baseball cap. He is the kind of storyteller created from many long nights sitting with one side to a campfire and the other to the dark. According to Marsteiner, about half of his clients at the Colorado Mountain Man Survival School tend to be ex-military, with a quarter of the remaining people from either the financial industry or the medical field. He has even trained a group of rocket scientists from California who had zero experience in the outdoors.

"I find it unnerving, a little, that I've had so many people from the financial industry: investors and bankers. So do they see some writing on the wall?" Marsteiner jokes.

The primary wilderness area used for his school was originally bought by his parents in the early 1980s, and he has since turned it into an outdoor campus where students can learn a host of survival skills.

When he was a child his parents, both Air Force veterans, moved to the remote spot near Cripple Creek, where they parked a small trailer and planned to live off the land—though he hesitates to call them "survivalists."

"I think the real term for it was: we were broke," Marsteiner says bluntly. Up until that time he and his sister had grown up in the city, so it was a unique difficulty in their new home to do simple things like take a bath when they didn't have running water. Instead the family stored water from friends who lived in town or went to a natural spring about four miles away that ran all year round and was used by the other mountain residents.

"So bathing was kind of inconvenient, I suppose," Marsteiner says. "We had a wood-burning stove inside the trailer and we would just boil water on that stove to bathe. And really, we used a wood-burning stove to bathe, to cook everything, and if you took water out of the stream you had to boil it to purify it—you couldn't just drink water out of a stream."

He adds that because the area was well known for its historic and modern-day gold mining operations, the heavy metal content of the local water source on their property was by default a little suspect.

"It was different. Most people were used to the showers and having running water. We just had to learn to improvise," Marsteiner says to me. "As a kid when your parents tell you that you don't have to bathe every day, you're like, 'Woohoo, sweet.'"

He tells me that a later legal issue with the large gold mine made it so the family had a difficult time accessing their property. They lived in town while they fought the issue in court, but even then they often received strange looks from their neighbors, from people at a liquor store and a Volkswagen repair shop, all because of a massive garden they owned and maintained.

"We had a huge garden that was the size of the parking lot of those two businesses," Marsteiner says. "So we grew most of our food, and we hunted. Even though we lived in the city, we went up to the mountains to go hunt. When we went to the store we only got bread and milk."

Even though they lived in town, the family burned wood for heat in the winter and raised chickens. Eventually the issue with the local mine was resolved and they could access their property again, but by then the plan to live there had mostly fallen by the wayside. Marsteiner says when he was growing up in the small town most of the other kids were into sports, but

Outdoor survival school instructor Jason Marsteiner
gives instruction to one of his classes. *(Photo by Ian Neligh)*

because he had a slight frame he had to focus his energy elsewhere and
spent his extra time in nature.

"On the weekends when everybody else was out playing sports,
I threw on my backpack and packed a little survival kit and some food and I
would go adventuring," Marsteiner says. "So that was my pastime. I would
just tell my parents, 'I'm going that way, going up that mountain... and
I'll either be home tonight or tomorrow,' and back then parents either didn't
worry as much or worry quite as much as I do now with my kid."

He would spend his time hiking, camping, and hunting for food
when necessary. There was always an inherent risk of going outdoors
especially with bears and mountain lions around, but he wasn't
overly concerned.

"There's danger involved. There's danger involved even now, being
an adult going out with Colorado's weather and how it can change,"
Marsteiner points out. "You get up in the morning and [it can] be sunny,
seventy to eighty degrees, and by midafternoon we've got a blizzard.
There's always that potential."

He learned to keep an eye on the weather, watch the clouds, and read the sky the way most people read a map. As an instructor he can tell his students when they need to get firewood ready and prepare for a serious storm. He believes weather almost always presents one of the most serious dangers.

"You can die in three hours from exposure," Marsteiner says. "Compare that to starvation. If you do not have food, you've got three weeks. You are not just going to fall over dead overnight because you're hungry—but if you're caught in a bad storm, you've got hours to live if it's bad enough. And it is really one of the leading killers of man when it comes to the outdoors."

In my time as a reporter for Colorado newspapers, I can attest to this. No matter the time of year I found myself always writing articles about hikers who bit off more than they could chew. A simple afternoon hike at an easy fourteener like Mount Bierstadt could turn into a life-or-death struggle. Even during the summer the nonprofit Alpine Rescue Team constantly responds to requests for help in finding lost, injured, or dead hikers. In his classes Marsteiner stresses the importance of finding and building shelter and learning to create a fire.

"Most people who go camping have a tent and a BIC lighter—both those items could fail very easily and people don't really realize it," he says. "When you know there are those inherent risks, I suppose you become more aware of your surroundings."

Even as a child Marsteiner was aware of his surroundings, walking quietly and listening to the woods around him. During the time of the Old West people traveling through the wilderness had to worry not only about the weather, predators, and environment but also about other people. Marsteiner tells me that anyone traveling through the wilderness in the area he grew up in might actually come across people hiding in the woods.

"You have to be careful about stumbling upon meth labs—you come across people like that and nothing good is going to happen," Marsteiner advises from personal experience. He had come across old meth labs and "weird little trailers" hidden in the middle of nowhere before.

When he was nineteen years old, he experienced his first legitimately dangerous situation caused by Colorado's weather.

After hiking for several days with a group of friends, Marsteiner was pretty far from civilization when a spring storm crept up on them.

"It started out a nice, sunny day and I had a raging headache—I get migraines, throwing up and the whole works—so I really wasn't paying too much attention," Marsteiner says. "I was just kind of trudging along with my heavy backpack and my three friends, and about two in the afternoon this freak snowstorm rolled in on us."

They decided to play it safe and hunker down until the worst of the storm was gone. However, the winds were so strong they couldn't put up their tents without them being blown away. The group sat in a circle with their backpacks behind them and dragged a tarp over their heads, tucking it in under them to make a small dome. They lit a small can of Sterno, huddled around the small flame, and waited through the worst of the storm. Six hours later when it was finally over, there was five feet of snow on the ground.

"We just sat there and rode out that storm, and I think that anybody who had not grown up in that situation probably would have perished," Marsteiner says. "But for us it was kind of fun, I suppose . . . that kind of stuff seemed to happen, not often, but when it did happen it was like no big deal. You just learn to hunker down and to stay put and to use your skills to make things better."

In those types of situations people tend to panic and stop thinking clearly—which makes a bad situation worse. Marsteiner also thinks that many tourists who come to Colorado to adventure often just don't know what they're doing.

"A lot of people plan for the best-case scenario," Marsteiner says. "I see people out hiking all the time with a little water bottle, a pair of shorts, and sandals in the spring—and in Colorado, the spring is one of our worst times of year for weather."

He says even for moderate hikes he can be found on the trail with a well-stocked backpack, which regularly earns him funny looks from other people thinking that he's some type of crazed survivalist. "I'm like, 'Well, as a matter of fact, I am. At least I'm going to make it home and there's the potential that you might not.'"

After high school he took some college classes but ended up working for the local gold mine where he did exploration for the geology department. The job essentially required him to do what he loved and travel into far-flung regions of the wilderness looking for gold. After a few years an old boss asked him to join working IT for a cellphone company. He took the job and for the next twenty years worked in what he describes as corporate America. "I absolutely hated it—but it paid pretty well," Marsteiner admits.

Then in about 2009 the survival industry became mainstream. Multiple television shows like *Survivorman, Man vs. Wild, I Shouldn't be Alive, The Colony, Out of the Wild, Surviving Disaster, Survive This, Alone in the Wild*, and a host of others featured people prepping for emergencies, the wilderness, and worst-case scenarios, and the public became interested in making "bug out" bags and seventy-two-hour kits. Outdoor survival became popular in a big way while Marsteiner wasn't even aware of the shift. One day one of his work colleagues asked him for help in eating the food from a seventy-two-hour kit that was about to expire.

"I was like, 'What the hell is a seventy-two-hour kit?' So he started explaining it to me and I was like...yeah, I carry one of those all the time and I've had it since I was a kid. I didn't even know it had a name," Marsteiner says. "Then I started searching around and discovered there were all these preppers out there and survivalists, [and I thought] 'Oh, so these people are basically my life growing up, and now it's a thing. Weird.'"

He started trying out some of the kits and found they were less than ideal, so he began making his own and found success selling them online. Marsteiner believes people were buying his kits because they didn't have the skills to survive on their own and were instead relying on the gear. This led to consulting work with his customers because they didn't know how to use the equipment they bought.

"Then I realized that I kind of enjoyed teaching people more than I did selling them stuff," Marsteiner says. In 2014 he went to a school in the Ozarks that specialized in training people to become survival instructors.

"Basically, I spent forty-five days out in the woods with ten items. For a week of that we were only allowed to use our knife. There were thirteen of us when we started out. By the time we were done, five people tapped out—which I couldn't believe because I thought it was so easy," Marsteiner tells me. Every one hundred feet he could find a pound worth of wild edibles; creating shelters and fire was also almost second nature to him. "It just had huge amounts of resources compared to Colorado," he says.

The next year when he was laid off from his job, Marsteiner decided it was time to begin teaching students how to survive full time. Since then he's taught a total of forty classes and never looked back.

"I've had stay-at-home moms come out, I've had people come down from Canada, I've had somebody come in from China, I've had people come in from the UK, I've had people from Colombia come out. People from all over our country," Marsteiner notes. "So my reach has gone pretty far globally, which is kind of surprising."

Learning the Ropes—Firsthand

It's one thing to write about the difficulties and general misery of living in a time when modern conveniences were essentially science fiction, but it's a whole other thing to force yourself to go without the day-to-day niceties such as heat—or sleeping accommodations without bugs. Most of us have about as much in common with those living during the Old West as the friendly-family Labrador does with a timber wolf. Frankly, that's how I prefer it. After all, who would intentionally pick a life of extreme physical hardship and misery when there is takeout pizza and movies to stream?

I wasn't a huge fan of camping myself and never found a way to make it anything other than a hellish experience. Even in the military where I had spent quite a bit of time in the field, I never got used to it. But if I'm to search for the remaining vestiges of the Wild West, learning the basics of survival in the outdoors is something that could only be experienced firsthand. Despite my reservations about camping, I had to try again. And what better way to gain a better understanding of life without modern conveniences than to spend a week with Marsteiner at his outdoor survival school?

DAY ONE
I arrive at the remote survival school without too much trouble. Driving into the small dirt parking area, I climb out to meet with Marsteiner at the school's rustic classroom comprised of several man-made shelters on a stretch of heavily forested land. Half a dozen collapsible camping chairs

surround a large fire pit in the center, and there's also a large community tent off to one side for those who don't want to brave trying out their own sleeping accommodations.

The first thing I do was set up my camp in a little clearing of trees with an old fire pit located just off to one side. There seems to be just enough privacy that I could enjoy a sense of being alone in the outdoors—but not so far away that someone wouldn't be able to hear me screaming if a mountain lion dragged me off into the bushes. Luckily, I still have a small cellphone signal, so I go on YouTube to look up a video on how to set up my new tent correctly. As far as really appreciating the importance of outdoor ruggedness and independence, I admit I may be off to a bad start.

There are other students here with me: a corporate executive, a father and his two children, and a more senior student who signed up for a fifty-day course out in the wilderness. We introduce ourselves and why we wanted to attend the week-long class. I joke that leaving my house to live in the wilderness is a bit like going off life support. Marsteiner then tells us about "the rule of three": you can survive three minutes without air, three hours without shelter in extreme weather, three days without water, and three weeks without food.

We begin with some basic skills. I work with a handful of other students on cutting down dead trees with only a knife so that we could fashion the wood into an assortment of useful tools such as clubs used for hammering and even fishing spears. It turns out a good knife and a club can also be used to make firewood—or anything you put your mind to making. We also learn about different types of plants and their uses, and which are edible. Yarrow could be used to staunch bleeding—something that would have been useful to know during the Old West as Band-Aids were in short supply. Willow bark could be used to make rope. Pine pitch and charcoal can make an extremely powerful glue, and adding deer scat, with its unique fibrous content, turns the pine pitch into something like fiberglass.

When the end of the day comes, I sit in my tent with my forearms sore from the constant knife work. No amount of vigorous keyboard typing can condition you for this type of activity. As I close my eyes, a legion of flies begins to bombard the exterior of the tent, filling the quiet somber evening with their buzzing insistence. Miraculously, the subtle mallet of exhaustion helps me to fall asleep anyway.

The author's sleeping quarters for the majority of the duration of his time attending Jason Marsteiner's school. *(Photo by Ian Neligh)*

DAY TWO

My morning is spent eating breakfast on a log in front of my tent just a foot away from the largest cow patty I've ever seen. It's nearly the size of a kitchen table, and how I missed it while picking a campsite the day before is beyond me. That, at least, certainly explains the flies.

Even though my camping site looks flat, it turns out it's actually on a slight incline, and so I had spent the previous evening sliding into the side of the tent, my face vacuum sealed against its side. At one point I had to pick up and move my sleeping pad back to the starboard side of the tent, which was when a squirrel began chittering at full blast next to my head. It's barely reassuring to hear I wasn't the only one plagued by the rodent in the night.

For most of the afternoon I work with the corporate executive to build an A-frame shelter, or a "jungle hootch." The little building looks a bit like a tree fort on stilts with an elevated bed about four feet off the ground and an old green canvas for a cover. In essence, it resembles a funeral pyre. Since I slept so terribly in the tent, Marsteiner barely needs to convince me to spend the night in the A-frame. Everyone throws around jokes about the dubious structure and my sleeping safety, so I am particularly mindful of checking my knots that would hold the thing together. It turns out that the Canadian Jam Knot is not the name of a lame college band but an exceptionally useful knot that can fashion pretty much anything together. Really, when in an emergency, a simple lean-to will do. What shape your shelter takes depends on the time you've got, how long you plan to stay in it, and the environment you're in.

The tent may have been uncomfortable, but the A-frame turns out to have its own unique brand of problems. Sleeping in a shelter you build yourself is impressive, but letting five dozen different types of insects climb on you while sleeping is a bothersome prospect. After deeming it safe and being wrong twice, I climb up into the sleeping pad and ready for the cold, rainy night to come. With my flashlight I spot what looks like a massive cricket with unusual and alarming coloring. I try to get it off the interior ceiling of my shelter, but it just falls into my bedding and I never find it again. Becoming indifferent to the entomology of your sleeping quarters is something the pioneers must have become exceedingly good at.

With the tips of both my head and feet sticking out of the ends of the A-frame, I stare at the ceiling of my wooden shelter and listen as pine beetles eat their way slowly through the tree my shelter is tied to. The pine beetles aren't that bad though compared to the hysterical noises of a nearby coyote. Marsteiner also said bears occasionally come into the camp. The thought of a bear grabbing onto my partly exposed foot and yanking me out of the shelter like it is a fancy taco is an alarming one. But the sound of hungry pine beetles eventually lull me to sleep. That is until the squirrel starts up again at about 3 a.m. like someone had set it on fire three feet from my head.

DAY THREE

The senior student kills the squirrel this morning to demonstrate skinning and gutting techniques. I wouldn't say it was karma but there is a little frontier justice in the act. I also learn that squirrel tastes like rubber and is harder to chew. But securing food, regardless of taste, is important to outdoor survival, regardless of personal culinary taste.

Yet finding shelter, in the short term, is even more essential. Marsteiner says making shelter and staying warm are the two single most important things you can do to better your chance of survival. Today we would learn how to stay warm. With my knife and a stick, I chop down a dead aspen tree and turn it into fire-making tools. The idea is to use a wooden bow, a Paracord rope, or your own rope made from fibrous plants, and a wooden drill to start a friction fire. For this to work I would hold on to the bow for dear life, moving it and the conjoining cord back and forth. This action rotates the wooden drill wound up in the rope which then causes the friction fire to start—or at least in theory. For me, this was unusually problematic. We hear some students never figure this out because of the high degree of difficulty involved with the practice, but this only adds to my urgency of getting it right. Making fire from nothing is as close to creating actual magic as it gets. Breathless, exhausted, and frustrated, I try again and again, without luck; but I am resolved to get this feat accomplished no matter what.

Another student joins our class today, a chiropractor who looks like he dabbles in professional bodybuilding. Cheerful, enthusiastic, well rested, and clean, he greets the class with vigorous high fives, meaningful life advice, and sincere encouragement to the students. He also creates fire without effort a dozen times, watching with genuine concern as the rest of us wheeze and sweat in extreme effort.

Being able to make fire could sometimes be the difference between life and death. I saw the bow back and forth as hard and as fast as I could for as long as I could stand it. This process spins the wooden drill, causing something like superheated sawdust to form on a patch of leather. With the right amount of heat and sawdust, small embers will begin to smoke and must be carefully blown and added to something that looks like a bird's nest built out of grass. Then the grass is added to small pieces of wood resembling a Lincoln log house to create a sustaining fire.

Fighting the exhaustion that comes with trying the physically demanding process more than one hundred times, I almost can't believe it when smoke finally appeared. Gently, I transfer the ember to the bird's nest and then to the miniature log house. Soon a fire blazes away. It really is magic. It's hard to explain, but when you can make fire from almost nothing it feels like you've leveled up in some profound way. It's like I joined some club I never knew existed but always wanted to be a part of.

As the day comes to an end and the sun sinks below the mountains, the father and the chiropractor earnestly discuss the problems with the country's insurance system. It soon grows dark and we tell ghost stories around an unlit fire. The fire has to stay out because of the state's recent fire bans. This makes the experience all the more chilling—literally.

I sleep better that night without a single paranoid thought of wandering bears, maniacs, or maniacs dressed as bears. The biggest problem is the ever-present threat of rolling out of my shelter and falling to the ground below. As I begin to drift off to sleep, I make a mental list of things that I ate that I probably shouldn't have: a squirrel, pine bark, ants, and a package of MRE meatballs.

DAY FOUR
There is something to be said for being the first person to greet the day in the camp. It's an accomplishment that lasts only as long as it takes for me to spot the chiropractor who woke an hour before I did to gather firewood and go for a quick jog.

Today we learn about traps and deadfalls for catching food. The only victim to my deadfall is my right hand, which is caught and crushed on numerous occasions as it's being set up.

Our small student group is about to become a little smaller. The two young boys and their father are leaving early. The father who said he had brought his children to the class to "become men" is tossing in the towel. They largely spent the first few days eating s'mores and accidentally cutting themselves with their expensive new knives, and now their father has decided to cut the week short and head back to civilization for a burger. At one point their father wanders off, leaving the two boys near the fire pit with the executive and me. One boy looks at us and says seriously, "You'd better keep an eye on us or I'll jump in the fire."

DAY FIVE
While sitting around the dead fire eating various odds and ends I brought with me, I realize that survival is about persistence and knowing what to do and when. How much of your time is spent making shelter, building fire, finding water, and hunting for food make up an equation that determines whether you'll survive or not.

This last day we make snares and water stills and do a host of other activities that make outdoor survival just that much more likely in an emergency. As we work, I reflect on how valuable a good routine is for life in the wilderness. In just a few days I learned that being outside in the cold and wet can be exhausting and calorie burning without a clear method and plan for conducting your daily activities. More than anything, the experience in the outdoor survival school gave me a more nuanced appreciation and respect for the mountain men, pioneers, and Native Americans who endured the fickle nature of the West's weather on a daily basis. After all, our predecessors had lived in a time where surviving in the Old West was more than just successfully enduring the dangerous turns in the weather. Starvation and dehydration could kill just as successfully as the bullet fired from a rifle.

As the day comes to an end and I pack up my gear, I understand that a week of outdoor training isn't enough, nor is a month, nor even a year. Knowing how to survive, or even thrive in the outdoors—that is a lifelong pursuit.

CHAPTER 9

U.S. MARSHALS
AND FRONTIER
JUSTICE

The West still has its fair share of fugitives today, and the U.S. Marshal Service is the best in the world at hunting them down. The country's oldest law enforcement service originally tracked down criminals under the directive of President George Washington, through the Old West and clear into modern times.

How much has this famous law enforcement service changed since its beginnings? I spoke with Dave Oney, the public affairs specialist with the U.S. Marshals, to talk about their work in the modern-day West. On average, the Marshal Service arrests 336 fugitives from justice every day. There is a total of 94 U.S. Marshals appointed by the president for each of the country's federal court districts, and each marshal has a host of deputy marshals working for them—a total of 3,571 deputies across the agency.

"We [also] have seven regional fugitive task forces that are congressionally mandated," Oney says. From the Pacific Southwest to the Caribbean, the task forces regularly assemble on missions to bring in fugitives. "We did the one in Colorado, we did one in San Antonio, then one in Houston—those are the most recent ones," he says.

One such operation netted 156 suspects wanted in connection with violent crimes, some of which are almost too disturbing to imagine.

This operation was carried out in just ninety days in Colorado. Termed "Operation Triple Beam Colorado," the multi-agency task force included multiple sheriff's offices, police departments, and law enforcement agencies and was spearheaded by the U.S. Marshal Service. Exactly like the posses of the Wild West, Operation Triple Beam Colorado saw the marshals make their fellow law enforcement partners into "special deputies" so they could work outside of their regular jurisdictions during the massive apprehension effort.

The agency conducted several similar operations in cities across the country in the last decade to round up those on the run from justice. Since initiating the state-hopping program in 2010, there have been 8,000 arrests and more than 1,800 illegal firearms seized. Drug dealers, gang members, and murderers have all found themselves netted in the Marshals' campaign to clean up the streets. The task force focuses on suspects and criminals with the most violent offenses, like homicide, rape, and gang activity.

"The people we're going after have already had their day in court and they didn't show up where they were supposed to or they cut off their ankle bracelet and fled, or they didn't check in with the people they are supposed to check in with," Oney tells me. "You really make a difference to pull that many people in, it is usually more than a hundred people arrested in a ninety-day period. They'll recover a lot of guns, a lot of drugs."

The Marshals aren't just tasked with fugitive recovery. They also contribute on asset forfeiture, prisoner transportation, witness protection—but their first and original mission is to provide judicial security.

"Judicial security is still the main [mission]. We protect the courts, we protect the facilities, we protect the judges, we have special protective details assigned to Supreme Court nominees," Oney says. "We protect the Supreme Court justices, when they travel outside of the metro DC area. There will be a team assigned to them. We protect people who are in federal custody of course and witnesses."

Judicial security, fugitive recovery—I remark that it seems that the agency's mission hasn't changed all that much since their creation in 1789.

"Nope," Oney agrees. "We go after the bad guys."

Rounding Up a Posse

The Marshals were started with the creation of the country's new federal court system—though President Washington didn't really know what to do with them.

"At first he didn't because he had a wide range of responsibilities— he was looking at the Marshals as kind of a catch-all for federal judiciary protection," says David Turk, the official U.S. Marshal historian and author of *Forging the Star*, a history of the U.S. Marshals. "One of our oldest and our primary function is the protection of the judiciary and the judges, U.S. attorneys, and witnesses." But Washington wanted more from the Marshals. He decided they should also be responsible for the federal census—a somewhat unusual job the agency held from 1790 to 1870.

"Our country was very young. You wanted to know where your wealth was, where the population centers were," Turk says. "We had a lot of other duties as assigned during this period. We had a very fluid period. We chased counterfeiters, we had our first federal execution in 1790." By all reports, being a U.S. Marshal wasn't a very lucrative job in the fledgling country. One of the first thirteen hired soon quit due to the poor pay. Turk believes being a marshal for many held more meaning than the job's meager salary, and those who stuck with it were clearly passionate about the job.

"And it was a lot of job," Turk says. "Washington was reported as saying, 'How important this job is, I know not,' but he was trying to figure out if they were more under the format of a French military model or the English admiralty court model—and I think he leaned more towards the latter." Understandably, it's fair to say there was something of a stigma attached to anything associated, even remotely, with the royalists— something Washington, no doubt, wanted to avoid. Each presidentially appointed marshal then had a handful of deputy marshals working for them and covering the ever-growing territory of the new country.

"That doesn't give you a lot of manpower and you've got a lot of acreage to cover," Turk says. "So you'd have to serve process for federal courts, subpoenas, you'd have to deliver federal prisoners sometimes over state and territorial lines, and there was a lot of business that you'd have to cover." Sometimes the job required deputy marshals to spend weeks in the field performing their duties, following judges as they went from one town to another and holding court.

"And you'd sometimes have to bring your own tools of execution—like a portable scaffold," Turk says. "There was probably a lot less crime committed than there is today but there was still a lot of territory." Lists were kept in different cities of people who could be relied upon to be made "special deputies" for a certain length of time to help the deputy marshals track down fugitives—for a paycheck, of course. This would later be known as a posse.

"It's part of the judiciary act of 1789...[a deputy marshal] can create special deputies and the special deputations would only last up to a year or until the end of that mission," Turk says. Some famous and rather unexpected characters were made special deputies to the U.S. Marshals during the Old West; and in a few cases, this led to a great deal of bloodshed and made determining who the good guys were sometimes exceptionally difficult.

Billy the Kid

The mission and reputation of the Marshal Service grew and became better known as their operations necessitated them moving ever westward into the territories. The federal territories didn't yet have something resembling state police and the marshals were tasked with the epic responsibility.

"Because they didn't have yet that state police, people had to rely more and more on us as their go-to police force," Turk says. "They only had a local sheriff and the military as other alternatives—and the military half the time was too emerged in dealing with other issues and the local police had their own problems."

Turk says that was why the Marshals are often mentioned in places like the New Mexico territory, Arizona territory, and even in Alaska until it became a state in 1959.

"Texas had the Rangers, so you didn't see us as much there, but often what would happen is we would work with them," Turk says.

This was a wild and often lawless time when men carrying the Silver Star traveled across the West, enforcing the laws of the federal government. Many notable Western personalities came to the forefront of history during this era because of their association with the service, including Pat Garrett and Henry McCarty, also known as William Bonney, also known as Billy the Kid. Turk holds deep passion for the story of the two famous adversaries and spent years studying the events leading up to the Kid's death. "Billy the Kid is a very complex character and a lot of people like to paint him as either a villain or hero. I don't think he was either one," Turk says. "I think he was somewhere in the middle."

Originally born in New York, Billy's family moved to Kansas looking for opportunity in 1862. After the death of his father, the family ended up in Silver City, New Mexico, in 1868 after his mother remarried. When his mother died, and in constant conflict with his stepfather, Billy struck out on his own. Almost as quick to laugh as get into a fight, the kid often found himself in trouble on the frontier as a rustler—and it wasn't long before his death toll started to grow.

While researching Billy the Kid, Turk came across letters in the National Archives surprisingly pointing to the Kid's brief time as a Special Deputy U.S. Marshal for a posse during the infamous New Mexico Lincoln County Wars. The so-called "wars" began when a young English rancher named John Tunstall challenged a ruthless merchandise and ranching monopoly in Lincoln County operated by J.J. Dolan and L.G. Murphy with his own business ventures. At the time Lincoln County was the largest county in the New Mexico territory. Concerned for his life, Tunstall hired bodyguards, one of whom was Billy the Kid. In 1878 the opposing faction's sheriff sent a posse to Tunstall's ranch, and the attack ended with Tunstall shot in the head. The murder of Billy the Kid's employer kicked off the war that helped create the Kid's infamous and tragic legend.

"The weird thing was the Marshals were kind of used during that whole Lincoln County war period," Turk remarks. "John Sherman Jr., who incidentally was the nephew of William Tecumseh Sherman of Civil War fame, was appointed marshal for the New Mexico territory in 1876." John Sherman Jr. was not thrilled to go to Lincoln County to deal with things hands on and decided to appoint two deputy marshals to help deal with the issues.

"Here's the problem: he appointed two deputies on either side of the Lincoln County War. So you had two Deputy U.S. Marshals on either side for several months in 1878," Turk says. "That whole thing was just a disaster."

Billy the Kid's side of the conflict soon lost the necessary political goodwill to continue. While Governor Lee Wallace gave amnesty to those enlisted on the losing side, the Kid was not among the pardoned, which effectively turned him into an outlaw.

Sheriff Pat Garrett

Pat Garrett moved west in 1869 at the age of nineteen to seek his fortune, leaving his family and a failing plantation behind in Louisiana. Cowboy, hired gunman, and buffalo hunter, Garrett eventually ended up in New Mexico where he was elected sheriff of Lincoln County in 1880 and also became a U.S. Deputy Marshal. He and Billy were allegedly former friends or acquaintances, but that didn't stop Garrett from relentlessly pursuing Billy for his crimes when the time came.

After a series of failed ambushes, Garrett finally captured Billy the Kid in 1880 for the killing of Sheriff William Brady and Deputy George Hindman. The Kid went to jail at the Lincoln County Courthouse and was sentenced to be hanged, and then famously escaped, killing two deputies in the process.

"As near as we can ascertain, Billy...watching his opportunity, slipped his handcuffs. He then knocked Deputy Sheriff [J.W.] Bell down and, snatching his revolver, shot the gallant young officer dead," reported one newspaper from the time. Billy then got a hold of deputy Bob Olinger's 10-gauge shotgun and waited. Olinger, who had a reputation as a ruthless killer himself, came over to the courthouse investigating the sound of gunfire when Billy the Kid shot him dead from a window on the second floor. The outlaw made good his famous escape, but just a year later Billy the Kid met his end while staying at the home of a mutual friend of his and Garrett's. The Kid's rather inglorious demise was reported in the *Fremont County Record* in 1881 as passed on to them by another newspaper:

> Sheriff Garrett arrived at Sumner on the evening of the 14th. Late in the night he went to Pete Maxwell's house and went in. Two men were left to guard the door. Garrett said to Pete, who was in bed, "I understand that Billy the Kid is here." Pete

answered that he was. Garrett was standing at the foot of the bed and there was but little light in the room. Billy just then stepped into the room in his stocking feet. He had a six shooter in one hand and a Bowie knife in the other. He saw Garrett standing at the foot of the bed and asked in Spanish "Who is that?" Pete did not answer but managed to indicate to Garrett that the other person was the Kid and jumped to the other end of the bed. Billy again asked, "Who is that." And as he did so Garret fired, striking the Kid through the heart, who fell back dead.

There is, of course, some debate as to whether Billy the Kid was armed at all when Pat Garrett shot him or if it was even he that Garrett shot. While the conspiracy theories continue to grow, so too will Billy the Kid's name in the West. Turk said Pat Garrett went on to become a Deputy U.S. Marshal a few more times in the years to come after killing the Kid, but he never again reached the same heights of fame. "[His career] was not as glorious [anymore] because there was no Billy the Kid to chase around," Turk says.

During the Old West the U.S. Marshal Service may have been less than exactly perfect in carrying out its sacred duties, such as deputizing people on both sides of a murky conflict. However, justice, such as it was, found Billy the Kid and ultimately put an end to the man— even as his legend lived on.

The Most Famous Gunfight of the Wild West

The U.S. Marshals had their fair number of famous names and faces from the Old West, but none quite as famous as that of the severely mustachioed visage of Wyatt Earp.

"He was actually a Deputy U.S. Marshal—but the thing was, he was a Special Deputy U.S. Marshal during Tombstone. A lot of people don't realize his brother Virgil Earp was actually the Deputy U.S. Marshal for two years in Tombstone," Turk says. "He deputized his brothers and Doc Holliday for the Tombstone battle that occurred with the Cowboys, which were a rustling group that was trying to infiltrate the town because cattle was like gold back then."

Wyatt Earp *(Public domain)*

The Tombstone battle was a gunfight that took place in less than thirty seconds, when thirty bullets were fired and ended with three men dead, three wounded, and the town of Tombstone, Arizona, going down in history as the location of the most famous gunfight of the Wild West—the erroneously titled Gunfight at the O.K. Corral.

On October 26, 1881, a confrontation erupted between the sometimes-lawmen Virgil Earp, Wyatt Earp, Morgan Earp, their friend Doc Holliday, and a gang of Cowboys, then a term synonymous with rustlers. The tension had been brewing for months, and almost from the beginning the Earps, who arrived in Tombstone in December of 1879 because of a rash of stagecoach robberies, began to clash with the local rustling gangs.

"I was asked to go to Tombstone in my capacity as a United States Marshal, and went. My brother Wyatt and myself were fairly well treated for a time, but when the desperate characters who were congregated there, and who had been unaccustomed to troublesome molestation by the authorities, learnt that we meant business and determined to stop their rascality, if possible, they began to make it warm for us," Virgil Earp said in an 1882 article in the *Arizona Daily Star*.

Unlike Virgil Earp who worked in law enforcement most of his life, his younger brother Wyatt started his professional life on the other side of the aisle. Wyatt was a gambler and often in trouble with law as a young man, which resulted in multiple arrests.

It wasn't until he was appointed to the Wichita police force in 1875 did he begin his famous on-and-off career in law enforcement. Three years later, while he was working a similar position in Dodge City and tracking a fugitive in Texas, his life was saved during an incident by John "Doc" Holliday, which started their famous friendship.

It's hard to say what one event, if there was just one, ultimately started the fatal turn of events leading to the famous Arizona gunfight, but the death of Tombstone's City Marshal Fred White may have been a factor. In an alleged drunken accident, the notorious outlaw "Curly Bill" Brocius of the Cowboys killed White in October of 1880 while White was trying to disarm Curly Bill. After the shooting, Wyatt Earp came forward and "buffaloed" or hit Curly Bill across the head with the barrel of his pistol, knocking him out so he could be more easily arrested. White died some days later and Virgil Earp took over White's duties as city marshal in addition to his job as Deputy U.S. Marshal.

Things continued to heat up between the two factions. Doc Holliday was later accused, without sufficient evidence, of robbing a stagecoach by Sheriff John Behan, who had aligned himself with the rustling gangs of the area. To add insult to injury, Wyatt had successfully courted an actress away from the arms of Behan and in addition was planning to run for Behan's position. Meanwhile, tension continued to grow between the Earps and other members of the Cowboys, including brothers Ike and Billy Clanton, and Frank and Tom McLaury. There are as many versions of what happened next as there are film and television adaptations—but perhaps the most accurate telling of the events comes from the *Tombstone Nugget* newspaper, which ran the tale of the incident the day after the infamous shootout: "The 26th of October will always be marked as one of the crimson days in the annals of Tombstone, a day when blood flowed as water, and human life was held as a shuttlecock, a day always to be remembered as witnessing the bloodiest and deadliest street fight that has ever occurred in this place, or probably in the Territory."

The trouble could be traced back to September of 1881, when Virgil Earp arrested Frank Stilwell and Pete Spence for holding up a stagecoach. In fact, Stilwell was also a deputy working for Sheriff Behan. Ike Clanton, a friend to both arrested men, arrived in Tombstone and posted bail for them. The paper reported that Clanton and Doc Holliday exchanged some words, and "when they parted it was generally understood that the feeling between the two men was that of intense hatred."

After a brutal overnighter spent in the saloons, Ike Clanton was spoiling for a fight the next morning with Holliday and the Earps. Clanton was more than happy to tell anyone who would listen to him about his plan to kill them, and people in the town saw him also wandering the streets armed with a rifle and a pistol. Given that there was a strict law in town against the carrying of firearms, not to mention the less-than-veiled threats against him and his brothers, Virgil Earp decided to take action. He found Clanton and acted before the man had time to register what was happening. Virgil took ahold of Clanton's rifle, and as Clanton then reached for his pistol instead, Virgil quickly clubbed him over the head with his own revolver. The blow caused Clanton to drop to the ground. Clanton swore retribution even as he was taken off to jail to be fined by a judge for carrying weapons. The fuel to the conflict between the two factions had just been lit and as a result many lives would be claimed.

"While in the Court room Wyatt Earp told [Ike Clanton] that as he had made threats against his life he wanted him to make his fight, to say how, when and where he would fight, and to get his crowd, and he [Wyatt] would be on half," the paper stated. "In reply Clanton said: 'four feet of ground is enough for me to fight on, and I'll be there.' A short time after this William Clanton and Frank McLowry [sic] came in town, and as Thomas McLowry [sic] was already here the feeling soon became general that a fight would ensue before the day was over, and crowds of expectant men stood on the corner of Allen and Fourth streets awaiting the coming conflict."

The recently released Ike Clanton and his brother, as well as the McLaurys, loitered in an empty lot off of Fremont Street, armed and ready. Sheriff Behan told Virgil that he would defuse the situation by asking the group to disarm. Virgil agreed and waited to hear back from Behan. When Virgil heard further reports from citizens that the men were still very much armed and showed no inclination to leave, he decided to take matters into his own hands. He gathered Wyatt, Morgan, and their friend Doc Holliday, and on their way over to where the Clantons and the McLaurys were waiting, Virgil handed Holliday a shotgun to hide under his long coat and in turn took Holliday's walking cane. The four then marched down the street to the inevitable confrontation.

The *Tombstone Nugget* reported, "The Sheriff stepped out and said: 'Hold up boys. Don't go down there or there will be trouble; I have been down there to disarm them.'" There's some question as to whether Sheriff Behan meant he had indeed disarmed the men or had attempted, unsuccessfully, to disarm them. But whatever the intention, the statement put the Earps at ease enough to holster their weapons. The Earps then came around the corner and faced their adversaries who still had their guns after all. The newspaper then reported the chaotic and bloody moments that soon followed.

When within a few feet of them the Marshal said to the Clantons and McLowrys [sic]: "Throw up your hands, boys, I intend to disarm you." As he spoke Frank McLowry [sic] made a motion to draw his revolver, when Wyatt Earp pulled his and shot him, the ball striking on the right side of his abdomen. About the same time Doc Holliday shot Tom McLowry [sic] in the right side using a short shotgun, such as is carried by Wells Fargo & Co.'s messengers. In the meantime Billy Clanton had shot at Morgan Earp, the ball passing through the point of the left shoulder blade across his back, just grazing the backbone and coming out at the shoulder, the ball remaining inside of his shirt. He fell to the ground, but in an instant gathered himself, and raised in a sitting position fired at Frank McLowry [sic] as he crossed Fremont street, and at the same instant Doc Holliday shot at him, both balls taking effect, either of which would have proved fatal, as one struck him in the right temple and the other in the left breast. As he started across the street, however, he pulled his gun down on Holliday saying, 'I've got you now.' 'Blaze away! You're a daisy if you have,' replied Doc. This shot of McLowry's [sic] passed through Holliday's pistol pocket, just grazing the skin. While this was going on Billy Clanton had shot Virgil Earp in the right leg, the ball passing through his calf, inflicting a severe flesh wound. In turn he had been shot by Morg[an] in the right side of the abdomen, and twice by Virgil Earp, once in the right wrist and once in the left breast.

As soon as the shooting broke out, Ike Clanton ran to Wyatt screaming that he wasn't armed. Wyatt replied, "Go to fighting or get away." Clanton ran into a saloon and out onto the street where he was then arrested and taken to county jail. His brother, unfortunately, was not so lucky. Billy Clanton died of his wounds an hour later in a house. All in all, the gunfight lasted no more than twenty-five seconds.

A trial was held and the court found the Earps had properly carried out their duty as law enforcement officers. But the ruling wouldn't be the end of the issue—far from it.

Vendetta Ride

In December, Virgil Earp was crossing Fifth Street between the Oriental Saloon and the Eagle Brewery when he was ambushed by three men armed with shotguns. The assassins hid but suspects included several Cowboys such as Frank Stilwell, Ike Clanton, Florentino "Indian Charlie" Cruz, and even possibly Curly Bill.

One paper reported many shots fired, with Virgil taking the heat of double-barreled shotguns. He was hit in the left arm and above the groin before it was all over. Despite the horrific injuries, Virgil got to his feet and found his brother. Wyatt telegraphed the U.S. Marshals asking to be deputized, since Virgil was wounded and possibly dying, and added that the local authorities including Sheriff Behan were not responding to the attacks. Wyatt was promptly made a Deputy U.S. Marshal. In quick order, he put together a posse of Special Deputy U.S. Marshals including Doc Holliday to search for the assassins. While the shootout between the Earps and the Clantons and McLaurys was unquestionably controversial among the townsfolk, it was clear to many that the Cowboys needed to be dealt with.

"Long ago the cowboy gang threatened the lives of Mayor Club, Judge Spicer, Marshall Williams, agent of Wells Fargo & Co., Earp and Holliday, and this is an attempt to carry the threats into execution. Intense feeling exists in the minds of all the better class of citizens at this dastardly attempt at assassination," one paper said. "The condition of United States Deputy Marshal Earp is critical...The doctor says there are four chances in five that he will die. The local authorities are doing nothing to capture the assassins, so far as known...Judge Spicer, Marshall Williams, Wyatt Earp, Rickabaugh and others are in momentary danger of assassination."

Virgil did not die, however, and the fight between the two groups wasn't over. Then in March of 1882, Morgan Earp was assassinated one evening while playing a game of billiards with Wyatt. Shots, likely from Frank Stilwell, came in through a window when Morgan's back was turned, hitting him in the spine, and one bullet landed in the wall above Wyatt's head. People rushed out into the street to hunt the assassins but found it empty. Morgan died moments later but not before asking his brother to find his murderers and to make sure Wyatt himself wasn't killed in the process.

Days later in Tucson, Frank Stilwell waited at the train station to assassinate Virgil Earp as he traveled out of state with his wife and Morgan's body. But Wyatt got there first, surprising Stilwell with a shotgun that he used at close range. This is considered the beginning of Wyatt's "vendetta ride" of systematically hunting down and killing anyone and everyone connected to the violence against his family.

"Before Stilwell died he confessed that he killed Morg[an] and gave the names of those who were implicated with him," Virgil later stated. The local law and newspapers turned against Wyatt and his posse, while the bodies of the alleged assassins of Morgan kept turning up.

"Nothing more has been heard from the Earp party since their killing the Mexican Florentino, in the Dragoon mountains," relayed a paper on March 24, 1882. "It is reported on good authority that they propose to kill three more men who they believe were a party to the killing of their brother, then they will leave the country or surrender. Two posses are after them—Sheriff Behan, of Cochise county, with eighteen men, and a party of cowboys from Charleston, numbering twenty-one."

Then on March 26, nine Cowboys attempted to ambush the Earp posse of six men, which resulted in Wyatt killing Curly Bill as reported in the *Tombstone Epitaph*:

> Not a man went down under this murderous fire, but like a thunderbolt shot from the hand of Jove the six desperate men charged upon their assailants like the light brigade at Balakava, and when within easy reach returned the fire under which one man went down never more to rise again. The remaining eight fled to the brush and regained their horses when they rose away towards Charleston as if the King of Terrors was at their heels in hot pursuit. The six men fired but one volley and from the close range it is supposed that several of the ambushed cowboys were seriously if not fatally wounded. The six men returned to their horses where one was found to be in the agony of death, he having received one of the leaden messengers intended for his rider. After the road was clear our informant rode on and came upon the dead man, who, from the description given, was none other than Curly Bill, the man who killed Marshal White in the streets of Tombstone, one year ago last September.

During the ambush of the Earp posse, everyone except Wyatt, bolted for cover under the intense hail of gunfire. Wyatt stood still in his saddle as bullets rained down and spotted Curly Bill. He raised his shotgun and killed the Cowboy before following his companions to find cover. Wyatt was completely unharmed. Longtime friend Bat Masterson later summed up Earp's vendetta ride: "They hunted down a Mexican named Florentine, whom they shot, and then one by one they got Frank Stilwell, Curly Bill and others who had a hand directly or indirectly in the war."

While the war wasn't over, it was indeed finally coming to an end. Men had died on both sides, and both sides had received the blessing of the law such as it was.

"So Wyatt was a full-time deputy marshal for all of four months," Turk says. "He went on that famous vendetta ride which, by the way, wasn't fully authorized." Turk adds that Earp and the others left Arizona and ended up in Colorado, never to return.

"That's because he never can go back—he was not fired but he was the next thing to fired. He basically has to quit because he got his marshal in trouble, and this marshal ended up getting fired because of irregularities in his accounts due to the vendetta ride," Turk says. "Wyatt was a great gunman and he was a fearless guy; the problem was he just didn't like to do paperwork and he didn't like going through the courts . . . and he got himself and his marshal in trouble."

While the vendetta ride made the history books and accomplished what Wyatt wanted, the U.S. Marshal Service doesn't consider the ride a success today.

"Not really, it was kind of a blunder," Turk says when asked. "He was all over the country and he was well regarded for his duties as a deputy marshal; no one is going to take that away from him—I certainly am not. But let's face it: I'm going to give Virgil his props for being the guy for two years—and he did the paperwork."

Given the authority of being a Deputy U.S. Marshal, Wyatt took the power to seek justice—even if it looked a lot like revenge. When law enforcement straddles both sides of a conflict, it further muddies the question of who the good guys actually are. If Wyatt hadn't won his vendetta ride, or if one of the many bullets fired at him had actually hit, history might look at him as a villain instead of the legendary lawman he's considered today.

CHAPTER 10

THE **GREATEST**
LAWMAN
OF THE **WEST**

During the often lawless and violent days of the late 1800s, the U.S. Marshal Service saw their ranks fill with notable Wild West characters such as Wild Bill Hickok and Bartholomew William Barclay "Bat" Masterson—but there was likely no better and more overlooked figure than former slave Bass Reeves. Some even consider Reeves to be a major part of the inspiration for the Lone Ranger.

In 1907 a reporter for the *Washington Post* sat down with the arguably greatest lawman who has ever lived. Described as more than six feet tall, sixty-eight years old but with the appearance of a man in his forties, Reeves worked as a deputy marshal for thirty-two years and captured a staggering three thousand criminals in the Indian Territory, which later became Oklahoma.

"During his lifetime Reeves has had some mighty close calls," the reporter said. "His belt was shot in two once, his hat brim shot away, a button on his coat was shot off, the bridle reins in his hand were shot in two, yet he has never had the blood drawn in a fight, though fourteen men in all have had their lives snuffed out by his deadly gun and in not a single instance did he ever shoot a man until the other fellow started the fight."

Reeves was born a slave in 1838 in Arkansas and brought into the Civil War by George Reeves, a Confederate colonel. During an argument that broke out after a card game in Texas, Reeves punched and knocked out George Reeves. This act ultimately necessitated his flight to freedom. He escaped and lived for a time with the Seminole and Creek Indians, learning their languages and how to track. After the machines of the country's war came rumbling to a stop, Reeves married and then raised, depending on the source, between eight and eleven children.

In 1875, "Hanging Judge" Isaac C. Parker was assigned to the Oklahoma Indian Territory where he appointed a U.S. Marshal to hire two hundred deputies in a massive effort to try and rein in the influx of outlaws in the area. Likely because of Reeves's fearsome reputation with a firearm, not to mention his ability to track and speak Native American languages, he was hired as one of the deputies. It would become a position he held longer than any of his peers. Working out of Fort Smith, Arkansas, Reeves used deception and disguises to hunt down and capture his targets. He worked as a deputy marshal until nearly two years after Oklahoma gained its statehood in 1907 and marshals were no longer needed to provide services for the state. During his employment, Reeves worked all of the Oklahoma and Indian Territory which were then under the jurisdiction of the Fort Smith court.

"Deputies from Fort Smith rode to Fort Reno, Fort Sill, and Anadarko for prisoners, a distance of 400 miles," said the reporter. "In those days the Missouri, Kansas and Texas Railroad running south across the Territory, marked the western fringe of civilization. Eighty miles west of Fort Smith it was known as 'the dead line,' and whenever a deputy marshal from Fort Smith or Paris, Tex., crossed the Missouri, Kansas and Texas track he took his life in his hands, and he knew it." The trails located past this "dead line" posted small cards threatening specific deputies with death. Reeves had a dozen cards posted just for him alone. "And in those days such a notice was no idle boast, and many an outlaw has bitten the dust trying to ambush a deputy on these trails," the reporter noted.

When on the road looking for fugitives, a deputy marshal brought along a cook and generally a Special Deputy U.S. Marshal, or "posseman." The deputy marshal also brought a specially reinforced wagon the captured fugitives could be chained to, which acted as a temporary prison.

Bass Reeves was a figure among the most
prolific lawmen of the Old West. *(Public domain)*

Generally the team and wagon stayed stationary as the deputy marshal moved around to hunt his quarry, using the wagon as a base camp during his time out in the field. The reporter said, "His only precaution was to prevent the prisoners from ever getting within reach of the six-shooters. This danger was ever-present."

While the job was known to be wildly dangerous, accordingly it was also possible for the deputy marshals to make a fair amount of money. During his trips, Reeves said that he never made less than $400 in a month on one of these outings. Over the years Reeves took different people along with him in support of his fugitive recovery efforts, including a Native American boy who acted as an assistant. It wasn't uncommon to see Reeves come back to civilization with his wagon brimming to overflowing with captured criminals.

"He went to Mud Creek and brought in sixteen prisoners at one time, and the fees amounted to $700, while the total actual expense to him was less than $100," said the writer. "The biggest killing he ever made was one time when he captured seventeen prisoners in the

Comanche country and took them into Fort Smith. His fees for that trip amounted to $900." In today's currency that roughly translates to Reeves bringing in a staggering $22,000 that month.

Those forays past the dead line obviously weren't without risk. Reeves told the *Post* reporter his most dangerous encounter came in 1884 when he went tracking fugitives in an area he described as the "Seminole whiskey trail." While riding his horse down the trail he was ambushed by the three "Bruner brothers"—the same men he was looking for. With their guns pointed at him, they ordered Reeves to dismount from his horse.

"He got down and showed them the warrants for their arrests and asked them to tell him the day of the month, so he could make a record to turn in to the government," the reporter said. "'You are just ready to turn in now,' remarked one of the outlaws, but they relaxed their vigilance for the merest instant, and that instant was enough."

Reeves drew his six-shooter and shot one of the brothers dead. Then he grabbed the gun of another to keep from being shot. The man fired three times while Reeves desperately held onto the weapon, keeping the bullets from hitting him. As he was struggling to keep the gun away from his body, he managed to shoot the third brother. Then he used his freed pistol to club the remaining brother to death.

"The bravest man I ever saw," Reeves told the reporter, "was Jim Webb, a Mexican that I killed in 1884 near Sacred Heart Mission. He was a murderer, I got in between him and his horse. He stepped out into the open, 500 feet away, and commenced shooting his Winchester. Before I could drop off my horse, his first bullet cut a button of my coat and the second cut my bridle rein in two. I shifted my six-shooter and grabbed my Winchester and shot twice. He dropped, and when I picked him up I found that my two bullets had struck him within a half inch of each other. He shot four times, and every time he shot he kept running up closer to me. He was 500 yards away from me when I killed him."

Other tales of Reeves law enforcement prowess could be found in the other newspapers of the time. One article reported that "one of the most remarkable examples of devotion to duty was furnished at Muskogee the other day when United States Marshal Bass Reeves while lying in bed dangerously sick with pneumonia, arrested a man and had him taken to jail." A man had chased his wife through the streets of the city with a knife, attempting to kill her, when she entered Reeves's home. The deputy marshal was in bed when the woman came in and the man followed behind her "flourishing the knife and continuing his threats, not knowing that he was butting into the domicile of a fearless deputy marshal." Reeves removed his pistol from beneath his pillow and told the man he was under arrest. While he kept the husband in his gun sights he sent the wife to bring back the police to make official the man's capture.

With fourteen men gunned down over the course of his duties for the federal government, there were times Reeves was tried for murder; but the courts always deemed his actions justified, and subsequently Reeves never failed to be acquitted of any wrongdoing. Bizarrely, on one occasion he was tried for killing his camp cook on an outing into Indian Territory. Multiple versions of the story proliferated, but Reeves stuck with the one of his accidentally shooting the man while trying to unjam a rifle. After a trial and defense that cost the deputy marshal a fair amount of his accumulated savings, he was again acquitted of any crime.

But the reporter for the *Washington Post* had heard a different version of the events: the cook had actually become angry about something and had thrown a pan of hot grease onto Reeves's favorite dog. In this version of the story, the act caused Reeves to shoot the man dead.

"[The cook] pitched forward into the campfire, and the deputy was so enraged that he let the body lie in the fire until it was charred. Reeves denies part of this story, but he stood trial for murder on account of it," the reporter said.

Stories of his dedication to his office were legendary. "Place a warrant for arrest in his hands and no circumstances can cause him to deviate," the writer added. "I saw him once arrest his own son charged with murder, take him to jail and place him behind bars. It was for a most diabolical crime."

In this true and tragic story, Reeves's son had murdered his own wife for an alleged infidelity. Reeves accepted the warrant for arrest without hesitation and set out to find and bring back his son.

The reporter said, "This was probably the most trying moment in the whole life of the old deputy. He walked into the office of Marshal

Bennett and was told that there was a warrant for his son for murder, and asked if he did not want some one else to serve it. 'Give me the 'writ,' was all he said." And true to his word, Reeves returned with the wanted man who served life in prison for his crime.

The reporter then asked the legendary lawman what he planned to do once he was no longer a deputy marshal, and Reeves replied that when the time came he was looking to become a farmer. He added he served under seven different marshals, but as Oklahoma was now a state he was finally planning to lay down his six-shooter. "For thirty-one years, going on thirty-two I have ridden as a deputy marshal... [soon] I am going to farming for a living," Reeves said.

Yet not long after the interview, Reeves became a police officer in Muskogee, Oklahoma. He held the job for two years before ultimately succumbing to Bright's Disease, a disease of the kidney, and died in his home at the age of seventy-one on January 12, 1910. He was never once injured in the line of duty.

"He killed fourteen men, but nothing more true could be said of him than he did his duty, and the Federal officers and ex-Federal officers in Eastern Oklahoma mourn the death of old Bass Reeves which occurred last Tuesday," one obituary said of his passing. "No history of frontier... [days] in Indian territory would be complete with no mention of Bass Reeves, and no tale of the old days of 'Hell on the Border,' could be told without the old deputy marshal as a prominent character."

For decades Bass Reeves was largely forgotten or intentionally overlooked in histories about that notorious time period and location because of his skin color. Twenty-three years after his death, stories emerged of a Lone Ranger who hunted criminals, often in disguise, and who always got his man. The tales of adventure captured the imaginations of Americans everywhere.

CHAPTER 11

THE LAST

GUNFIGHT

Abeautiful and vertical hiking trail above the City of Glenwood Springs, Colorado, ends abruptly in a graveyard. Tombstones going back to the late 1800s stand like unusual toadstools among the area's many gnarled and twisted junipers. The Linwood Cemetery overlooking the town was established specifically for its unique depositing status in 1887. The location was chosen after the city leaders determined its original cemetery was in a natural water runoff, which understandably raised a handful of alarming health concerns.

Following the trail markers and signs, I make my way through the mostly empty cemetery to the gravestone of John Henry "Doc" Holliday. The white-and-gray–streaked marble marker rests on a weathered pad of concrete which itself is littered with tributes to the famed Old West gunslinger, dentist, and steadfast friend of Wyatt Earp.

Coins, playing cards held in place with rocks, two shot glasses filled with what once was probably alcohol, and a staggering variety of used brass handgun cartridges litter the area around the marker. Doc Holliday died in the town below on November 8, 1887, in his hotel room at the Glenwood Hotel due to complications associated with his long-term battle with tuberculosis.

It's clear based on the amount of directional signage, the worn trail, and colorful array of offerings that Holliday's resting place is well visited—

The memorial for gambler and gunslinger John Henry "Doc" Holliday in Glenwood Springs, Colorado. *(Photo by Ian Neligh)*

even if he's not really located there. Just a few feet below the headstone in the center of a patch of dead grass is another marker that read, "This Memorial Dedicated to Doc Holliday Who is Buried Someplace in this Cemetery."

The vague but honest statement refers to the fact that any records associated with where Holliday actually lies in the cemetery are now long gone. It's even possible that because of his lack of funds, he may have been buried in the potter's field conjoining the cemetery and further to the east. If that were the case, a standard wooden marker identifying his last resting place would have completely disintegrated over time.

In the 1950s the town's chamber of commerce erected a tombstone in an ideal location for Holliday, tapping into the gunslinger's renewed popularity from the wave of Hollywood movies depicting his and the Earps' adventures. The town updated the marker in 2004 to have more accurate information about the gambler turned gunfighter.

There's something about Holliday that still lures people up to the cemetery. He was a man who, perhaps even more so than Wyatt Earp, straddled that shifting line between being an outlaw and a peace officer.

Some sources attribute Wyatt Earp saying, "Doc was a dentist whom necessity had made a gambler; a gentleman whom disease had made a frontier vagabond; a philosopher whom life had made a caustic wit; a long, lean ash-blond fellow nearly dead with consumption, and at the same time the most skillful gambler and the nerviest, speediest, deadliest man with a six-gun I ever knew."

Holliday was flawed, controversial in his own time, and he became something of a hero in ours. This is likely due to the tales of his often unblinking friendship and loyalty to Wyatt, his almost eager willingness to put himself in harm's way on behalf of his friend, and his reputation as being quick and accurate with a firearm.

Legendary Old West lawman Bartholomew William Barclay "Bat" Masterson was less favorably inclined toward Holliday when discussing some of the major gunslingers of his time that he knew: "Speaking of the picturesque characters, I guess Doc Holliday stands in that category. I never liked him and few persons did. He had a mean disposition and differed from most of the big gunfighters in that he would seek a fight. He was a consumptive and physically weak, which probably had something to do with his unfortunate disposition. He was of a fine Georgia family and was educated as a dentist."

In spite of these words, evidently Masterson was impressed enough by Holliday that he and Wyatt Earp came up with a plan to get Holliday out of a spot of trouble in Denver in 1882. They presented a bogus arrest warrant for fraud to move Holliday from a Denver jail after a con-artist falsely claimed to be a peace officer and had him arrested. The clever maneuver got Holliday out of jail, into Masterson's custody, and away from extradition to Arizona for a murder charge connected to Wyatt Earp's vendetta ride. "Holliday is not so black as painted," Masterson told a Denver paper. He had been in full damage control mode after the dentist's arrest, adding that Holliday had served as a law enforcement officer in Arizona. "He is simply being persecuted and run down in order that he may be placed in the power of the cowboys of Arizona, who hate him and desire his death."

While Holliday may only be responsible for a handful of deaths in shootouts, his reputation preceded him all along the frontier. He was slick with a gun and often ran afoul of the law before and after his time with the Earps. William Kight, the executive director of the Glenwood Springs

Historical Society and Frontier Museum and the local expert on Holliday, tells me that the question of whether Holliday was one of the good guys or bad guys is a tricky one because Holliday imbibed both characteristics frequently over the course of his life.

"I don't think either one," Kight responds to me. "I think we tend to make heroes or villains larger than life, then we can either look up to them or down on them because it just makes it easier for us." In fact, Kight personally identifies with Holliday because the man was eclectic—and he's not alone. Over the years Kight has met men who have started calling themselves "Doc Holliday" for one reason or another. While reporting in the Rockies, I, too, had met a couple of characters who opted to go by the unusual moniker, and as far as I could determine, none were actually doctors.

"There's just a lot of people that hang onto his coattails for whatever reason, I'm unable to figure out [why]—and they identify with him," Kight says. "I think they're trying to identify with someone in particular. To them, it gives them a look into the past in a certain way. I think we all romanticize the West, while not looking at all the hardships they had."

For his part, Kight says he respects Holliday given what he was able to accomplish enduring those hardships. Holliday suffered from an ultimately fatal case of tuberculosis while traveling the West on horseback.

"For him to survive that long, I think, is probably an anomaly," Kight says. Holliday lived to the age of thirty-six, in spite of both his serious illness and the risks of his profession. "But I think that in itself is what draws people. What was he made of that he could survive that long? . . . I don't know how he did it. That kind of strength is what draws me to want to know more about him. Not his gunslinging, supposedly, not any of that other stuff. Just that—he was one tough guy. That's part of the real Wild West as far as I'm concerned." Kight adds that he believed the West was tamed a bit after the 1881 shootout at the O.K. Corral and the accompanying vendetta ride. Holliday ended up in Colorado, like Wyatt Earp, after the events in Arizona as he tried to avoid further legal troubles caused by their actions.

But his history and reputation followed him like his shadow, often causing him trouble.

One Final Stand

Holliday lived in Leadville, Colorado, in 1884, trying to make a quiet living as a gambler when his notoriety once again caught up with him. Tensions between him and a group of local tough guys continued to ratchet up until a violent conclusion was all but inevitable. Then on August 23, the famed gunslinger took part in his last gunfight.

"Holliday claimed that there was a certain clique of gamblers and hard men who had sworn to take his life. The feud dated back into the troublous days in Arizona in 1881, when several of the element here were residents of Tombstone," reported a writer for the *Carbonate Chronicle* newspaper. "Several tragedies ensured [sic] and two factions were formed. Holliday, accused of murder, fled the territory to meet some of the ringleaders among his enemies here. Holliday, weak, out of health, spirits, and money, slowly dying...considered that he was imposed on, and several times notified the police that there was a plot on foot to kill him."

The police didn't react to his complaints and often searched him for illegal carrying of a firearm. They never found one—but also didn't do anything to alleviate his growing concerns. During one incident at Hyman's bar, several of the men antagonized Holliday to "pull his gun." Holliday told the group he didn't have one and left, but not before being insulted and harassed on his way out the door. This type of behavior continued often enough to frustrate Holliday who just wanted to spend the remainder of his days peacefully.

"Next day he told the writer, tears of rage coming to his eyes as he talked that they were insulting and humiliating him because they knew he could not retaliate. 'If I should kill someone here,' he said, 'no matter if I were acquitted the governor would be sure to turn me over to the Arizona authorities, and I would stand no show for life there at all. I am afraid to defend myself and these cowards kick me because they know I am down. I haven't a cent, have few friends and they will murder me yet before they are done.'"

The situation further escalated when the much larger, sometimes law enforcement officer and ally of the gamblers Billy Allen said he loaned Holliday $5 (the equivalent to $120 today) and intended to collect by whatever means possible, even to "do him in" if he didn't pay

Doc Holliday, a trained dentist, traveled the West
while slowly dying of tuberculosis. *(Public domain)*

by a certain date. The minuscule amount seemed unlikely justification
to beat and possibly kill a man already dying from tuberculosis, and
Holliday saw it as a setup. In any case, Holliday couldn't pay the debt in
the time Allen wanted.

The day the money was due, Allen began hunting for Holliday,
some witnesses later testifying with a gun in his pocket. Tired of being
harassed and unwilling to be found unarmed, Holliday collected his
single-action Colt revolver and stood behind a bar in one of the town's
popular establishments. With the gun placed under the bar, Holliday
waited for Allen to find him.

Once Allen stepped into the building, Holliday immediately fired
the first shot. "The ball struck [Allen] below the muscle of the right arm,
passing through the arm, emerging near the shoulder and shattering the
upper light of the folding door," one reporter said. "Allen fell at once,
uttering a loud scream, and Holliday, rushing behind the cigar case, leaned
over it and fired again. The bullet missed the prostrate man's head by a
hair's breadth and buried itself in the door sill."

One of the bartenders grabbed the gun from Holliday to keep him from firing a third and likely fatal shot. The *Buena Vista Democrat* reported that a local editor was walking outside at the time with a prominent businessman when the shooting occurred: "They were startled by two pistol shots and the whizzing of a couple of bullets in close proximity to their cheeks. The murderous missiles grazed the merchant's [face] and captured a lick from the editor's auburn growth of hair. The victim simultaneously fell in bloody gore before them, none other than the unfortunate Billy Allen at the hands of Doc. Holliday."

The bullet had hit one of Allen's arteries, but he recovered in time, and Holliday was taken to jail to wait for a trial. The reporter for the *Carbonate Chronicle* raced to the jail to interview Holliday just moments after the shooting occurred. He noted that Holliday was "perfectly cool and collected."

"It was not about the $5. That was taken as a pretext. It is the old trouble, and Allen was picked out as the man to kill me," Holliday said.

"Please describe the shooting to me?" the reporter asked.

"Well, Allen had told me he intended to do me up this evening. I was standing behind the counter when he came in and [I] saw that he had both hands in his pocket and that the handle of a pistol protruded from one of them. Of course, I couldn't let him murder me so I fired."

"What has Allen got particularly against you?"

"He is the tool of the gang," Holliday said.

"How do you account for no pistol being found on him?"

"Was there none found?" Holliday asked.

"No."

"His friends spirited it away—that's all."

"How about your trouble in Arizona?"

"I lived there for three years, was part of the time a peace officer, and all I ever did was forced on me and I was tried for and honorably acquitted of," Holliday said. "There are people in town who desire to murder me for notoriety. They know I am helpless and have spread the report that I am a bad man to protect themselves when they do the work. I defy anyone to say they ever saw me conduct myself in any other way than as a gentleman should."

Holliday was found not guilty after the jury convened for only a short time after the trial. Witnesses testified to seeing Allen carry a firearm right before his confrontation with Holliday, and the shooting of Allen was considered self defense. It seemed Allen and the gamblers left Holliday alone from there on.

Finally at Rest

Holliday traveled the state a bit more before heading to Glenwood Springs, a resort town well known for its hotels and healing hot springs. At this point the ailing gunslinger had already stayed in communities located at high altitude, which was no doubt difficult on his struggling lungs. "I can't imagine riding on a rough stage with [tuberculosis] like he had and knowing that he was dying . . . " Kight says. "He pretty much knew when he came to Glenwood he was going to die."

Holliday must have hoped the area's famed vapors would help him, but his health took a sudden turn for the worst. He died in his hotel room on November 8, 1887. He was thirty-six years old.

"I think him wanting to come to Glenwood Springs was his last hurrah in a sense that it's been a resort town . . . so I think he probably felt safe here," Kight says. "He didn't have to prove himself here and hopefully the water would be healing to him. I think this gave him some respite and some rest that he probably wouldn't find elsewhere."

In death, Doc Holliday has continued to live on in the people's memories and conceptions of what the West was—and still is.

"It's hard to really pin him down," Kight acknowledges. "Was he a good guy? Is he an outlaw? Well, there's a little bit of outlaw in all of us. I think people tend to see what side of him they want."

Perhaps one of the most apt descriptions of Holliday's character came from Virgil Earp who wrote, "There was something very peculiar about Doc. He was gentlemanly, a good dentist, a friendly man, and yet outside of us boys I don't think he had a friend in the Territory . . . He was a slender, sickly fellow, but whenever a stage was robbed or row started, and help was needed, Doc was one of the first to saddle his horse and reported for duty."

Doc's story shows the West held redemption for those looking for it. Even someone with a criminal past, with more than a few questionable deeds under his belt, could still be considered one of the good guys.

CHAPTER 12

GUNS

OF THE

WEST

On the basement level of a high-end Western apparel store in Glenwood Springs, where the original Hotel Glenwood once stood, sits a small Doc Holliday–themed museum, dedicated to the famed gambler and gunslinger of the Old West. In the center of the little museum, with its walls covered in paraphernalia, a glass case holds a nickel-plated 1866 Remington Derringer with mother-of-pearl grips. The small firearm has a simple and elegant design, making it the perfect companion for a smoky frontier game of faro as it could easily be hidden in a pocket or up a sleeve. Engravings on the derringer's backstrap read: "To Doc From Kate." The derringer is believed to have been a gift to Holliday from Mary Katherine Horony-Cummings, also known as Big Nose Kate, another famous Western personality. The gun draws Old West enthusiasts from around the world to get a look at it, trying to find a closer connection to its legendary owner.

Famous gunslingers of the West have brought name and fame to their firearms, making the guns nearly as iconic as their owners. Like King Arthur's Excalibur, some notable weapons of America's colorful history reach legendary status even to warrant their own names. There's Buffalo Bill Cody's Springfield .50 caliber trapdoor needle gun "Lucretia Borgia," David "Davy" Crockett's "Old Betsy," and John Baker "Texas Jack" Omohundro's rifle the "Widow." Many would recognize James Butler "Wild Bill" Hickok's twin Model 1851 Navy Colt custom revolvers, the pistol butts famously worn outwards. They'd know John Wesley Hardin's Smith & Wesson .44 American Model, or Jesse James's Remington Model 1875.

Similarly, the engraved Remington Derringer in the museum now sits behind a glass case for its possible ties to Holliday. Reportedly the derringer was discovered in Holliday's hotel room and ended up in the possession of the hotel's owner, who used it to pay for Holliday's funeral. Documents and other pieces of evidence point to its legitimacy, but the waves of time have obscured any absolute certainty of its true origin. Still, the weapon's likely connection to one of the Wild West's most famous residents gives the pistol a certain historical degree of gravity. Despite the simple practicality and uses the gunslingers treated toward their guns, today the firearms are the closest tangible relics that best represent that time.

Lawman Bat Masterson said in a 1910 interview of the weapons used on the frontier that there was an evolution as new technologies presented themselves. "The first gun we had out there was the old cap and ball six shooter. There was a little steel ramrod fastened alongside the barrel . . . It was necessary to put in the powder then the ball and then ram down the charge. Some were pretty quick at it, but naturally it was slow work at the best," Masterson said.

Because speed was essential to the difference between life and death in a gunfight, Masterson said many of the people he knew carried two guns.

"We could use two guns at once, shooting equally well with either hand. The caliber of those old guns was .36 and .44. The modern .46 Colt did not come in till about 1870, when the calvary introduced it—just when it was needed."

When recalling the art of killing someone quickly during the Wild West, Masterson said a little modification was also necessary to get a firearm just right. "We used to file the notch off the hammer till the trigger would pull 'sweet,' which is another way of saying that the blame gun would pretty near go off if you looked at it. Some of the boys used to file the notch entirely off so that the gun would go off simply

An 1866 Remington Derringer reportedly given to Doc Holliday is on display in a small museum in Glenwood Springs, Colorado. *(Photo by Ian Neligh)*

by pulling back the hammer and letting it go. The filed notch finally became the mark of the bad man or the would-be bad man, but the real gunfighters—the better class, I mean—didn't file the notches off, even though they generally did the next best thing. Many used to carry in addition to a gun in the hip holster another swung under the armpit. In this way they could draw on an adversary while he was waiting for the familiar motion towards the hip."

One gun or two, modified or not—the firearms of the West tell us not only about the time but the people who chose them and why. Understanding their choices in firearms gives us a peek behind the curtain of many of the time's greatest conflicts and characters.

The Right Price

Stories of the popular gun brands used on the frontier point to well-known manufacturers such as Winchester, Colt, Smith & Wesson, and Remington—all who were too happy to take on starring roles in the retelling of the West in the decades to follow. However, the history of firearms used in the West may have a humbler, and far more affordable, origin story.

"A lot of guns that were used on the frontier were not just Winchesters and Smith and Wessons and Colts—they were cheap European copies of those brands, as well as post-war weapons [or] surplus guns from the Civil War that had been modified," says Cody Firearms Museum curator Ashley Hlebinsky. The Cody Firearms Museum is one of the largest museums of its kind in the world and is part of the much larger Buffalo Bill Center of the West, which is a complex made up of five museums and a research library. An expert in the field, Hlebinsky admits her own interest in the history of firearms came about in an unconventional manner.

"I didn't grow up around firearms," she says. "I actually got into the study through ballistics. I wanted to be a doctor and had an interest in battlefield medicine. On a Civil War medicine tour, I heard about how the advancements of weapons technology altered medical technology on the battlefield. I got an internship at a military museum and had to identify over two hundred different types of firearms and became fascinated by them, not only as objects of technology but the different roles they have played in society and culture."

Hlebinsky has a master's degree in American History and Museum Studies and has spent years researching the Smithsonian's Institution's National Firearms Collection. The twenty-nine-year-old talks and thinks about firearms and history in a rapid-fire manner that gives a lasting impression of her knowledge and profound enthusiasm for the subject as well as her appreciation of caffeinated beverages. As I talk to Hlebinsky, I can't help but notice we are only steps away from Buffalo Bill's Lucretia Borgia, John Jeremiah "Liver-eating" Johnson's cherished .56 caliber Hawken Rifle, as well as seven thousand other historically significant firearms.

"For six bucks you could buy a military gun from the Civil War because of the surplus," Hlebinsky says. She adds that popular firearm manufacturers often elevated their own status, intentionally or otherwise, to legends in Wild West shows, film, and later television serials. "So the idea that Winchesters were the only guns available in the West is not true—but they were popular with Buffalo Bill and the early Westerns."

At least for Winchester, the rifle's myth was something carefully crafted to speak to the nostalgia of the country's vanishing time of the frontier. The firearms manufacturer created a famous marketing campaign in 1919 calling their Model 1873 Rifle "The Gun that Won the West."

"They put themselves as this kind of mythical company of the American West, and yes...Buffalo Bill had Winchesters and obviously they were popular in the West—but they were expensive on the frontier," Hlebinsky says.

The same went for all the other famous firearms manufacturers. While they were certainly available for the right price, that cost generally proved too steep for the average person.

The Scattergun

Most times, weapons used on the frontier were just as likely something passed down in a family for generations such as flintlocks. Hlebinsky tells me that the most common type of firearm used in the Old West wasn't necessarily the classic six-shot revolver but rather the simple and somewhat inelegant shotgun.

"I think that the shotgun always kind of references the real gun that would have been the most accessible," Hlebinsky says. "It was a good multi-purpose tool. And it is still used like that today. The shotgun is used by the military for breaching doors, riot clearing—it's a multi-purpose gun that you can use for many reasons."

Unlike the careful construction and fine tuning that went into engineering a rifle for long distance or the revolver for up-close accuracy, the shotgun was a simpler weapon. It was created to send out a medium- to close-range cone of devastating lead shot—hence the nickname "scattergun." If a shotgun was rugged enough, literally anything could be fired out of it, including coins. It was powerful and cheap, and if the goal was to hit the target and cause the most amount of damage, the shotgun was often the right tool for the job. Its versatility was no doubt the key to the weapon's success. Simple, somewhat crude, but wildly successful in the right circumstances—of which many ultimately presented themselves.

In an interview with a well-known sportsman Sol Shaw in 1889, a reporter for the *Rocky Mountain Sun* asked if he'd ever had the opportunity to kill a bear. Sol replied, "Wait till the bear gets right up to you, and then [with a shotgun] you can blow a hole right through him as big as your arm.'" While the sportsman may have been pulling the reporter's leg somewhat, the shotgun's violent reputation during the Wild West was well earned.

The shotgun's success proved itself over and over again, making it a popular—and bold—choice throughout the West. Perhaps most famously, U.S. Deputy Marshal Virgil Earp handed a short-barreled shotgun to his friend Doc Holliday, which he used on Cowboy member Tom McLaury during the legendary shootout at the O.K. Corral in 1881. For his part, legendary lawman Wyatt Earp used an absolutely brutal Stevens 10-gauge double-barrel shotgun during a shootout to kill Curly Bill Brocius in 1882. Infamous Civil War veteran, mercenary, and Austin city marshal Ben Thompson carried a breech-loading, double-barrel shotgun made by Braddell & Sons of Belfast, Ireland, to enforce the Texas rule of law. Henry McCarty, also known as William H. Bonney or "Billy the Kid," famously shot and killed lawman Bob Olinger with his own Whitney 10-gauge shotgun while escaping from the Lincoln County Courthouse in 1881. Of course, the shotgun didn't guarantee long-term victory: the Kid was later killed by Sheriff Pat Garrett in 1881 at Fort Sumner with a Colt Frontier Model single-action .44-40.

Assassin and outlaw James "Jim" Brown Miller, known as "Deacon Jim" or "Killer Miller," preferred the use of a shotgun for his many executions because of how effective it was. Miller largely worked as an assassin for hire and was well known for his impeccable manners, excellent choice in clothing, and his devotion to the church. Oftentimes the testimony and support from the religious community helped sway a jury in favor of acquittal when he was tried for murder. Having claimed to kill as many as fifty people, Miller found himself facing a criminal trial again after killing U.S. Deputy Marshal Gus Bobbitt in Oklahoma with a double-barreled shotgun. As in the past, members of the church sent in letters of support for the man they could not believe was the monster he was charged with being. But then a lynch mob broke him and several other suspected criminals out of jail and dragged them to a livery stable. The other three were hanged from the rafters and Miller was last to go. With a rope around his neck he reportedly yelled, "Let 'er rip" before enthusiastically meeting his death.

For as simple, cheap, and effective as the shotgun was, the rope that killed him was just as quick—and maybe even more efficient.

Collective Memory and Firearms

Some argue that many of the myths of the Wild West and the associated guns of that time were created not long after the Civil War in 1865 in part to help the country mend its steep division.

"The Civil War ends, and you've got kind of a fractured country. You need nation building," Hlebinsky said. "Ideas of collective memory and how you build an identity, an American identity, and that American Western mythology was the identity for a long time and firearms played a role in that." The myth of winning the West was an attempt to take the tragedy of the Civil War and find a way to create a shared triumph, she said. "Even though today we can look back and some can question the frontier image, that is a lot of the mythology that people were looking for in that time period," Hlebinsky says. "At the same time, firearms became a lot more of a consumer product."

She believes that late-nineteenth century consumer culture and availability of firearms turned target shooting and firearm ownership into a national pastime. "By the 1880s machine guns were available, by the 1890s semi-automatic pistols were becoming popular—so it is a really weird time," Hlebinsky says. "A lot of the things that you associate with the American West and the Frontier is almost nostalgic."

Names like Winchester and Colt still bring back visions of an untamed land filled with gunslinging cowboys and rifle-wielding horsemen. In fact, many of the famous gun manufacturers of the Old West still exist today—but often not as they once did. In Winchester's case, the firearms manufacturer looked to playing up the nostalgia of the Wild West after World War I. The iconic reputation was a successful marketing stunt but the company ultimately went bankrupt in 1931. "The Winchester brand today is actually made by Fabrique Nationale. They are made abroad and license the name from an American company,

Olin Corporation—but it is very, very different than what you imagined," Hlebinsky says.

She notes without hesitation the firearm of the modern Wild West is the Glock. The Austrian polymer-framed semi-automatic pistols were developed in the 1980s and quickly grew in popularity. Just as the Colt was considered the point-and-shoot gun of the Old West, so too is the Glock considered the point-and-shoot gun of the Modern West. The Colt didn't have a safety feature, and not dissimilarly the Glock has a series of internal passive safeties rather than an active one. Glocks are also considered affordable, accurate, easy to use, and virtually indestructible, making them a popular choice in the Modern West. And like the Colt, Hlebinsky said the Glock has even entered the modern Western mythology and is often featured in contemporary Western television dramas. Between 60 and 70 percent of police officers carry a Glock in the United States, ensuring its placement as the firearm of the modern Wild West.

"Someone on the show always carries a Winchester, someone always carries a Colt, whether it is a semi-auto or single action, or Smith & Wesson—but somebody carries a Glock and it is usually a younger person," Hlebinsky says. "If you look at our town, our cops, they're carrying Glocks...I actually did a lecture here about how Glocks are the new sidearm of the American West."

Despite the advancements of the firearms industry, the desire for the basic single-action revolver has not gone away. In Hlebinsky's museum sitting inside a glass case is a massive revolver made by Wyoming gunsmith John Linebaugh, who makes some of the most powerful handguns on the planet.

Bullets in the Walls

The sun is still making its daily summit across the polished Wyoming sky when I arrive at the house and workshop of legendary gunmaker John Linebaugh. He carries one of his revolvers he planned to test-fire when he comes around front to meet with me. In his early sixties, wearing glasses, a long-sleeve button-up shirt, and a baseball cap, the famed gunsmith looks more than a little like an engineer, which is appropriate given his unique calling. Linebaugh is often hailed as a pioneer in his field of custom firearms, notably for his world-famous .50 caliber single-action revolvers. When Clint Eastwood's celluloid-chewing Dirty Harry snarled his classic line about the .44 Magnum being the most powerful handgun in the world, at the time it actually wasn't anymore. Gunsmiths were quickly developing larger and more powerful calibers for handguns. In the '80s when Linebaugh developed the .500 caliber, which would bear his name, it would literally be twice as powerful as the famed .44 Magnum. "I never stepped into this to become popular or famous; I stepped into it to build a bigger and better mousetrap," Linebaugh says.

Originally from rural Missouri, he came out to Wyoming in 1978. Growing up, Linebaugh lived in a household that didn't allow firearms.

"My dad had a friend who had his eye shot out with a BB gun when they were little kids and we didn't have guns—couldn't buy them—so we built them." Linebaugh says, taking a seat at a table on his front porch. "We did a lot of shooting, a lot of testing. We built a .458 [caliber rifle] when I was seventeen years old just because we thought we ought to have one." When he moved to Wyoming in the late '70s, he met people trying similar things that helped set him on his course.

"So then we started experimenting with ballistics and more powerful guns," Linebaugh says, adding he followed in the footsteps of fellow Wyoming gunsmith legend Dick Casull, who created the ferocious .454 Casull cartridge. "Basically Dick Casull did when I was in diapers in the mid '50s what we tried to do in the early '80s."

During that time, Wyoming was the perfect place for innovation and creation for Linebaugh. "This was a totally different world here. The mindset was unlimited, the thought patterns were laid-back and relaxed. It's not 'how can we do it' or 'can we do it?'; it's 'just go do it,'" he says. The mentality of the area encouraged divergent thinking for gunsmiths like Linebaugh. They came out to the state to push their industry in new directions and in the process changed it forever.

He believes this no-nonsense, determined type of problem solving allowed the original pioneers to come into the West and scratch out an existence. "It's a tough country. Even if you have the luxuries of wealth and money, it is still a tough country," Linebaugh says, looking around. "This is the last frontier right here."

The Western Mentality

According to Linebaugh, the story behind the massive caliber bearing his name came about, essentially, because the state was just allowing handguns for use in hunting during the mid '80s.

"They set up a panel of experts ... and they set up a list of cartridges that were legal, or not legal, to use on big game animals," Linebaugh says. "You couldn't get the .454 Casull at that time because it wasn't in production. They were very close to it, and they wouldn't let us use the .45 Colt ... so we made our own. The [firearms] industry was almost as much in the dark as we were ... the handgun field was wide open to serious experimentation and development."

Linebaugh tested, evaluated, and continued to work on his firearm projects. "We shot guns to destruction. We bent 'em, twisted 'em, broke 'em, blew 'em up. And then had all that data tested and substantiated." His idea was to create a cartridge that shot a bullet at 2,800 psi. Considering the size of the bullet and other similarly sized rounds, this may be considered slow—but he said faster projectiles have far less penetration.

"It's like an arrow. 'I want a carbon shaft and I want an overdraw and I want wheels on it and I want all this stuff'—just get you a longbow and shoot a heavy arrow, it shoots through stuff. When we got onto this theory, that's when we made our push, that's when we made our drive," Linebaugh says. In the process, he made firearms history. His .500 caliber pistol was featured on the front cover of Guns & Ammo Magazine in August of 1986, and ever since there have been constant orders. There is currently a two-year backlog and it takes him about a week to build a gun. He's made about 1,600 revolvers for customers over the years, each of which generally cost between $3,800 and $7,500.

Linebaugh says living in the West makes people think differently about what is possible. He's adamant the Western mentality helps people to think, create, and innovate.

"There's nothing holding you back, there's nothing you can't do if you're big enough to do it. You've got to think differently," Linebaugh says. "To me, it makes a person more rounded, self-reliant—the very things this country has lost. That's what I love about it so much."

Inside his house there is a buffalo head mounted on the wall. He can point to where a bullet was lodged in a horn. Not far from there sits an old cowboy hat that was gifted to him after its owner fired one of his revolvers without being careful and the front sight kicked back and hit him in the head, punching a hole through the hat. He shows me his workshop, then we step out to the back of his property.

"There's your target." He points to a distant white stone, then hands me a revolver. I slip on hearing protection and raise the handgun. The sun is now directly over us, reaching high noon. I aim, thumb back the hammer, and pull the trigger.

CHAPTER 13

CALL OF THE
WOLVES

With the three timber wolves now captured, the people decided some sport should be had with them. The wolves would be released in something termed a "wolf chase," a new sport imagined as a take on the idea of the classic European fox hunt—but with a dangerous Western spin. About three hundred men, women, and children arrived to take part in what was expected to be the day's thrilling event. Tourists staying in a nearby town followed along in a wagon during the day's bloody spectacle. The year was 1900, and the idolization of the American West was fully underway by both those who viewed it across the Mississippi and those living within its confines.

For years a war was being orchestrated against wolves by Western cattle and sheep stockmen who were afraid of the continued losses in revenue from one of the country's few large natural predators. In some areas, a lucrative bounty on wolves ranged between $10 and $20 apiece, no doubt a strong temptation for those with the skills and aptitude for trapping and killing the animals. It was probably only a matter of time before the general adventuresome spirit, fictional or otherwise, of the Wild West found its way into the time's prevalent, systematic eradication of the country's wolves.

"Western sport more exciting than following foxes and hares," exclaimed the *Herald Democrat*, a paper located in Leadville, Colorado, said of the wolf chase, which was likely in Wyoming or Montana. "Chasing foxes or hares is too tame for sportsmen of the west. Wolves are more to their liking." Besides the large crowd, there were also thirty dogs enlisted in the mighty effort. Rumors swirled around that some of the dogs loaned to the wolf chase might be by none other than Buffalo Bill Cody himself. The reporter went on to explain the three large captured timber wolves were far from docile despite their many days in captivity, "with mighty jaws lined with shining sharp teeth that snapped ominously when anyone came near them. They are not cowards, those timber wolves."

The three wolves were brought out ahead some ways of the party of dogs, men, women, children, and tourists to give them a sporting head start. Right off the bat, things did not go as planned, and the heroic chase was delayed.

"At first they laid down as if hopeless of escape and absolutely refused to budge," the writer said. "Even kicks failed to arouse them. Finally, the smallest of the trio got up and started off with a limp, and the others followed him a moment later. They did not run fast at the start . . . "

Before long the hounds were set loose in a deafening chorus to their madcap, scrambling effort to track down the animals. The writer assumed the wolves, injured as they were from being captured in metal traps, would soon be caught by the dogs. However, it appeared as soon as the wolves could hear the baying of the approaching hounds, they sped up.

The journalist admitted he and others were afraid that with the wolves' newfound speed, such as it was, they might indeed escape. If that were to happen, no fox hunting–like tail trophies would be distributed to the participants. But whatever advantage the wolves had in their temporary boost in speed turned out not to last long. The writer reported, "So far [the hounds] had been running by scent, but soon they caught sight of the fugitives. Then the chased assumed a different aspect, and the wolves might as well have tried to race an express train."

The dogs came in fast and aggressively, knocking down the wolves. The wolves tried to make good their escape before being bowled over yet again by their pursuers. The pack soon fought with two male wolves while the female wolf ran. The reporter referred to the fight as being similar to a "scrimmage on a football field." After killing five dogs, the wounded wolves were finally taken down for good. The she-wolf hadn't made it too much further away before the dogs and people caught up and formed a circle around her.

Dogs came up to the wolf and snapped at her but she didn't pay them any attention. The reporter noted that none of the dogs were willing to attack the wolf. Then: "Finally a dog with more of the bloodhound than the others led the assault. The old wolf woke up and killed him instantly."

After that, the rest of the dogs refused to follow suit and attack. Some in the crowd thought their hesitance was due to some type of canine chivalry for the wounded female wolf. An awkward pause in the day's sport followed as people stood around watching. If there was sport to be had by chasing the animal, it seemed the party was having some difficulty in finding it. At last the coach carrying the tourists rumbled up and asked them what the holdup was. On hearing of the hunt's unexpected development, one man said his vicious thirty-pound female bulldog would be up to the task of killing the wolf. The writer said, "He was advised against the course, but he insisted, and his [bulldog] was unleashed."

The tourist's dog immediately attacked the exhausted wolf. Again and again, the wolf barely responded to the bulldog's attacks. The dog finally clamped its teeth on the wolf's throat, and only with great effort was she able to shake the bulldog off—who promptly came back again. This time the wolf made quick work of the dog by crushing its head between her jaws.

"The lifeless body was thrown aside with contempt. A bullet from a cowboy's six-shooter then ended the old wolf's career, and the crowd rode home, trying to figure out whether the game had been worth the candle."

In many respects the early settlers were at war with nearly everything they came in contact with to carve out a new life on the frontier. They fought the elements, the environment, the indigenous tribes, even each other; nothing was an exception, including the wildlife—and especially the wolves. As a result, the wolf was erroneously considered a serious threat to life and business and hunted to the edge of extinction.

The Big Bad Wolf

Wolves have had bad reputations among humans for centuries. Justified or otherwise, tales of their monstrous behavior have appeared in everything from fairy tales, where they ate grandmothers, to mythology, where they helped bring about the end of the world. Europe was filled with stories of the slavering jaws of wolves tearing apart people and eating children. When settlers began streaming across North America looking to start new lives, the stories of the malevolence of wolves continued. While these animals can be violent and extremely dangerous, it is important to remember that these tales were the result of an ecosystem out of balance. In many cases the wolves were starving to death or trying to protect themselves.

W.J. Gidley, the manager of the stage line between Gillette and Buffalo, Wyoming, recalled to a writer in 1892 his most harrowing experience of a battle with wolves in Dakota years before. Gidley said he was driving a team of six horses and had a full load of passengers. It was winter, the snow as high as two feet, when a pack of wolves ambushed them. The stagecoach driver said for three hours they fought a desperate assault on their lives, shooting more than thirty wolves in the process. Gidley knew something had to be done, so he tied the reins to the coach's brake and leaped out onto one of the running horses. As he worked to untie the horse from the team, he said wolves jumped and snapped at him, trying to drag him to the ground. Once freed, the horse ran off in another direction and drew the wolves with it, and Gidley was then able to get the coach and its passengers back to safety without further issue.

Just the year before, a Minnesota periodical told the tale of how a group of 125 wolves had gathered together because of a forest fire not far from Saint Paul. Apparently, the three children of Audre Gulick came across the pack of wolves after wandering away from their home in the woods and were promptly devoured.

That same year a missionary among the Native American tribes, then living near Lake Winnipeg, wrote that a camp was attacked by a band of wolves numbering about one hundred. The members of the tribe fought for their lives, shooting and cudgeling wolves left and right. One man climbed a tree to get away from the onslaught and shot twenty wolves from his precarious vantage point. Another man was yanked down to the ground from his fighting spot and systematically torn apart. The wolves were eventually driven off, but many of the Native Americans living in the area panicked about another such attack. The missionary said the tribe members believed the wolves acted in this unusual fashion because there were no longer deer in the area to hunt.

My personal favorite tale of an alleged wolf attack was reported in the *Cañon City Record* in 1904 when two men, Frank Perry and C.K. Chapman, were attacked while operating a sleigh. Only five miles outside of town, five timber wolves came out of the forest and attacked the men and a frenzied chase began. Before long, the horses became winded and the wolves were getting ever closer. One man resorted to using a horsewhip to keep the wolves from leaping directly into the sleigh with them. Again and again, they tried to get aboard. The situation looked hopeless.

"Perry then produced a well-stocked lunch box and threw a few morsels of food to the wolves. They devoured it, spending a little time quarreling over the donation. Again they came on, and again they were treated to sandwiches. These delays enabled the horses to slow down and save their strength and wind."

Soon the sandwiches ran out, but by then the men were close enough to a town that they were saved from an ignominious death.

Whether it's a close call or unceremonious end, based on a true story or a tall tale, encounters with wolves have always left a harsh mark on people's minds, which eventually led to extreme measures.

War with the Wolves

As ranchers and free-ranging cattle operations blossomed in the West, wolves soon grew to become a serious issue for their bottom line. Unlike the native prey of the indigenous wolves, European imports like cattle and sheep didn't know how to defend themselves. As such, they became easy pickings for the wolves, and people decided something needed to be done. But trying to hunt wolves was not an effortless undertaking. As reported by the *Herald Democrat* in 1892, tired of attacks on their cattle and sheep, a group of miners and stockmen gathered together to engage in a wolf hunt in Idaho. "It was a great success from every point of view, eleven wolves being killed," a writer exclaimed, then somewhat surreptitiously added, "and nine men, more or less, [were] seriously injured."

Often ranchers resorted to using any means possible to rid themselves of the area's natural predators. In 1896 near Sioux Falls, South Dakota, there were large systematic efforts to rid the state of gray wolves for harming the operation of stockmen. During one such hunt some thirty hunters were engaged to kill eighteen big gray wolves. A writer noted that a special breed of hound would be brought into the country specifically to drive wolves from the state for good. People organized group hunts, offered payment in exchange for dead wolves; others, it seems, had more novel approaches to the perceived wolf problem.

One newspaper in 1893 reported that J.M. Campbell, "the most extensive sheep man in western Texas," lost 22 percent of his flock in one year. Campbell had killed off more than one hundred wolves on his property but decided he needed a more permanent and total solution to his wolf problem. "He has...hit upon a novel scheme for exterminating every wolf in western Texas. It is by the inoculation of disease among them," the paper said. Campbell caught ten wolves and trapped them in with a dog afflicted with mange, and once the disease caught he planned to release the wolves. Campbell hoped the disease would spread among the wolf population and exterminate them for good. Sadly, these types of tactics weren't regulated just to the animal populations. Biological warfare had also been used by colonists on the indigenous people in the form of small pox–infected blankets. As it was, disease was certainly common during the Old West and was especially devastating to Native American societies, which were, sometimes, completely wiped out as a result.

Surprisingly, not all methods of ridding the wolves ended with death. Others came up with more colorful ways to rid the country of wolves. Colorado's *Brush Tribune* detailed a new invention to scare away wolves from grazing cattle in 1901. The invention, already being used by sheep-growing districts, was described as an "automatic gun" which fired at regular intervals to keep the wolves away. "It consists of a sort of box which contains a clockwork attachment with a small steel barrel projecting from one end," the newspaper said. "Wolves do not attack sheep in the daytime, and the gun needs to be in operation only from sunset to sunrise ... It may be that the wolf, which is a decidedly intelligent animal, may learn the deception after a while and realize that the automatic gun has not a man behind it."

With all these combined efforts, in time wolves were pushed out of and eradicated from the Mississippi West. Colorado was the first state to put an official bounty on the animals in 1869 and the last wolf was finally killed in 1945. By 1978, U.S. Fish and Wildlife Services considered the gray wolves an endangered species.

Chinook the Hybrid

I'd spent years of my childhood with my face pressed up against car windows trying to catch a glimpse of a wolf while traveling through Yellowstone National Park. It was like trying to spot a ghost. Years later now, I would finally get an up-close look at some of the only wolves that still live in Colorado.

Between the towns of Florissant and Divide sits the Colorado Wolf and Wildlife Center, a nonprofit organization and the only wolf refuge in the state certified by the Association of Zoos & Aquariums. On the way to the refuge the early morning mists stubbornly cling to the thick surrounding forest, but once I step out of the truck I hear them. There's something about the forlorn howl of the wolf that awakens a dormant part of the brain, like a buried line of computer code that comes to the surface with a little voice reminding you that humans aren't the only predators in town. I can't see them yet but one howl joins another, and in the foggy morning weather they sound like they are standing next to me.

The organization's founder Darlene Kobobel has her hair in a ponytail and wears a gray shirt, khaki shorts, well-worn hiking boots, and a smattering of silver jewelry. We sit down to talk about how the refuge started and how a girl from California, afraid of wolves, became one of their fiercest advocates, dedicating her life to their protection. Kobobel admits that growing up she never gave much thought to wolves or their plight in the West.

"When I was a little girl my biggest fear in the world was actually a wolf," she admits. "The reason for that was because of the stories that you would read and watching cartoons or movies that portrayed the wolf as this vicious mean animal coming out of the woods with these glowing eyes and tongue hanging out ... so it was like the wolf is kind of a bad and scary animal."

She never thought in her wildest dreams that one day she would actually be rescuing wolves. Kobobel moved to Colorado in the early 1990s and began volunteering at a local animal shelter. Her job was to take the dogs that couldn't be adopted and try to find them a family at a large pet supply store in the neighboring city of Colorado Springs. For the dogs, it was their last chance to get off death row.

Kobobel would stand there in front of the many aisles of dog supplies and try to show off each animal's best side. She knew that if she returned with them back to the shelter, there was a good chance that they would be euthanized. One day she took three dogs with her down to the store and realized with a start that she'd forgotten their water dishes. Kobobel drove back to the animal shelter and while looking for the dishes came across a wolf-dog hybrid named Chinook in a cage hidden in the back.

"There was this beautiful wolf-dog that was there and she stood about thirty-two inches at the shoulder. She was almost five and a half feet from nose tip to tail," Kobobel says. "Silver gray, absolutely gorgeous, and she looked at me and I looked at her and she starts literally jumping up and down like, 'Please get me out of here.'"

Kobobel learned from the animal control officer the wolf-dog couldn't be adopted because it was against the law to allow adoption of any type of wolf hybrid. Depending on how much wolf they have in them, the wolf-dogs might not be the kind of animal to sleep peacefully by the fireplace or, in some cases, to come into the house. Wolves do not make good pets. She says, "So, unfortunately, a lot of people who get them, no matter what wolf content they have, it is still estimated that out of two hundred fifty thousand that are born, every year 80 percent will never reach their third birthday ... If you have a wolf-dog and you take it to an animal shelter or humane society and you're like, 'I have to surrender my wolf,' then it is usually euthanized with[in] twenty-four to forty-eight hours unless it can be adopted to a sanctuary."

She comments that the other issue is that most sanctuaries in the United States operate beyond capacity and can't take any more of these animals. After she appealed to the animal control officer, he reluctantly agreed to let her have the dog—if she got back from adopting out the other dogs before Chinook was euthanized.

Motivated, she adopted out two of three dogs. The last one wouldn't stop barking, no matter what she tried. Finally, Kobobel found a lady who said she rather liked the fact that he barked because she was a trucker. The woman said she needed a dog that would keep people away from her rig but she couldn't afford the adoption fee. Kobobel paid the adoption fee and raced back to the animal shelter, hoping she would make it in time.

"I opened up the door to the shelter and they were marching her into the backroom to euthanize her. So he looks at me and said, 'If you want that wolf, you better take her now,'" Kobobel says. "So he hands over the leash to me, just gives her to me. I didn't tell him I didn't really have a place for her. I had a one-bedroom cabin with two other dogs—but I thought, you know what, if there's a will there's a way."

Kobobel decided as she started to learn more about wolf-dogs, wolves, and the issues they face that she would start a rescue center. She admits that at first she didn't have any idea what she was getting herself into. She had a sign put out that announced she was running a wolf hybrid rescue center and was almost immediately inundated with people dropping off their dogs.

"My first week I ended up with seventeen animals, and I had a five-acre enclosure . . . back in the day, I could barely afford to feed myself. I lived very poorly," Kobobel says. "To support not only myself but to feed them and to take care of them, I took on three jobs."

In addition to taking care of the wolf hybrids, Kobobel worked in construction, waited on customers at casinos, and cleaned houses. People driving past her rescue center would stop in and ask questions about the animals, so education also became a large part of what she did as well.

"There were times where I was like, 'I can't do this anymore.' There was one time where I was so desperate financially I thought, 'I don't know if I can do this.' I was exhausted. I thought maybe I just have to give this up and maybe find someone who can take it over," Kobobel recalls. "Then I went to the post office and there was a letter, and this lady said, 'Thank you so much for what you do for the wolves.' Right there I got up and dusted myself off, and was like, 'We're going to do this.'"

Ten years later she decided to move to a larger location that she leased for several years before the landlord told her he was no longer interested in her business. She was able to secure a loan for a new spot in 2006 though. She began offering tours and expanded from thirty-five to seventy acres. Today she has Arctic wolves, timber wolves, Alaskan interior wolves, Mexican Grays, two species of fox, and a family of coyotes—along with seven employees and ten volunteers.

"The passion in my heart will always be—every day when I get up and breathe, it is to be a voice for these animals," Kobobel says. "I look at them and look at how they've been persecuted. I watch them when they run and when they play and how they're a family together."

What the Future Holds

Whether wolves should be brought back to Colorado or not is a highly controversial topic. Essentially the argument pits a damaging nuisance for stockmen against an essential part of the ecosystem needed to keep burgeoning elk and deer populations under control. The state does a lot to regulate and control herd animals, but advocates for wolf integration argue a natural predator would not only help to cull burgeoning populations but also to move herds around to keep them from overgrazing.

Kobobel believes wolves belong in the present. "We have an overpopulation of our ungulates... they are out of control. Even the parks and wildlife give out extra hunting license because there're so many of them. Look at how many of them get killed by cars and the impact people have on injuries and totaled vehicles because we have so many of them here."

Motorists in Colorado hit an estimated three thousand animals, including deer, every year. From my own perspective, I think that the deer population is so large it seems like they literally rain out of the sky. I've known multiple people who have hit deer with cars and witnessed several such accidents. In some places there are so many deer fearlessly standing in large numbers in the roads, yards, and driveways that it feels a little bit like a low-budget horror movie titled *Night of the Ungulates*.

"Colorado is out of balance and there is something that is missing—and that is the wolf," Kobobel says.

The few wolves that have come to Colorado from the reintegration project in Yellowstone National Park have died. One was hit and killed by a car not far from the mountain town where I worked for a time as the editor of a newspaper. Another was mistaken for a coyote and shot and killed.

Kobobel says wolves should be reintroduced in Colorado and that the state shouldn't just wait for them to come back naturally. She believes there is little chance that a wolf can successfully make the trip from Yellowstone by itself.

"They'll never make it," Kobobel says. "There will never be enough who will get here to be able to make it alive and then sustain a pack, because the ones who have filtered through here have either been shot or killed or hit by a vehicle." She tells me the life expectancy for a wolf in the wild is only between three and six years. Life is sometimes difficult for a creature that only has the use of its jaws to survive.

"In Yellowstone, the wolves that die, or have been killed, they do a necropsy and most of the wolves had busted ribs, they had broken jaws—it's a hard life," Kobobel says. "They have jaw power, but unlike a bear and unlike a cougar where they can grab and hold their victim, [wolves] have a small snout and it is harder for them to take down prey. For a lot of them, starvation is really big."

Wolves are also social animals and have the best chance of survival in packs. They hunt together, keep watch together, and protect one another. The lone wolf that reaches the state by itself has a steep road to travel—and it's usually filled with cars and ranchers who see coyotes.

"The amount of domestic livestock that is taken down is just so minimal, and there are ways to be able to coexist with wolves," Kobobel says. "First of all, they're not going to come around humans; they're deathly afraid of them, they're very elusive. They don't hunt people, they don't eat people."

Not generally, that is. While any animal is certainly capable of becoming dangerous in the right situation, in the last sixty years there are only three known cases of wolf attacks in North America. One tragically occurred with wolves kept in captivity. Another death occurred in Saskatchewan, Canada, in 2005 when a man's body was found surrounded by wolves. In that case, the coroner ruled his death was indeed caused by the wolves—but an expert in wolf biology said he thought it was more likely the death was caused by a black bear. Lastly, a young woman was

Colorado Wolf and Wildlife Center founder Darlene Kobobel spends time with one of the wolves at the center. *(Photo by Ian Neligh)*

killed in 2010 while out running near Chignik, Alaska. Ultimately, DNA evidence was used to link her death to a wolf attack.

In contrast, more than sixty people have been killed in the last one hundred years by black bears in the United States. In Yellowstone, thirty-eight people have been injured by grizzly bears since 1980. Horrifically, man's best friend looks positively homicidal compared to both wolves and bears. It is estimated that four million people are bitten by dogs every year. From 1979 to 2005, on average about nineteen deaths have occurred every year from dog attacks. By comparison, modern-day predatory wolf attacks in North America are almost nonexistent.

"These animals want to be left alone and they want to do their own thing, and if you leave them alone, they're not coming after you," Kobobel says. "Food and babies are the two main things they want to protect."

Kobobel then takes me outside for a look at some of her residents. In many ways, the wolf refuge is like a retirement home for the giant carnivores, with large outdoor enclosures holding two wolves at a time. I'm struck by how large the wolves are in person, and while I was not expecting something that acted like a labradoodle, what assumptions I did have quickly vanish. Wolves look and act differently, and behind the uncanny yellow eyes, there is an intelligent brain that operates in a distinctly different fashion than a dog's.

"I believe that we can coexist together . . . if you look at a healthy ecosystem, you have to have your predator and prey to make that balance to make a healthy ecosystem," Kobobel says. "Without wolves, we have more coyotes—because the competition is not there. [Coyotes] are having bigger litters and if you have wolves, the wolves keep them in check and run them out of different areas."

There is no tail wagging, no eager vying for treats. The wolves display only a clinical, if skittish, interest in my activities and behavior. With dogs, there's a type of familiarity, a shared recognition in the eyes. My own dog would leap through fire for a treat but couldn't survive an afternoon on her own.

Not so with wolves. Kobobel tells me to step toward the enclosure where two wolves keenly watch us. In perfect unison, they leap back to keep their distance from me. For a species that was almost eradicated, I can't say I entirely blame them. In the 1990s gray wolves were reintroduced into Yellowstone National Park after almost having been wiped nearly seventy years before. While their numbers have fluctuated wildly over that time, today there are almost a hundred living in the wild and that number is growing.

Considered a keystone species in Yellowstone, wolves have direct and indirect effects on other wildlife populations. In the 1930s after wolves were eliminated from the park, elk populations soon grew to uncontrollable levels. Predators no longer pushed them along in the winter and as such overgrazed areas, damaging plants and the local wildlife dependent on those resources. Since the gray wolf's introduction into the Yellowstone ecosystem in 1995, a series of unexpected but positive changes occurred throughout the park. The wolves are now moving the elk along, which gives areas time to recover from overgrazing, which in turn allows species, such as the beaver, to come back. With the return of the beaver there has been an increase in strong plant, fish, and bird habitat and the further developing of a more complex and robust ecosystem. Clearly there is a need—and the wolves have answered the call.

CHAPTER 14

BARE-KNUCKLE

BOXING

A rowdy line snakes out from the entrance of the Cheyenne Ice and Events Center under a heavy, early evening sun. The intermittent waft of marijuana smoke swirls across the crowd to mingle with the cigarette haze. A young woman covered in tattoos tries to get those passing by her table to enter a drawing for a new Harley-Davidson motorcycle. Some listen to her earnest pitch—but many have their eyes resolutely set towards their destination: glass doors, flanked by bald men in black shirts with handheld metal detectors. The crowd hums with anticipation for the coming event. Soon the gates will open to admit those in line to the first-ever state-sanctioned bare-knuckle boxing contest in the history of the United States.

The historic meeting of modern-day pugilists takes place on June 2, 2018, just across the border from Colorado where I make the three-hour trek to witness the unusual display of fisticuffs firsthand. The last time this sport was even close to an acceptable practice was when the Old West was still alive and well. Bare-knuckle boxing was a rather popular form of entertainment specifically during the late 1800s. This style of boxing consists of two competitors in a ring, trying to score the most devastating hits to the head and body of their opponent with their bare fists. Originally the rules also said the number of rounds in a fight were often determined by how long a fighter stayed on his feet. Because of its dubious legal status, for a time many local authorities turned a blind eye to the bloody sport, which often found its way into the West's resilient mining towns and districts. The last fully sanctioned bare-knuckle heavyweight championship bout occurred almost 130 years ago, when in the aftermath of the world-famous battle authorities promptly put both fighters in jail.

The Most Anticipated Fight in the World

The year was 1889 and bare-knuckle boxing was illegal in every state. Yet newspapers across the country were breathlessly reporting on their front covers the details of the upcoming heavyweight championship bout between John L. Sullivan and Jake Kilrain. Every detail about the upcoming fight—the location, the time, the date, everything—was a secret except to just a few. But soon details of the fight began to spread to those interested in attending and placing their bets. Authorities across the country promised that anyone involved would be found out and arrested.

The conflict between the two men had been building for years until finally they decided to step into the ring and settle their long dispute over who was the greatest heavyweight bare-knuckle boxer in the world. Sullivan, from Roxbury, Massachusetts, was arguably the first major sports celebrity in the United States and, many would consider, the heavyweight boxing champion of the world. A massive fighter, Sullivan often shaved his head and mustache before a fight so that his opponent wouldn't be able to find an opportunistic purchase during their bout. Sullivan had his fair share of troubles largely because of his well-documented love affair for hard liquor. After his last large championship fight, he spent from 1883 to 1884 traveling the country and offering $1,000 to anyone who could last four rounds with him. "His success was marvelous," reported one paper at the time. "In several trips through the country he knocked out no less than sixty of the largest, most powerful and skillful pugilists to be found."

Often the local police would step in and stop these bloody one-sided contests from going too far, afraid Sullivan's foolhardy opponent would be killed or seriously injured during the process of being beaten to a pulp. *The Colorado Daily Chieftain* announced one such visit to the City of Pueblo in 1883: "Everyone who has ever read of the exploits of

John L. Sullivan, of Boston, the champion pugilist of the world, has felt a keen desire, no doubt, to see the man who is capable of withstanding and conquering the hardest hitters of his day." He was considered unbeatable and at the top of his game.

In contrast, Kilrain was a quiet family man from another Boston suburb. He seemed to be very much Sullivan's opposite but was also considered by many to be the true heavyweight champion of the world. Kilrain had often challenged Sullivan to a fight to settle the matter and was regularly rebuffed.

After a thirty-nine-round draw in England, Sullivan came back to the United States and nearly died due to kidney and liver collapse, no doubt related to the enormous amount of alcohol he consumed on a regular basis. Many assumed Sullivan would die or that at the very least his fighting days were behind him, like a long line of empty whiskey bottles. However, not for the last time, he ignored his detractors and managed to pull through. Surprising everyone one more time, he also accepted Kilrain's challenge. With the type of contagious anticipation that many of the country's newspapers were soon to be afflicted, the *St. Paul Daily Globe* announced:

> A prize ring battle for the largest stake ever fought for is to take place at a point within two hundred miles of New Orleans on the 8th of July. The contestants will be John L. Sullivan "The champion of champions," and John Killian, more commonly known as "Jake Kilrain." They are to fight for $10,000 a side ($20,000 in all) and the diamond studded gold champion's belt...worth about $1,500; so that, altogether, $21,500 is involved in the result of this pugilistic contest...This fight will differ materially from the majority of those which have taken place in America in the last eight years, as it will be conducted under what are known as "the latest rules of the London prize ring."

London Prize Fighting Rules for boxing differed from the more commonly accepted Marquess of Queensberry Rules in that it would be fought bare fisted and allowed wrestling throws. For his part, Sullivan admitted he was not a fan of London Prize Fighting Rules, preferring

SULLIVAN AND KILRAIN IN THE RING.

An artist's illustration of the historic bare-knuckle heavyweight boxing match between John Sullivan and Jake Kilrain. *(Public domain)*

rather to fight with gloves if given the opportunity. He said, "The London Prize-ring Rules allow too much leeway for the rowdy element to indulge in their practices. Such mean tricks as spiking, biting, gouging, concealing snuff in one's mouth to blind an opponent, strangling, butting with the head, falling down without being struck, scratching with nails, kicking, falling on an antagonist with knees, the using of stones and resin, and the hundred other tricks that are impossible under the Marquess of Queensberry rules, are under the others practiced almost openly."

To get ready for the fight, Sullivan reportedly swore off alcohol and worked on a farm in upstate New York, performing strenuous outdoor chores to get his body back into fighting shape. To be sure, it wasn't an easy or quick process, and Sullivan was evidently so tired from his labors that he didn't have the time or energy to partake in drinking alcohol. Because of his poor health, many considered Sullivan the match's underdog. Meanwhile, at the secret location of the fight in Mississippi, a wealthy farmer prepared his land for the title match.

Men worked in secret and often at night to prepare the spot for the historic spectacle. Officials again redoubled their threats to arrest anyone connected to the fight, and the governor of Mississippi promised to pay $1,000 to anyone who spotted either fighter entering his state. And yet, so anticipated was this match that no one turned in either fighter.

Tickets to the fight included passage on one of three trains that would take spectators to the secret location. Altogether about three thousand people were transported to the secret location of the fight. "The anxiety to see the fight amounted almost to a frenzy, and those who were without the means to pay $10 or $15, the price of transportation and admission, took the chances of losing their lives in attempting to steal a ride," one reporter noted. "Just before the $15 train started from New Orleans it was discovered that scores of men and boys had concealed themselves on the cross-beams connecting the wheels, while others hung on the long iron rods connecting the trucks. The greater number, however, were perched on the roofs of the cars. They were driven off with difficulty."

The specific difficulties, as reported by the *Pittsburg Dispatch*, included an alarming amount of gunfire. The paper said that the trains cleared off freeloading riders from the roofs and trucks. Angered, some people took to their guns. "Many of those put off were very vengeful, and they fired a number of shots at the engineer of the train. This caused the passengers to duck and scramble as close to the floor of the cars as possible. Not less than 15 to 20 shots were fired, and that someone was not hurt was a little short of miraculous."

That didn't stop people from clambering onto the roof of the train again and squeezing into any and every spot they could find to get aboard, regardless of their own safety. "After passing the 28-mile trestle over Lake Pontchartrain, it was discovered that at least three dozen men were hanging on the trucks, in momentary danger of falling off and being killed, and the train was stopped and they were permitted to get on in regular fashion . . . " Allegedly, many stowaways decided not to climb inside the train because there just wasn't any room. An armed group of law enforcement officers also tried to get the train to stop at one point, but the engineer ignored them and continued past at forty miles per hour to the fight's location in Mississippi.

Both Sullivan and Kilrain had given the authorities searching for them the slip just the day before and slept in nearby houses overnight. Apparently the local sheriff showed up and warned the assembled crowd not to participate in an illegal fight. According to one reporter, $250 and the suggestion that he might be needed elsewhere in his county happened to be enough to put the issue to rest.

The temperature continued to rise like the crowd's growing bloodlust, and soon it was well above one hundred degrees. Two thousand spectators crowded into the hastily constructed stands while another thousand watched from the sides. A writer for the *St. Paul Daily Globe* noted the crowd was largely friendly; but they were also tired, thirsty, and hungry, and the only thing to eat came from a man selling cheese sandwiches of dubious quality. While looking at the notable people in the crowd, one newspaper writer near the boxing ring spotted none other than lawman Bat Masterson and fellow gunfighter Luke Short.

When the time came, the two boxers entered and disrobed. Depending on the account, Sullivan looked either healthy or overweight, and Kilrain looked either pale and sickly or perfectly fit. The two men shook hands and readied for the match. Kilrain and Sullivan advanced to the center of the ring, the latter said to be wearing a confident smile while Kilrain looked rather serious, and the world championship match began.

Sullivan vs. Kilrain

In the first round of the fight Kilrain rushed Sullivan, feinted a punch with his left, then suddenly grabbed Sullivan and threw him heavily to the ground. In the second round Sullivan struck back with a left punch and caught Kilrain in the ribs. They clinched, and then Sullivan threw Kilrain to the ground. Again the crowd went wild. By round eight Sullivan came up bleeding from a cut on his ear. It was the first time blood was spilled, and money for bets was exchanged. Sullivan took on "the appearance of an enraged bull" and rushed Kilrain with a massive right hand punch to the mouth, sending him to the ground. When the tenth round came, reporters noted Kilrain looked serious now. "Realizing that [Kilrain] had undertaken a huge contract, and as he showed no disposition to come to the center of the ring, Sullivan impatiently exclaimed: 'Stand up and fight like a man, I'm not a sprinter; I'm a fighter.'"

Over the course of the two-hour fight, things began to go downhill for Kilrain. While he did score some good hits on his beefier opponent, he largely spent his time trying to avoid getting hit and often took a knee to give himself time to recover from the attacks. At one point Kilrain used the spikes on the bottom of his shoes to tear up the top of Sullivan's feet. With swollen fists they traded blows, but Sullivan landed heavier and more effective shots. Everyone heard one hit to Kilrain's ribs in round nineteen. He slipped and dodged and kept just out of Sullivan's reach, prompting Sullivan to yell, "Why can't you fight like a man?"

By round twenty-three Kilrain was fully in retreat with Sullivan in pursuit. Sullivan landed another heavy hit on Kilrain's ribs, and the two clinched and fell to the ground. It was at this time Sullivan put his knee across Kilrain's throat. It wasn't the first or last foul from the fighters, which was conveniently overlooked by the referee. Kilrain made several more good attacks and even threw Sullivan to the ground for loud cheers, but the end was just around the corner. By round thirty-four Kilrain immediately went to the ground from a severe blow to the mouth. In round forty-two Kilrain fell from a light blow, likely to catch his breath. In round forty-four Sullivan "commenced vomiting freely, whereupon Kilrain told him he would not hit him while vomiting. Sullivan blurted out: 'Come on; I'm ready.'" For the rest of the fight until the seventy-fifth round, Kilrain tried his best to avoid Sullivan and often fell to the ground to avoid further punishment.

"The brutality of the crowd increased with Kilrain's discomfiture. In the sixty-fourth round they yelled to Sullivan to 'finish him,' and some shouted 'kill him,'" reported one paper. "Sullivan fought the battle of his life... He also took punishment like a Spartan, and never lost confidence or nerve. One finger on either hand was broken in the fight, but no one discovered it but his seconds."

After a half-hearted bluff to get Sullivan to agree to a draw, a bloody sponge was tossed from Kilrain's corner to the center of the ring, signaling the end of the fight.

"The champion is only a little the worse for wear, while Kilrain bled profusely and was badly worsted, despite the fact that he didn't stand up to take much punishment," said the *Pittsburg Dispatch.* "The battle was the hardest ever fought between big men in this country, but from start to finish Sullivan had decidedly the best of it. . . . The day was intensely hot, and this added to the punishment of the men."

With Sullivan jubilant and Kilrain reportedly weeping despite receiving a post-fight shot of morphine, both fighters were hurried off to their trains before the law could intercept them. Apparently, not long after the fight, militiamen caused Sullivan to climb out a train window and hide in the nearby woods until they were gone. Officers had warrants out for the arrest of both the fighters. Sullivan was eventually arrested in Nashville as he was boarding a train but was released the next day after posting bail. He was sentenced to a year in jail but appealed and got off with a $500 fine. Kilrain was on the run a bit longer, but he was also found and arrested in Baltimore. He was sentenced to jail for only two months but was "hired" out by the wealthy farmer who owned the location of the original fight and spent his time essentially recuperating.

Sullivan and Kilrain's fight was the last of its kind for a while. While bare-knuckle boxing still existed and could be found illegally or unsanctioned in warehouses and barges, the big championships became a thing of the past as authorities cracked down. Gloved boxing rose to prominence, fully eclipsing its bloodier sibling and leaving it to the pages of history. That is, at least, until David Feldman came along.

The Sweetest Science

Today the public filters into the Wyoming events center to watch the return of bare-knuckle boxing and the first heavyweight championship match of its kind since Sullivan and Kilrain. Sitting near the boxing ring, I watch a yellow spotlight drift apathetically across the walls and ceiling as people file into their assigned seats. American and Canadian flags hang from the wall behind the empty boxing ring, a tribute to the hockey games hosted in the facility most nights. But tonight a very different game will play in the stadium.

Simply sitting in a seat and drinking a beer during the fight is, if certainly not extraordinary, then at the very least significant. The last crowd to attend such a milestone fight of this variety had to take secret trains to an undisclosed location in Mississippi. Today's crowd gradually warms like an early model Chevy on a winter day, and soon it is spitting flames and roaring.

Two men come out into the ring and stare each other down. The anticipation builds until the bell rings, and then the men advance forward, fists swinging. Blood begins to flow almost immediately. The fighter bleeding from a gash pantomimes an amused look and the fight continues.

Bare-knuckle boxing's return and newly found legal status as a sanctioned sport is actually the work of fight promoter and former boxer David Feldman. The son of Philadelphia Hall of Fame boxing trainer Marty Feldman (not to be confused with the famous comedian), David Feldman fought to revive the lost sport for almost a decade. When I ask Feldman why he decided to bring bare-knuckle boxing back from the dead, he explains how personal it could be for people.

"One of my fighters who fought for a couple of world championships is actually an Irish Traveller, and he started telling me about the bare-knuckle fights they used to do over there in the fields and it's how they solved family problems," Feldman says. "It's called 'fair-and-square fights.' We talked about it for a little bit and it just really intrigued me."

Feldman says he started looking into the concept of bare-knuckle fighting and decided one day he wanted to try and bring it back. The fight promoter had his own firsthand experience with the sport. Not only was he an accomplished boxer in the welterweight division, but also he experienced a bare-knuckle fight himself in the ring, though it wasn't exactly intentional.

"I was promoting an underground fight and I got called out by one of the guys, and I was actually like, 'Nah, I really don't want to fight. I'm a promoter now,' and he just started trash talking a little. Aggravated at that, I'm like, 'All right, let's do it.' So it only lasted like a minute I ended up hitting the guy with a really nice right hook to the ribs and breaking his ribs—so that was the end of that fight," Feldman tells me.

Now that he's in his late forties, fighting isn't really something that he wants to do anymore and prefers to avoid it if possible. "At my age now, I really don't want to get hit again ever," Feldman laughs. "I've been hit about a half a million times in my life and I just don't want to get hit again."

In 2011 he held an unsanctioned bare-knuckle fight at a casino on an Indian reservation as a test run and was intrigued by both the turnout and response to the event. He spent the next seven years trying to get the sport officially sanctioned before finding a willing partner with the state of Wyoming. "This is the twenty-ninth state that I approached on this," Feldman says. "I got turned down twenty-eight times."

After a major setback in trying to bring back the sport, Feldman decided to quit for a time. As luck would have it, he spoke with a writer for *Rolling Stone Magazine* who was familiar with his previous effort and told him he thought the sport would be huge—if it ever got off the ground. With the added motivation, Feldman decided to keep pushing. But during a fight at an event organized by the most popular mixed martial arts promoter in the world, the organization's owner told him bare-knuckle boxing would never be sanctioned.

"And I was so furious I tapped him on his shoulder and I said, 'Listen, my man, isn't that what they said to you? I'll see you at the top.' And I walked away and I was like, 'Did I really just say that to him?'" Feldman says. "He gave me the fuel to keep doing this because I'm a fighter and the worst thing you can ever do to me is tell me no."

Despite the pushback and the regular rejections, Feldman kept fighting for the lost sport. In a way, it became his obsession. He says that a lot of people wrongly have the perception that bare-knuckle fighting is essentially a backyard street fight and can't be a sport that is safely regulated.

"It is something they do in warehouses, it is something they do in bars, and it's not a regulatory-able sport, and I just said, 'You're wrong.' I said, 'It's safer,'" Feldman says.

To Feldman's way of thinking, fighters without gloves are more careful about how many times they punch or can get punched. "If I take a brick and hit you in the head, I'm going to knock you out," Feldman explains. "I wrap the brick in padding I hit you in the head five, six, seven times and knock you out—what's better? One concussive shot or five, six, or seven? Very simple: one concussive shot is better. That's bare-knuckle boxing. In bare-knuckle, you won't take the continual pounding. Boxing is called 'the sweet science' and I call this the sweetest science because you have to take your shots, you have to throw [punches at] guys—this isn't just defense."

Ultimately the Wyoming Combat Sports Commission approved sanctioned bare-knuckle fights and has since helped with sport's rules, regulations, accountability, and standards. Chairman of the commission Bryan Pedersen counted there to be six to ten unsanctioned fighting events occurring every year for the last five years, so to be able to monitor these fights and help bring the safest outcome for all the fighters was a step in the right direction.

Feldman considers his fighters as pioneers, and as such many of them will be remembered long after their fights in Wyoming. He adds that a lot of the fighters don't know what to expect when they sign up but know they are getting the chance to be a part of history. But what Feldman really wants is for the people to be wowed by the return of the classic pugilist sport.

"From a historical standpoint I really want them to say, 'Man, that was everything I thought it was going to be,'" Feldman says. "The combat sports world is due for something new and here it is. It's the oldest and newest form of hand-to-hand combat."

Wyoming's Only Bare-Knuckle Boxer

One after another, boxers enter the ring before the excited and raucous crowd, doing their best to defeat the opponent across from them. Some fights go on for several rounds while others finish after the first punch. Undefeated boxer Bobby Gun defeats his opponent in forty-one seconds with a single hit to the stomach, crumpling his opponent like a newspaper to the mat before the astonished crowd. "I want to tell everyone we made history here tonight," he shouts into a microphone after his win.

Then Nick Mamalis, the only fighter that evening hailing from Wyoming, climbs into the ring, and the home crowd roars.

Nick Mamalis grew up in Green River, Wyoming, where he still lives and works as a miner 1,600 feet underground in the "Trona Capital of the World." Trona is a mineral used in making soda ash, which goes into everything from laundry detergent to glass.

"I'm from a smaller town and wrestling is big here," Mamalis told me some weeks before the fight. "That's what led me to MMA and eventually to this bare-knuckle boxing."

Mamalis wrestled from the staggeringly young age of six all the way through college. At first glance, the father of five looks and sounds more like a young college professor than a fighter built from a lifetime of competitive matches—but looks are deceiving. Mamalis is an accomplished mixed martial artist with several wrestling honors under his belt. His mixed martial arts career began one day when he came across a flier pinned up at his college. It announced there would be a fighting tournament and the victor would take home $1,000.

"That first one was a no-weight-class tournament, talk about Wild West—just whoever signs up is in," Mamalis says. "In college that sounded like a lot of money, and so I signed up for that and kind of fell in love with the sport of MMA," Mamalis says. "There's a lot to learn and a lot that intrigued me by it."

He thought he stood a good chance and entered his name into the martial contest. It was just after his college wrestling season had come to an end and as a result he was in great shape.

"I felt pretty confident, and then when I got there and saw some of the guys who were signing up, I thought, 'Oh shoot, these guys are a lot bigger than what I was expecting,'" he says.

Mamalis usually fights at 125 pounds but he says most of the other fighters signing up for the same event were massive. In fact, during the final round he ended up fighting an opponent who weighed about 350 pounds.

"It was over pretty quick," Mamalis says. "I got lucky. I threw one punch, he tried to punch back, I slipped it, and the next thing you know I was behind him, choking him out."

Mamalis won the fighting tournament. Predictably, it wasn't long before he found himself in more competitions. With his extensive wrestling background he won the majority of them. "I've always been kind of into that sport and just kind of the gladiator aspect of it." he says.

When the bare-knuckle fighting championship was announced, Mamalis was eager to toss his hat in the ring. While certainly an accomplished fighter, he says he didn't have a lot of experience specifically with striking or boxing.

"Other than maybe getting into a fight here or there that I shouldn't have been in, I don't have any bare-knuckle boxing [experience]." He says the closest thing he came to that was when growing up he made his own gloves because his father refused to let him buy boxing gloves. "I made some boxing gloves out of milk jugs, then my friends and I beat each other up with them," he laughs.

He admits he wasn't surprised when the resurrected sport came calling in his home state, adding that Wyoming is often the first to embrace things considered to be a little on the edge. "That's how it is here; if it was going to happen somewhere, it might as well be here," he says. "It just fits in. Everyone has that idea of the Wild West and this state with the rugged cattle towns just fits in, you know?"

To prepare for the tournament, and since Mamalis couldn't choke out his opponent, he needed to brush up on boxing. He started attending classes in a nearby boxing gym and trained with some of the younger members. "Since then I've obviously worked on striking and other facets of the game, and this [competition] kind of fell together in my home state," he says. "I definitely wanted to be a part of it. I thought it was going to be a pretty neat history-making deal and so I jumped at the opportunity when it rolled around."

Mamalis vs. Bedford

Nick Mamalis stands in his corner as his fight song "Blaze of Glory" by classic rocker Jon Bon Jovi thundered through the events center. He waits as it finishes, preparing for the arrival of opponent Johnny Bedford, a former UFC fighter and experienced boxer from Ohio, and currently hailing from Texas.

The referee directs the boxers forward from their respective corners and tells them to put their hands up. "Buckle up," he adds. The bell rings and Mamalis and Bedford approach one another.

Quick as a viper, Bedford smirks as his punches comes in hitting Mamalis again and again. In time Bedford, confident in his ability, and of the presumed outcome of the fight, doesn't even bother to raise his fists to ward off any attacks. He clowns around the ring, taunting the Wyoming native. Mamalis takes a hit on the nose without flinching, but he still gets in several good strikes on Bedford just before the bell rings, ending the first round.

When the second round starts, Bedford comes out in a fury, sending Mamalis to the mat after a series of heavy hits. Dazed, Mamalis takes a moment to get back up to his feet in front of the cheering crowd. Blood now runs freely from a cut under his left eye, painting half his face red.

Undaunted, he gets back into the fight with Bedford. With thirty seconds left in the second round, Bedford brings Mamalis down to the mat for a second time under a flurry of stunning hits. Bedford walks away, pantomiming that his job was done. Mamalis fights back to his feet—but the referee takes one final look at him and calls it. Mamalis loses his first bare-knuckle fight.

"The fight obviously could have gone better," he admits to me later. "I'm not real comfortable on my feet, wrestling is my background, so that was kind of a fish out of water [scenario]. It was a good experience though. I had fun." Mamalis tells me his injuries are minor compared to other sports he's participated in such as wrestling.

"I'm definitely going to fight MMA again," he says. "I think that's where I'm most comfortable—but the bare-knuckle boxing? I don't think jumping back in there is out of the question. I think I need a little bit of a redemption fight after that one."

For the rest of the night I watch one boxer take on another with greater or lesser degrees of difficulty. The bare-knuckle fight between Australian Bec Rawlings and Denver resident Alma Garcia stuns the crowd with its technical prowess, easily besting many other conflicts of the evening. The tattooed women battle before Rawlings wins with a technical knockout in the second round. During the last fight of the evening, two heavyweight fighters ponderously trade punches to the head. Like two heavily armed battleships, they launch devastating salvos at one another, neither one yielding to the onslaught of knuckle-to-face punishment.

The night ends, and many of the fighters are richly bruised and battered. A least one contestant finishes his night with beer bought for him by the audience and enthusiastic slaps on the back and hearty congratulations. Still covered in sweat and blood, the fighter wanders happily from one group hailing him to the next. He lost badly to his opponent earlier that night but understands he took part in something historically significant.

Bare-knuckle boxing is a sport that vanished with the eventual expiration of the Old West. The night no doubt was awash with much of the same sort of excitement and cheers as the Sullivan and Kilrain fight in 1889, except for one thing: all fighters could be rest assured the law wouldn't chase them down and have them arrested for their match in the days to come.

CHAPTER 15

REENACTING
THE WEST

The tiny roads in and around the small mountain town of Bailey, Colorado, are packed with cars and tourists. Flip flops, sunglasses, and strollers parade past the idyllic mountain scenery in an ocean of unsettling colors. Strained past the point of friendly endurance, local cops grit their teeth at people as they wave family after family safely across the highway cutting the town in half. The Bailey Day event, a popular annual summer festival, draws massive crowds to meander up and down a blocked-off street filled with local food, beer, and various entertainment options. In the sea of people I drift like an errant barge, keeping my eyes peeled for a man named Jim Myers.

Myers previously told me over the phone that all I had to do to find him at the festival was search for anyone dressed in clothing from the 1880s and simply ask them to point the way to him—which is exactly what I do. I come across a man walking through the crowd dressed like an Old West deputy sheriff, six-gun attached to his belt, and relay to him my instructions. After a moment he nods and bids me to follow. He meanders through the crowd to a little park just off the main thoroughfare, which includes a recreated storefront of an Old West town. An audience is gathered to watch actors play through various scenarios that always end in a shooting. "That's him," the man tells me. I follow his outstretched finger across the crowd and see another man who looks just plain villainous.

As the founder of the Park County Regulators' Old West reenactment group, Jim Myers dresses in period clothing but is dirty, unshaven, and looking a little vicious. He and all the other reenactors seem like they could have stepped out of the grittiest Western ever filmed. Their Old West certainly isn't one that included Roy Rogers or Gene Autry.

"We're trying to recreate the Old West today, so we are very much into authenticity," Myers tells me. That includes authentic weapons, clothing—right down to the smallest detail. "No jeans, nothing polyester; it has to be cotton, silk, canvas, what they would have worn in that time." Myers says he's even working with his team to turn all their buttons over to metal, mother of pearl, or wood because plastic wasn't being used yet.

Getting into Old West reenactment isn't cheap. For women, it costs more than $1,000 to get a period-appropriate costume. For men, it's a little more affordable at $700 for the outfits and guns. Myers tells me their goal is to look like they stepped right out of the 1800s and I say they were successful. To me the men look grungy, a little menacing, and like they're in need of a good delousing.

"It is still funny that people who see us are intimidated by the look, and particularly kids," Meyers says. "We'll walk up to them and they're getting behind their mom even though we're not trying to be mean or intimidating—just, we're dirty, we've got guns on our hips, and that's just kind of what happens. It's like, 'Whoa, you guys look at little bit more real than I was expecting.'"

I watch with a crowd of onlookers as the group competes in a quick draw contest and performs a humorous scene in which two women in an argument over a man end up shooting the man instead of each other. While the story is obviously fictitious, the group does partake in reenacting more realistic historical activities such as train robbing. For the last few years, the Park County Regulators have been called on to rob train passengers of fake money at the popular tourist attraction the Georgetown Loop Railroad. The outlaws, including Myers, would go down the train cars playfully harassing the riders before getting into an obligatory gunfight with lawmen.

"The biggest problem we have is people trying to take our guns and our knives out of their sheaths and holsters, and they've succeeded more than once," Myers says. "I had my gun pulled out of my holster, fully loaded with blanks because we were going to do a gunfight shortly thereafter, and I turned around and they were passing it down the aisle."

The fourth person who was handed Myers's gun wasn't in on the joke and was trying to figure out why someone just handed them a massive revolver.

"They're like, 'I don't know what to do with this,' so I just took it away. Thankfully they are single action, so you have to cock it and fire it, you can't just pull the trigger," Myers says. "But I was still afraid someone was going to do that, so I'm quickly trying to grab it. I told the railroad...they have to announce every single train ride, 'Do not touch the guns and knives of the reenactors because these are real knives and real guns.'"

All their weapons can be dangerous. Guns loaded with blanks often can be quite deadly, especially at close range. Knives, of course, can cause harm or injury. Myers marvels at how often members of his team have had people pull knives out of their sheaths. "You turn around and the guy is like, 'I've got your knife,'" he says. "And these are adults, not kids. Adults every time [are] doing this." Reenactors not only have to put on a show, but they must monitor the adults and children watching to make sure no one gets hurt.

Finding Authenticity

As far as authenticity goes, Myers and his group work hard to stay as accurate as they could to the time period. "There are [reenactment] groups that have been around a lot longer than we have that have their guys wear jeans and stuff like that. That's not period correct and it could be that they just don't care about that kind of thing," Myers tells me with more than a little professional pride. "We actually go and make an effort to watch other groups perform to learn from them, what they're doing well, what we wouldn't want to do—but there's always something we can learn one way or the other."

In addition to reenacting, Myers owns a local business called The Sasquatch Outpost, which is where I visit him. The store offers outdoor gear and other essentials while providing a ton of Sasquatch-themed merchandise, and there's also a colorful museum dedicated to the legendary creature. As people come in and out of his store expressing their appreciation to him for all things Sasquatch, I look around at his other interest and ask why he decided to start a reenactment group dedicated to the Old West in the first place.

"Who doesn't want to be a cowboy? What grown man doesn't want in his heart to get to play cowboy and not be made fun of—and actually do it well?" Myers asks. "To me, it is just romantic and exciting. I'm sure at the time in the Old West when it was normal, people would think it was foolish to think one day people would dress up like them just for fun. And it was dangerous because people would get shot all the time and they carried guns for a reason as opposed to why we're carrying them."

It's a fair point. Reenactments are certainly a spectacle to behold but I always thought they were maybe a little silly or at worst insincere. Once for a newspaper article I'd dressed up as a Civil War newspaper correspondent in Arkansas for the reenactment of the Battle of Prairie Grove. Not being in the usual blue or gray costume made things a little weird in my experience. Besides getting odd looks from local high school students, who thought I was maybe play-acting as a period-accurate homeless person, I basically stood around taking notes. That and doing my best to avoid being trampled by horses, large families, or anyone with a massive digital camera.

So what was the point of dressing up in period clothing and pretending to shoot others? To be completely honest, it feels a bit like going to a renaissance festival with an obsessive focus on history and its accompanying suffering, and less on the more whimsical arena of dragons, turkey legs, and flagons of mead. Yet this love for nostalgia and glory isn't new.

Reenacting has a long and storied history going back at least as far as the Civil War. In some cases, battle reenactments took place just months after the actual battles were fought and the war was still raging across the country. These recreations or "sham battles" of famous conflicts were prominent and popular attractions at many festivals, holidays, and celebrations. Even the veterans of the Civil War itself were recruited to take part in reenactments of battles they participated in for a likely surreal and

Old Trail Town in Cody, Wyoming, is a recreated Old West town,
using historic buildings brought in from other locations. *(Photo by Ian Neligh)*

troubling experience. One reporter in 1904 wrote about a reenactment of
the battle at Manassas that included twenty-five thousand soldiers and
four to six thousand state militiamen. "The ground includes that on which
both the battles of Bull Run were fought, and it is said to be the intention
of Major General Corbin, under whose command the maneuvers will be
held, to duplicate as far as possible the fight of the rebellion."

Reenactments have always strived for a high degree of realism
and accuracy, but sometimes they have unintentionally become just a
little too real.

Lethal Turn

Four years ago Myers's Old West reenactment group just barely
escaped tragedy when a firearm loaded with actual bullets was fired
into the ground during a performance and ricocheted into the groin
area of another actor. It was not a life-threatening injury but almost
ended the group.

"We made the decision to give up reenacting at that point, but the town kind of rallied behind us and said, 'No, it was a foolish mistake, it never should have happened, but we don't want you guys to stop,'" Myers says. "We're not positive how we had a live round, but it could have been catastrophic. It could have been one of our guys or the crowd."

Speaking of injury, while we speak someone comes into the store looking for a first-aid kit for a local who is bleeding after a recent hip surgery. Myers digs around and pulls one out from underneath the front counter.

"Thank you, sir," the man says as he hurries off.

This was the West still, where injuries are unpredictable sometimes. Myers resumes saying that two months after the shooting accident the same thing happened in Tombstone, Arizona, to another Old West reenacting group.

In this case, the actor was running late and didn't get his pistol checked before stepping into the performance, not far from the actual location of the Gunfight at the O.K. Corral. Subsequently, two people were hit with bullets. One actor was shot but not fatally, and a woman was grazed as she was walking nearly seven hundred feet away. Two live rounds thudded into buildings.

"What happened to them, like what happened to us, is they got a little lax on their safety protocol, and you just can't," Myers says. "You can never let up on your safety protocols." For Myers and his group, the incident changed how they approach every event. Now guns used in reenactments can never be used for anything else until the actor has left the group. Additionally, they have a real deputy on hand inspecting the loading of the firearms with blanks.

"So we've had four years of safe record and no incidents, and I think it is just a testimony to our town who wanted us to continue— and to our safety protocols," Myers says. "But what saved the day for us is that we never fire at each other, we fire towards the ground. The crowd never notices because it is just loud with [lots of] smoke but we fire towards the ground. It was a ricochet that hit him, not a direct hit. It saved his life. We do it because we don't even want gunpowder hitting each other, so we're always firing down."

Jim Myers of the reenactment group the Park County Regulators gets ready
to put on a show for visitors in Bailey, Colorado. *(Photo by Billie Diemand)*

As long as there have been reenactments, there have been
similar injuries and sometimes deaths. In the 1980s in the City of
Idaho Springs, Colorado, a man was killed during an Old West–style
shootout. Even as far back as 1885, a Colorado newspaper reported
that a Lieutenant Stolbrand was both injured and lost a pocket watch
worth $126 during a sham battle in Denver. "These sham battles are
dangerous things; almost as dangerous as real ones," the
paper concluded.

Injuries of this sort are extremely rare, but they do happen
regardless of the era or decade the reenactors recreate. In 1998 a
twenty-two-year-old Confederate reenactor was shot in the neck at the
reenactment of the Battle of Gettysburg by a .44-caliber ball from
a revolver. Luckily, he survived. The shooter turned out to be a reenactor
from France who arrived for the 135th anniversary of the battle.

In 2008 a man playing a Union soldier was shot in the back
and wounded by another man dressed as a Confederate soldier in Suffolk,
Virginia. A video of that incident had to be played to see who it was who

fired the offending firearm. The reenactor was not fatally wounded but did receive a massive .44 caliber ball in his back for his trouble.

Most recently a man was shot in the stomach during a 2015 World War II reenactment in Texas. The man, playing a Nazi soldier, was hit with a .30-caliber carbine round from an M1 rifle. He survived and promptly announced his intentions to continue to participate in war reenactments despite his close call.

It's not really war, and yet reenacting can still be dangerous. But regardless of the risks, the lure of living through a specific moment or era of the past proves again and again to be a powerful motivator for historical enthusiasts of all types.

For Love of the West

"We've had a blast, no pun intended, performing the last four years," Myers says. Myers grew up in Kenya where his parents—and later Myers himself and his wife—were missionaries. "I have spent more time outside of the U.S. than in the U.S.—but when we moved to Colorado that part of my soul came to life, I guess. I just love doing what we're doing," he says.

He originally created the group when the town needed something to spice up the Bailey Day event. At the time he was responsible for organizing the annual festival. "Bailey Day used to be just a street fair and a drunken brawl basically and . . . I thought, you know, what Bailey Day needs is a theme. To give it life again," Myers says.

That first year he invited a reenactment group to perform and said they did a tremendous job, but the subsequent year he found they were no longer available. As Myers thought about the problem, he realized that he knew enough people who might be interested in creating their own team of reenactors. The group started with six actors but over the years has more than doubled in number.

"I love the Old West. I love everything about the Old West. I always dress in cowboy boots and cowboy hats—long before we did the reenactment team. My bucket list is to act in a Western and I'm hoping that will happen one day," Myers says with a smile.

But one thing a spectator probably won't see is Myers playing a lawman anytime soon. "I never liked to play lawmen. I have to twist our guys' arms behind their back to make them play lawmen. They all would rather play an outlaw," Myers confides. "It is much more fun." I can only guess why.

CHAPTER 16

THE **TREASURE**
HUNTERS

A half hour west of Cañon City and maybe forty minutes up Texas Creek into the Bull Gulch area, the pickup truck finally stops its slow, unsteady progress up the washed-out path of the steep canyon. Finally the long and tortuous climb is over. We grab our backpacks and pile out, ready to begin hiking.

It's no secret the Spanish came into the West looking for gold hundreds of years even before the first American prospectors stumbled across the Rockies. Some believe that early Spanish miners left behind markers and monuments that point the way to Spanish mines and treasure caches. I'd first heard about contemporary fortune hunters in search of lost Spanish treasure in the West just a few years ago while interviewing an old gold miner. Before, I thought treasure maps and treasure hunters belonged in old Westerns—but here I am now.

On my hands and knees, negotiating a dense thicket of brush with my head, I do my best to follow Sydney Moon and her husband, Boyd. In their late sixties and early seventies, they move across the rugged landscape with the practiced ease of a pair of mountain goats. Out the other side, we pause, looking around at our surroundings. Steep canyon walls flank us on both sides and the breathtaking valley opens up in front of us to the north.

"That's a damn big black bear," Boyd says, gesturing nonchalantly in front of me to a massive pile of fresh scat. A little shaken from my close-up view, I look up to see the two set off again. I take a sip of water from my canteen, amazed that anyone would have made it this far back into the wilderness for any reason. But gold has, and perhaps will always, draw people to the very edges of the Earth. I come down a slight incline and catch up to Sydney to see her looking up and off to the right.

"Do you see it?" she asks.

Faces in the Stone

Sydney Moon's treasure hunting story begins with her father Edward Burks. He came back from World War II seriously injured during a friendly fire incident. While recovering in Colorado he spent time exploring the West.

He began to find gold and other rare earth minerals during his many outings. On one trip during the 1950s while exploring near the Continental Divide, he came across an old miner in his eighties who invited Edward to stay the night at his camp. The dwelling turned out to be a mining camp or small ghost town, complete with perfectly preserved buildings, including a saloon. The old miner worked in a nearby mine and lived there alone with his burro among the empty houses. He showed Edward pictures of the residents long ago left behind.

"Dad said there were player pianos and all kinds of stuff up in those buildings, and he let him stay in one of the old cabins that still had the beds and all the old personal possessions," Sydney says.

Apparently, the little town was empty because one winter in the 1800s a rockslide made it impossible for the residents to leave. They either starved or froze to death.

"Others came and got the bodies out over the rockslide," she tells me, but mentions that everything else was left intact because of the extreme difficulty in removing the deceased occupants. Her father went back once more in the 1960s and found the town was still in immaculate condition, but he never took anything with him, deciding to leave it there untouched. After her father's death in the late '80s, the town's location was never discovered, once again lost to history.

For Sydney's father, the West was a vast playground filled with similar discoveries, treasures, massive gemstones, and wild tales of its past. She tells me that as a kid she and her sister weren't interested in joining him on his backcountry adventures, but once he passed away that all changed.

"I was going through all kinds of his maps and stories and notes, and I sat there and was like, my gosh, you think about all this stuff and there are so many cool places here," she says. Sydney and her sister spent the next ten years carefully researching and taking trips on horseback to hunt down as many of the things their father had discovered and written about in his notes. She self-published a small book in 2000 to share as many of those locations and stories as she could with anyone interested in trying to trace her father's footsteps.

During one trip while trying to find a waterfall he had written about, she and her sister cut across one trail to another and in the process came across a boulder carved into a giant face, with very clear eyes, lips, teeth, and a chin. "I didn't know what this was at the time. I just knew that it wasn't natural," she says.

She began looking into what the stone face could have been and came across the work of famed treasure hunter and author Charles "Chuck" Kenworthy. Kenworthy had found a host of treasures decades before and had even gone on a trek for sunken treasure with John Wayne in 1975, off the Santa Catalina Island on the actor's boat named *Wild Goose*.

Kenworthy was convinced that the Spanish had left monuments or markers pointing the way to various important locations involving mines and treasure. There's almost nothing out there to substantiate that these types of monuments actually exist in North America, but Kenworthy believed in them and there is a small army of supporters who agree. Sydney was positive this was what she had found and begun hunting for them herself. She says the monuments were constructed to help supplement the maps made by the Spanish. If a map was lost, then the monuments could also be used in a pinch to find the valuable mines or treasure storage sites because they all had a shared code or set of designs. Guard dogs, lions, growling bears, frogs, turtles, rabbits, lambs, snakes, lizards, human faces, or various saints could mean a variety of things to someone who knew what they were looking for. For instance, a dog could mean it is guarding a treasure, so someone looking for it needed to look

Near Cañon City, Colorado, a massive stone structure resembling a lizard might point the way to hidden Spanish treasure or a lost mine. *(Photo by Ian Neligh)*

behind the dog. A snake or a broken heart or a heart with a lightning bolt through it meant that the treasure site was booby-trapped.

Sydney tells me she has one such secret spot in Utah that she believes holds a massive cache of treasure. Presumably the Spanish would gather the gold or silver they were mining from one or many locations and store it in "a treasure room" or location where it would be safe until it could safely be transported back to Spain. Of course, if a site had a booby trap, it was holding something of extraordinary value. She says she almost triggered a trap during one such exploration. She hasn't yet found any Spanish gold but has spent years doing research and crawling around underground in search of it, adding that finding treasure has become not only her passion but her full-time job. "That's basically what I do," Sydney says.

As Sydney waits for my answer, to be honest I don't see anything at first. Before me was the natural geography of the area contrasted with the deep shadows of the morning sun; but after a long minute, my eyes focus on an unusual stone shape. It was looking out over the canyon, had eyes and a mouth. It could have been naturally forming, a trick of the light, but from where the valley floor looking up, it does look like something rather unnatural, like a massive stone lizard. Sydney keeps moving, and I follow my guide further into the valley.

Cans of Gold and a Severed Head

Stories of Spanish gold and other treasures circulated the West as fortune seekers, successful miners, and famous outlaws roamed the land. One legend many have gone in search for spoke of a buried treasure stolen and hid in Colorado by a band of Confederate stagecoach bandits before they were killed. This was the famed treasure of the Reynolds gang, who made their mark not only with the violence of their time on earth but also with rumors of what they left behind in death.

The gang's name came from Jim Reynolds and his brother John who came from Texas to Colorado in 1859 during the first year of the state's gold rush. They were to try their hand at mining near the South Platte River. However, just a few years later they were arrested as part of an effort to sweep up Confederate sympathizers. As luck would have it, they were broken out of confinement and went to Texas where the brothers became Irregulars in the Confederate Army in Northern Texas. Jim Reynolds apparently wanted to return to the Rockies with the grand ambition of overrunning the state and sacking Denver in the process.

They hoped to take a group of about fifty men from Texas back to Colorado to rob stagecoaches, ranches, and anything else they could get their hands on to help build their small army, while enlisting further help from the mining camps. Gang member Thomas Holliman later said in a statement after his capture, whether to please his jailers or not, that he and the others had actually been trying to avoid being drafted into the Confederacy, which is why they had come to Colorado: "I lay hid in the brush in Texas with many others, about three months, to avoid being conscripted into the confederate service. Jim wanted us to go with him to Colorado, where he said he had formerly lived, that it was out of the war; times were good there and we could make money and not be molested by the draft."

Holliman later admitted that it was Jim Reynolds's ambition to become Colorado's version of "a second Quantrill." Quantrill's Raiders were Confederate-allied guerrillas who operated in Missouri during the Civil War. Among their members were famed outlaws Frank and Jesse James. The group from Texas, however, set off for the Rockies raiding along the way—but the plan started to fall apart almost as soon as it had begun.

"[We] took rations for a few days only, as we feared the confederate authorities would suspect we were going out of country and detain us; lived on game, and when that failed lived on horses; killed and ate two pack horses. Had several fights with Indians; fought them at one time two days [which were] mostly Apaches. Got very weak for want of provisions," Holliman said.

Reynolds's company dwindled the closer they got to Colorado. Soon they lost even more men who felt the money they'd taken should be equally split among them and not just under the watchful eye of their captain Jim Reynolds. Before too long there were only nine members left including the two brothers, but they vigorously kept up their activity in the name, if not the spirit, of the Confederacy.

On July 26, 1864 they robbed a stagecoach about ten miles from the town of Fairplay. They took $400 and a gold watch from the passenger Bill McClellan, the stage line's superintendent, and fifteen cents from the stagecoach's driver Absalom "Abe" Williamson. The gang also forced open an express trunk revealing $6,000 in gold dust and gold amalgam worth about $2,000. They opened letters miners had sent back home containing money for a total of $10,000, claiming it all for the Confederacy. Jim Reynolds later told the captives that he and his group were just the tip of the Confederate iceberg that was sweeping up into Colorado from Texas.

Once the Reynolds Gang had left, McClellan apparently "stayed in the saddle almost night and day for over a week, and in that time had the whole country aroused. His energy and determined fearlessness probably saved many lives and thousands of dollars worth of property." He would not let the Reynolds go without a fight.

While they continued to grab money and valuables from ranches and travelers, the gang soon found large groups of armed men on their trail. Perhaps sensing the end was near, they decided to hide the bulk of their treasure and split up. The two brothers hiked up near the head of Elk Creek and found a prospecting hole to hide their money. The band later made camp that day at a thicket of trees on Geneva Gulch. As evening approached on July 31, 1864, they prepared food and Jim Reynolds divvied up what was left of their spoils when suddenly a hail of gunfire hit the camp.

A posse had found them. Gang member Owen Singleterry was killed outright and Jim Reynolds was struck in the arm. The ambushing posse later removed Singleterry's head from his shoulders, and legend has it that the gruesome trophy was displayed at various public locations floating in alcohol for a number of years. The rest of the gang scattered and were later captured in the days to come. The only two who escaped were John Reynolds and Jake Stowe, the latter later killed for stealing horses in New Mexico.

Denver lawman Dave Cook tried to get now jailed Jim Reynolds to reveal where they'd hidden the stolen gold and money, but without success. The gang was tried and quickly convicted in a closed trial and sent off to be incarcerated at Fort Lyons, but they would never make it to their destination. Once robbed by the gang, Absalom "Abe" Williamson was also on that trip, not as a driver but now as a sergeant and in command of the prisoner's guard. Legend has it that despite the unwillingness of his men, Williamson personally saw to it the gang members were executed while tied to a tree.

In his account of the events that happened, Cook said one of the bandits named John Andrews survived a bullet wound to his chest. He made his way to New Mexico to meet up with John Reynolds and Jake Stowe but was later killed by an avenging posse when the men tried to steal horses from a ranch. By the late 1870s anyone associated directly or indirectly with the Reynolds Gang and their treasure was dead.

Bandit Cache

But knowledge of the treasure lived on. Cook recorded in his autobiography, *Hands up; or, Thirty-five years of detective life in the mountains and on the plains,* an interview with a prisoner named Albert Brown, who was locked up for robbing a stagecoach and stealing a team of mules. Brown told Cook he was originally in Colorado searching for the treasure hidden by the

Reynolds Gang in a secret location given by none other than the last surviving member of the gang, John Reynolds. Brown and Reynolds were stealing horses in New Mexico when Reynolds caught a lethal bullet. As he lay dying, he made Brown promise to bury him, then told him about the treasure. Cook dramatically retells the scene in his book:

> I've got over $60,000 buried not fifty miles from there in the mountains, and I could go right up to the spot where Jim and me buried it in 1864. But there's no use in me wastin' breath, for I'm to the end of my rope now, an' I'll tell you just where it is, so that you can go an' get it after you've planted me deep enough so the coyotes won't dig me up an' gnaw my bones. Jim an' me buried it the morning before the fight at the grove on Geneva Gulch. You go up above there a little ways and find where one of our horses mired down in a swamp. On up at the head of the gulch we turned to the right and followed the mountain around a little farther, an' just above the head of Deer creek we found an old prospect hole at about timber line. There was $40,000 in greenbacks, wrapped in silk oil cloth, an' three cans of gold dust. We filled the mouth of the hole up with stones, an' ten steps below struck a butcher knife into a tree about four feet from the ground an' broke the handle off, an' left it pointing to the mouth of the hole.

Brown told Cook he had gone to the area to look for the treasure with some help but couldn't find it because the area had changed so much due to a forest fire. Years later, Brown escaped prison and was ultimately killed in a Wyoming bar fight. With him went the last connection to the gold raised to help the Confederacy claim Colorado.

But rumors, legends, and Cook's own account helped drive interest in finding the hidden money. In 1906 the *Park County Bulletin* reported the story of two miners who had discovered treasure associated with the Reynolds Gang: "Buried plunder aggregating in value [of] $18,000.30 was uncovered by two prospectors . . . in an abandoned shaft about three miles from town on the Horseshoe road Wednesday. The treasure is for the most part in gold dust, although some in paper money." The newspaper said the two men were tightlipped about the details and only told their story after they tried to use some of the money in town and a merchant charged that they were trying to pass counterfeit bills. It guessed the gold dust and money was a portion of the larger treasure hidden by one of the gang members fleeing from the posse in 1864, but not the original treasure hidden by the Reynolds brothers. That treasure still called to fortune hunters.

"Many searched for this [treasure], but a forest fire swept that country soon after the breaking up of the marauders and the face of the country has been changed beyond recognition, all the landmarks being obliterated," the paper went on to add. That didn't stop treasure hunters from coming out in force to find the rest and larger share of the treasure hidden by the brothers. The same year the *Herald Democrat* claimed the discovery started a rush of people in search of the "bandit cache" to enter the city of Fairplay. Yet despite the renewed focus on finding the buried wealth, the treasure was not found that year—or in the subsequent decades that followed.

The Right Mindset

When Matt Dambrosky built the room on his garage dedicated just for his maps, artifacts, and rare discoveries, he knew his obsession for finding hidden treasure had gone to the next level. It's a passion that he fully embraces. Often when he travels to an area he'll do research on the local history and use detective work to hunt for a lost treasure. It could be a lost stagecoach carrying silver in Colorado's Black Canyon of the Gunnison, or a trip through California panning the historic goldfields. Precious minerals, stones, lost treasure, or even the rare antique candle picks used by the Rockies original gold miners can become something that Dambrosky studies and ultimately goes in search of. On and off for the past ten years, Dambrosky has had one treasure in particular that he's tried again and again to find. He says one day he plans to be the one to unearth the lost treasure of the infamous Reynolds Gang.

Matt Dambrosky got into treasure hunting after someone played a prank on him. It wasn't particularly cruel but it changed his life forever. Twenty years ago when he moved to Park County, Colorado, he met a neighbor who panned for gold. Intrigued, he also found out at about the same time that his aunt's new husband also looked for gold, and they invited him along on a trip. Their destination was a stream in Como, Colorado, not far from where the Reynolds Gang robbed the stagecoach carrying Bill McClellan and the vengeful Absalom "Abe" Williamson. It didn't take too much work, and he saw a lot of gold in his pan.

"I caught the fever and started to learn to do the little prospector dance," Dambrosky says. With short dark hair, plus a hint of a youth spent living just outside of Chicago still in his voice, he wears a black baseball hat and a gray shirt announcing he's a professional chimney sweep. While we sit in chairs at his place of business, a cat rolls around on the table between us as Dambrosky sips coffee from a giant mason jar. Dambrosky says finding that gold in his pan propelled him forward to continue searching at an obsession-like level.

He attended prospecting groups on the Front Range and offered his help to the older members, such as carrying heavy supplies while out in the field, so he could learn about areas rich in gold.

"Then it exploded from there," he says. "It was like, 'Wow, this gold thing is really cool, let me find out how it gets to where you find it.' So I started studying a lot of geology, wanting to know how gold got to where it was."

At the same time, Dambrosky poured over books detailing stories of hidden treasure and then went in search for them. What he didn't know was his aunt and uncle had "salted" his pan during that trip to look for gold. Salting is a term used to describe someone intentionally placing gold at a location to trick a prospector or investor into thinking the area has wealth.

"Like four years later they finally admitted it, and I think they were starting to feel guilty because I actually built an addition onto my garage that was solely for gold prospecting and treasure hunting," Dambrosky says. "I just had to laugh. You know? It worked."

Since then Dambrosky has found gold, precious stones, and all types of items that could be considered treasure. He came across the story of the Reynolds Gang while researching some semi-precious minerals, called epidote, located above where he lives.

"And just started really reading about [the treasure] and, wow, this could be in my backyard. Because I live at the headwaters of Deer Creek, and Elk Creek where the treasure is said to be," Dambrosky says.

By taking the clues from the stories about that time and overlaying a series of maps, Dambrosky believes his method eventually will point the way. One map might tell you about the geology of the area and where a miner might dig a hole looking for gold—the same hole the brothers buried the treasure. Another map might show timberline, the approximate location of where Jim and John Reynolds found the prospecting hole—with consideration that a subsequent forest fire may have altered that landmark.

"We have a little peak in the back there called Bandit Peak, and in all my research I can't find out why it's been called Bandit Peak, and that would have been right in the spot," Dambrosky says. "A lot of it is keeping your eyes and ears open for details."

A decade has passed since he first looked for the treasure of the Reynolds Gang and one day he plans to find it.

"Every time I go out in those woods, I'm looking for it," Dambrosky says. But it's far from the only treasure he's obsessed with finding. In fact, he says if there's one he spends all of his free time obsessing over, that he and his twelve-year-old son regularly pick a spot after much research to look for, it is the treasure of Forest Fenn. In fact, "Fenning" is actually something Dambrosky and his son do together on their birthdays.

The quest to find it has taken Dambrosky to long-forgotten cemeteries. He has used drones to scour canyons and pours over pages for hidden meanings, secret codes, or obscure references to latitude and longitude. He's not alone. It's estimated hundreds of thousands of people have gone hunting for Fenn's Treasure, and between four and six people have even died in that search.

Fenn's Treasure

Somewhere in the Rocky Mountains, there's $10 million in gold, valuable gems, and artifacts hidden in a chest. Unlike many of the treasures hidden in the myth of the Wild West, this one is from modern times and its creator is an art dealer, Vietnam veteran, and millionaire who lives in Santa Fe. Forest Fenn was eighty years old in 2010 when he hid the treasure with clues sprinkled throughout his autobiography *The Thrill of the Chase*.

In his autobiography, Fenn added a poem, also found in multiple places online and in newspaper articles, which is supposed to lead the way to the treasure with cryptic stanzas. For almost a decade people have scoured the Rockies hoping to find the treasure without any success and without Fenn revealing any of his secrets. It is a mystery that not even his wife knows and one he'll happily take to his grave. Intrigued by both his inspiration and motivations to hide $10 million and further add to the legend of the modern-day Wild West, I contact the enigmatic art dealer to hear more. It's clear that Fenn has a profound appreciation for the Rockies.

"My father was a schoolteacher in Texas, so we had summers off," Fenn tells me. "I spent nineteen of my first twenty summers in Yellowstone or West Yellowstone. That was starting in 1930. I feel like I grew up in the Rockies, under pine trees."

Fenn says the discovery of an arrowhead when he was just nine years old propelled him to a "road of adventure and discovery." Apparently, Fenn originally had the idea to bury a treasure for others to find when he was diagnosed with cancer.

"I had cancer in 1988 and was expected to die. I told myself if I had to go I would take some of my things with me," Fenn says. He ultimately beat cancer but years later decided to carry out his plan anyway, hiding the chest laden with treasure in a place sentimental to him.

"It's something I'd imagine people daydream of doing but few actually accomplish," he says. Ultimately his goal is to give people something exciting to go and do outdoors with their children, very much like what Dambrosky and his son experience.

"I wanted them out of the game room, off of the couch, and away from their electronic gadgets," Fenn says. "Also, we were in a recession. People were losing their jobs and despair was everywhere. I wanted to give some hope to those who were willing to go looking for a new life." Of course he means for the search to be within reason. There have been accidental deaths associated with the search for the treasure, and in subsequent interviews Fenn has urged caution to anyone spending time in the outdoors, adding the treasure is not in a dangerous location.

"When looking at your legacy and famous hidden treasure, what do you want people to remember about it and your reasons?" I ask him.

"The treasure story will remain because so much has been written about it, but my name will have an asterisk beside it—and that is the way it should be," Fenn says. "I hope others will pick up my idea and expand on it. We must get our young people outside again."

Considering how well he hid his treasure, I ask if he is comfortable with it never being found.

"It will be found some time," Fenn says. "The Rosetta Stone was buried two thousand years before it was found."

Joining the Hunt

Driving through the great dark spaces of Wyoming at night, I am entirely unconscious of the fact that my fists are gripping the steering wheel ever tighter, squeezing out whatever life it may have had. In that swirling ocean of empty darkness only the antelope greet the way. They stand at the edges of the road watching me as I pass, a suicidal honor guard, ever threatening to leap in front of my vehicle.

The unreadable and slightly sinister ungulate faces spread out before me in a sporadic parade along the empty miles. Their eyes light up in my headlights like small stars that whisk past me back into the dark. Thankfully I finally see through my bug-spattered windshield building structures in a galaxy of color. Signs with Buffalo Bill Cody's likeness appear everywhere. I have arrived in Cody, Wyoming.

I pry my fingers free from my vehicle's helm and check into the hotel. Only while settling in a bed that almost fits into the shoebox-sized room do I finally make up my mind: I would search for Forest Fenn's treasure. After consulting friends and family and remapping my travel plans, I find a possible location.

It is as good a spot as any, and honestly I don't really expect to find anything. Sometimes the journey itself is worth the destination, unless there's undue suffering involved. The location I decide on is just near Yellowstone National Park, north of Gardiner, Montana, near the Devil's Slide, which matched one of Fenn's clues mentioning a "blaze." The slide is a massive red stone streak cutting vertically down the side of Cinnabar Mountain. I don't expect more than an interesting hike along the Yellowstone River though. Knowing that my chances of coming upon some fabulous wealth that eluded countless others is ridiculously narrow, I half-talk myself out of making the daylong detour. The next day, after being properly furnished with a cup of morning coffee from Wyoming's surliest drive-thru coffee attendant, I am ready for a day of adventure. My trip takes me on a predictably breathtaking drive through Yellowstone before I arrive in Montana. The sun just begins its gradual downward slide across the horizon when I spot what I am searching for.

Parking a few miles from Gardiner at a pullout along Highway 89, I get out and look down a cliff-like embankment to the Yellowstone River below and ask myself, "Is this something an eighty-year-old man would do?" Possibly. If there is an easier approach to the riverbank, I don't see it. All I could discover is a vertical, nasty-looking dirt trail. So naturally, I head directly for it.

It doesn't look so bad from the road; a little steep maybe, but not too difficult. I decide not to bring any gear, which probably saves me the awkward experience of impaling myself on a camp shovel. Sometimes you have to be thankful for the little things. If Forest Fenn buried his treasure six feet underground, then someone else with more resolve and a high-end metal detector would probably have to find it.

The path I choose soon becomes a waterfall of fine dirt, flowing out from under my feet to shower the bank far below. I reach out to grab something, anything, to slow my momentum and am awarded a cruel fistful of a prickly bush. Perhaps the best course of action is not to cry out in dismay but to work my way back up to the vehicle—if that is even still possible. But the insistence of gravity and my disappearing footholds are all the motivation I need to continue onward.

Plus, the prospect of a motorist taking a break from the road and looking over the side to see me looking back up as I dangle over the bank, a fistful of thorns and an associated look of abject misery, is more than enough to inspire my journey forward. I slide in a rather undignified fashion down to the bottom and find a beach covered in cannonball-sized boulders. As I walk across them they slide and shift under my feet, squealing as the marble-smooth rocks grind into one another.

Under every rotted tree stump and log, I find a growing excitement for the possibility of coming across Fenn's treasure chest, although admittedly I might instead find some long-lost rafter. It reminds me of being a kid and the epic adventures I went on hunting for imaginary treasures—the potential of discovering a sun-dried mummy aside—but the best part of this is that this treasure is real. There really is a fortune in gold and jewels hiding out there.

I spend longer than I should digging behind old weather-beaten tree stumps with my hands when I spot the sandy beach. It's small, beautiful, located under a fallen tree long ago bleached bone white with something like an "X marks the spot" formation in its fingerlike branches.

Poison ivy also surrounds it on all sides. I carefully take a path largely free of painful dermatitis-inducing horror to reach the little beach. It looks like a perfect spot to bury a treasure. I have no shovel or metal detector, so I lean against the dead tree, rubbing dirt and sweat from my forehead, and look out across the Yellowstone River to the Devil's Slide on the other side. Maybe the treasure is here, and maybe it isn't, but I found what Forest Fenn hid after all. Steeling myself for the return journey, I brush the dirt off my pants and head back the way I came.

CHAPTER 17

BUFFALO
BILL'S
BODY

You're the ones that have his body," says the man dressed like an Old West sheriff after asking where I am from. He stands behind a counter piled high with self-published Western fiction and waits for my response. He knows, as well as I do, where the body is—or at least where it's supposed to be. I look at his badge, then meet his eyes and respond, "I guess we do." But it's hardly as straightforward as that. When it comes to William F. "Buffalo Bill" Cody's body, it is never that simple.

The location of Cody's final resting spot has long been a contentious issue, and from where I am standing I'm in the epicenter of the hundred-year-old debate. Well, actually I stand at the entrance to a tourist attraction called Old Trail Town, a recreated Western town and the original location where Cody himself created the townsite for Cody, Wyoming, in 1895. The site today is a collection of historically significant buildings from the Old West, which were moved there in the 1960s to resemble a classic Western town. Many of the structures were originally built during 1879 to 1901, boasting some kind of historical significance. Some cabins were reportedly used by Butch Cassidy and the Sundance Kid. The town is very much a beautifully recreated tombstone of the Old West—but buildings aren't the only things taken from elsewhere and planted in Old Trail Town. In the area's small cemetery there's the gravesite for John "Liver-Eating" Johnson whose body was brought over from Los Angeles in 1974 with the help of a group of local students. There are also graves for buffalo hunters, frontiersmen, and more all taken from other locations and buried in the little cemetery throughout the '70s and '80s. One body the town doesn't have is that of its founder— but not for lack of trying.

Lookout Mountain

On a freezing morning on January 15, 1917 the doors to the Denver capitol were opened to the public. Governors, delegations, members of the armed services, fraternal organizations, veterans of the Civil War, and thousands of children came to see the old scout and performer. A line stretched out the door and out under the winter sky as people waited for their chance to say farewell.

"Goodby, old pard. Goodby, Bill," a reporter overheard people saying as they marched past his open casket.

It was estimated by one newspaper that some twenty-five thousand people came to see Buffalo Bill one last time. Drawing a crowd even after death, Cody likely would have been proud at the tremendous turnout. After giving the public a chance to say farewell, a procession headed out of the capital through the streets of downtown Denver led by police officers and followed by Cody's casket and the many service attendees. At the very end some seventy cowboys came with Cody's riderless horse McKinley.

At age seventy-one, Cody went to Glenwood Springs on January 3, 1917 to partake in the town's healing waters, as advised by his doctor, to help him overcome some of the many ailments he was suffering, including chest pains. Two days after visiting Glenwood Springs, he collapsed and became delirious. In this state he apparently told people he planned to bring back his show, making it better than ever. Doctors sent him to his sister's house in Denver; it was apparent to them he was dying. On January 10, William "Buffalo Bill" Cody followed those who had already taken their last trail ride into the history of the Old West.

It was originally thought when Cody died he would be buried near Cody, Wyoming, but his wife said he had changed his mind in the end, requesting to be buried on Lookout Mountain overlooking Denver

William "Buffalo Bill" Cody died in 1917, but his legacy like that of the Wild West he helped create lives on. *(Courtesy of the Buffalo Bill Museum & Grave)*

and the Front Range to the plains beyond. This beautiful spot looks out on the land where he first began building his legend. Soon, however, the trouble began. Legend has it that as many as one hundred residents of Cody went to bring back his body before it was buried and were turned back by the National Guard at the state line.

As early as 1921 there was another attempt to take back Cody's body, but it was speculated to have never made it any further than a bar in Casper, Wyoming. In 1926 there was talk in local newspapers about an effort to raise money for the transport. By 1948 the war over Cody's remains grew to the point where the Cody American Legion offered a $10,000 reward for the return of his body to the town. The *Casper Star Tribune* in 1948 said Denver's response to the bounty on Buffalo Bill's body was: "Not a chance."

Apparently the Cheyenne American Legion trumpet and bugle corps swore it could secretly travel to Colorado and forcibly remove Cody's body and return it to Wyoming. As such, Cody American Legion's commander J.F. Fitzstephens said the reward would be paid to them if they could indeed fulfill their promise. That year an editorial in the *Great Fall Tribune* wished the trumpet and bugle corps well in their coming attempt to return Cody to Wyoming. The writer said Cody was still being used to draw crowds for Denver and this was profoundly irritating to Wyoming. The editorial went on to say the entertainer wished to be buried on Cedar Mountain above the town named for him. He added over the years many attempts were made to bring him back, calling Denver's hold on Cody a "noose" around his neck that Wyoming must break. It's unclear what happened during that foray to Colorado, but it wasn't the end of the fight over the body. According to the *Los Angeles Times*, in 1950 a group of citizens from Cody headed out once again to retrieve the body but were met with the Colorado National Guard at the gravesite and quickly aborted the attempt. A story in the *Billings Gazette* reported that a tank was ultimately parked on top of Cody's grave to dissuade any would-be grave robbers. The people of Denver then decided to dig up Cody and rebury him under even more cement.

In 1985 the feud between the two states over the dead performer was still very much alive. Wyoming Senator Alan Simpson demanded on the senate floor that Denver return his body to Cody. However, Colorado Senator Bill Armstrong vowed there was no way that was going to happen. This issue was brought up again, perhaps tongue-in-cheek, in 2006 in the Wyoming House of Representatives when state legislators discussed ways of funding a raiding party to bring the body back.

To make matters even stranger, there are theories that Buffalo Bill isn't actually buried at Lookout Mountain at all, and that he is indeed buried in Cody. This version of the story gets its foothold because of the weather-related delay in Cody's actual burial. Because of the January freezing conditions in Colorado when he passed away, the hardness of the ground made burial and access to Lookout Mountain impossible, so Cody wasn't put into the ground until June. The theory goes that a couple of Cody residents and an undertaker went to Denver and snuck his body out of the funeral home it was waiting in without anyone noticing. They brought with them a dead cowboy who had a striking similarity to the dead performer and left him in Cody's place at the funeral home.

With all these doubts and speculation swirling around, no one can really know for sure where Buffalo Bill's body is unless the grave is dug up and a DNA test is performed to positively identify Cody. Despite the legends and rumors, the people who run the Buffalo Bill

Museum and Grave on Lookout Mountain are convinced he is still resting quite peacefully there and has done so since 1917.

When I ask Betsy Martinson, the program administrator for the Buffalo Bill Museum, about the subject, she references a trip Cody previously took to the location. "He commented at the time that this would be a good place to be buried because of the view," she says. "When he was dying he happened to be here in Denver . . . he was talking with his wife and the priest and said, 'Bury me on Mount Lookout.' That's their story, that's our story, so we're sticking with it."

Martinson says in a previous will Cody had stated he wanted to be buried in Wyoming, but ultimately he changed his mind, leaving it to his wife's discretion in an updated will written in 1913.

"People did witness him say he wanted to be buried here," Martinson says. "Unfortunately, at that same time somebody who [Cody] owed $10,000 to said, 'Go ahead and bury him in Denver and we'll relieve that debt.' So now people are saying, 'Oh, she sold the body to whoever paid her $10,000.' So there's this whole contingency that said, 'Well, actually they just sold the body,' but that's not accurate either. I'm sure there were many factors that led to her decision. The strongest being [him saying] 'bury me here.'"

I stand beside his presumed final resting place, looking over the small fence that surrounded it and the piles of coins visitors placed next to his grave. I toss a coin onto the grave, which bounces off a stone and rings loudly in the early morning air drawing the scrutiny of several who are nearby, surprised at the unexpected sound. I think Cody would have liked the attention.

As the man who created our concept of the original Wild West, many consider Cody a fundamental piece to legitimizing today's West. Ultimately, his final resting place shouldn't matter to anyone but his descendants, historians and writers. As in life, so too in death, he was the crown jewel of a bygone era. The feud over where Cody belongs has cooled a little over the last one hundred years—but will probably continue in some form for at least another century.

There may be debate about where Buffalo Bill's body is or should be, but there's little mystery about where his spirit can be found today. The view from his memorial site offers a stunning view of the Denver

Front Range, and just off to the south a little ways one can make out the training grounds for the Colorado Westernaires.

The Westernaires

With Lookout Mountain looming large in the distance, hundreds of students train in Western riding, dressage, and precision drills at the Jefferson County Fairgrounds as part of the Colorado Westernaires. The nonprofit organization, started in 1949, teaches suburban children how to ride, care for, and perform with horses. The program is the only one of its kind in the United States, with upwards of one thousand students at a time, ranging in age from nine to nineteen. Complex horsemanship drills, reenactments, and trick riding—the students learn the importance of maintaining the Western traditions and have performed in towns across the West, fully embracing aspects of what made Cody's Wild West show so legendary.

Walking alongside a group of young children who just finished one of their first trail rides, I cut through the massive parking lot filled with students and their horses to one of four indoor arenas used by the organization. Inside, the all-girls Precisionettes team races at high speed around the arena, performing a series of impressively complicated drills with their horses while a small group watches from the stadium seats.

"Tighten it up," calls out Kris Maikranz, chief instructor of a training division of the Westernaires and an instructor of the Precisionettes. Maikranz stands watching the girls from a balcony above the arena grounds. The hooves of horses thundered beneath her as she analyzes every movement of every student. Maikranz was first involved as a student of the program in 1979 and is now in her thirty-second year of instructing.

"We all believe very strongly what these horses bring to kids," Maikranz says. "You'll hear repeatedly out here that the outside of that horse is good for the inside of that kid."

The Westernaires allow students to rent horses for as little as $30 a month, making the opportunity an affordable option for children with little or no equestrian experience or access. Westernaires instructor Richard Rollings says he spends part of his time with the younger horseback riders and that most of his students have no experience with horses when they come to him.

"They're interested, but the opportunities just are not out there anywhere. This gives them the opportunity and they fall in love with it," Rollings says. "There's nothing like this out there, anywhere."

Over the years, the Westernaires have performed at the Calgary Stampede, at Mile High Stadium for the Broncos, and even with the Canadian Mounties.

"You take away some responsibility that you don't get hanging with your high school friends when you're out here loading a horse at three in the morning," Maikranz says. "They're not dealing with sports, they're not dealing with home, they're not dealing with boyfriends. I get them and a horse. I get them doing what they love. When they come out here, it all falls away."

It's stunning to watch the speed and intricacy of the drills as the students weave in and out of each other, their horses kicking up clods of dirt in their wake.

"Okay, ladies, that was a really good first drill," Maikranz says, which elicits enthusiastic whoops and hollers from the riders. "We're going to set the stopwatch on the second drill."

"I would tighten up the mariner's cross and thread the needle a little bit too—because I think you guys could tighten it up a little bit and make it more dramatic," Don Hawkinson, another instructor of the Precisionettes, says.

"He likes to scare the audience," Maikranz jokingly tells me over her shoulder.

"I do," Hawkinson agrees, playing along.

"Line up. Let's do it again, my dears," Maikranz tells the team, prompting more enthusiastic cheering. "Let's just step it up a notch. By degree, my dears, by degree." And they're off again. Lines of riders rumble past, through and around other lines. Each rider carries a colored flag, which ripples out behind them.

"When you think about it, the Westernaires has probably produced thousands of high-quality, excellent riders for kids that would have never been on a horse," Hawkinson says. Hawkinson, who was also in the Westernaires as a student, remembers the thrill of performing on a horse for large crowds. "I still remember the pitch-black arena. They put the spotlights on, the smoke, the horses jump through the smoke, and you're

Colorado Westernaires instructors Don Hawkinson and Kris Maikranz
coach the all-girls Precisionettes team. *(Photo by Ian Neligh)*

running in darkness going, 'Turn on the lights, lights, lights,' going at a
dead run as you make it through," Hawkinson says. "[It is] kind of a thrill
to do stuff like that."

As he watches, Hawkinson leans over to me and tells me the team is
"threading the needle." To me, it doesn't mean anything other than an
attempt to describe the tying of a complicated knot the riders were making
with their dizzying patterns across the arena—like synchronized
swimming at high speed on horseback. The students must memorize
every position in the drill, able to swap out in any spot.

"All it takes is one person slightly out of position like that and you
could have a collision. That's why it is very dangerous and why we practice so
much." Just as Hawkinson says this, two girls collide at high speed with one
girl being knocked out of her saddle. Maikranz shouts out a command and
all the riders come to a complete stop, without trampling the fallen rider.

"They came in too fast and made the horses knock each other.
They didn't come in smooth, they came in too hard and made a
sharp turn," Maikranz explains.

The team and a small audience in the arena applaud the girl as she gets up, dusts herself off, and walks out of the stadium, sore but not seriously injured. After more drills, the girls ride out of the arena on horseback, much the same way Cody's own performers probably did more than a century before.

After the training, I go down to the arena and speak with a couple of the students. I listen as eighteen-year-old Miranda Granillo tells me how she got involved with the Westernaires. As a young child, she watched them perform at the National Western Stock Show in Denver and thought it looked amazing. Going to school and practicing several times a week year-round isn't easy, but she stuck with it over the years because of the community she built with her fellow team members.

"The one thing that has held me is how much it is a family out here," Granillo says. "Westernaires is so unique in the fact that everyone out here is a volunteer, everyone wants to be here . . . there are so many people that help you and encourage you along the way and just want to see you succeed."

The sense of community I hear from her and the others reminds me of my own research into Cody's Wild West show. It is easy to see both the past and future of the West in that moment.

As I drive away from the training grounds, out of my windshield I see Lookout Mountain, the resting place of Buffalo Bill Cody. At the same time from my driver's side window I hear the sounds of equestrian training carried in by a warm fall breeze. I brake to a stop as a small procession of students and horses cross in front of me. From here I could see the end of one generation of the Wild West and the beginning of another.

Epilogue

The February sky glows hazily above Colorado, with low-hanging purple and gray clouds obscuring most of Mount Silverheels. The sun, a gold coin in an icy river, peers through a small gap in the gloom to light up the snow-covered landscape like a freezing desert of bleached bone. With temperatures near the single digits, the white expanse is broken only by small patches of short grass cleared of snow by the ceaseless, bitter wind. Resting in a field in the shadow of the mountain whispers the legend of a mysterious dancer who had once nursed a dying town before disappearing forever.

Untangling truth from legend is a tricky prospect, especially when considering the deeds of those who lived during the Old West—the pioneers, cowboys, and gunfighters. One such story, and its spectral epilogue, can be found in the unseen town of Buckskin Joe, its remnants no longer present to signify the community that once existed. Only a general store stands, moved from the townsite in the late 1950s to an area outside of Cañon City. Plans for a Western town, also called Buckskin Joe, to be constructed for numerous movies including the original *True Grit* instead ended up becoming a Western-styled theme park with regular cowboy shootouts for tourists. Then the park was purchased in 2010 by a billionaire Western enthusiast who planned to move the town to his private ranch outside of Gunnison, Colorado. What he did with his own private ghost town is anyone's guess.

But though the real Buckskin Joe is long gone, the legend of its beautiful dancer endures, outlasting the citizens and the town's many buildings, which were worn away to almost nothing by the harsh mountain weather.

No one is sure of the dancer's real name, although there is still much speculation with some positing that it might have been Gerda Bechtel or even Josie Dillon. What is universally agreed on is that she arrived to town one day on the stagecoach. The year was likely 1861 when the young woman first stepped foot in gold-enthused Buckskin Joe, then a tough community working desperately to become more than just a hardscrabble mining town.

Buckskin Joe was the county seat for a time. There was an attempt to rename it the more flattering Laurette—but the name ultimately didn't stick, and until it became a ghost town in 1873 it was simply called Buckskin Joe, named for its founder who was apparently fond of wearing animal skins. Stories say that one day he had traded his holdings to settle his bill at the local saloon and for a horse, and then he left town for good.

The town of Buckskin Joe quickly grew and soon boasted its own saloons, a newspaper, theaters, a hotel with luxuriously carpeted rooms; in those early days of the Colorado frontier, it was clear it had more aspirations than it was destined to be. At the local dance hall, the beautiful young dancer amazed audiences with her skill and grace. She wore slippers with silver heels, either brought with her or donated by a benefactor, and hence she was given the nickname Silver Heels. Men came from far and wide just to get a glance at her face, such was her stunning beauty.

While being interviewed in his nineties, well-known frontiersman Frank Mayer said when he was a young man and marshal of the town he remembered the dancer's famous performances. He was able to recall them in detail still—but as he would have been eleven years old at the time and living on the other side of the country from Colorado, this seems like a rather fanciful claim.

In the 1860s smallpox ravaged some of the mining communities in the area, including Buckskin Joe, and took with it a fair number of victims. Legend has it that while residents fled the afflicted area, the dancer refused to leave and instead nursed the smallpox victims. She worked relentlessly to help those stricken with the infectious disease, even contributing her own money to bring in more help. In time, the smallpox passed from town—but not before she, too, contracted the virus.

The dancer recovered, but the disease left her horribly scarred. She would never be able to dance in front of a crowd again. Thankful for its angel of mercy, the town raised as much as $5,000 to show the dancer its genuine appreciation. But by the time the townspeople went to her cabin to give her the sum, she was gone. Her items were packed and missing, and she was never seen again. The legend says the money was redistributed to its donors and the nearby 13,822-foot peak overlooking the town was named Mount Silverheels in her honor.

But though her name may be lost to history, her presence remained. Stories claim a woman with a black veil covering her face was seen placing flowers at the graves of those who had died during the epidemic. When approached, she had hurriedly disappeared into the surrounding woods. As if her duty to the town's residents and the price she paid wasn't enough, there are some who believe a specter in black still visits the graves of the smallpox victims in the town's surviving cemetery.

Tales of the Wild West continue generation after generation, finding new life in audiences eager for exciting stories of menace and adventure. But even the occasional melancholy yarn of self sacrifice and accompanying hauntings can find a cozy spot around the campfire. Similar to a good ghost story, legends of the American West never truly die.

While the Old West is gone, ever fading into the obscurity of history and the nostalgia of daydreams—the region itself is still very much alive. It is, as it has always been, a place where the air is a little colder, clearer, and the horizon stretches a little further. Where men and women still saddle their horses to get in a day's work, where bandits are still hunted by those with badges and sometimes without. Where ghostly dancers still retain their haunting charm. The West lives on in its ranches, farms, and small-town rodeos.

In some places wolves still howl and buffalo roam. It's a region where the legends of the past came, made names for themselves, and as often as not, surrendered their spurs to a new generation. More than anything, the Wild West is an idea. The idea was, and still is, that anyone can do something extraordinary. From trick shooting to saving wolves, to learning to ride with the skill and devotion of a Westernaire. Those who still embrace the strengths and passion of a Western lifestyle help make the region and its communities what they are today. Despite adversity, Americans of all eras and backgrounds have shown a boundless capacity for generosity, resolve, and an indomitable spirit.

While the West is limited by geography and the Old West restricted by its place in history, I don't believe the spirit of the Wild West is limited to any one place or people. It's less a region and more a way of thinking, not so much about the past—but the future. It's still a place where someone is judged by their tenacity, bravery, and grit and, occasionally, by how fast they can draw their pistol. It's evolving, always becoming something new, but more than anything the West is still wild.

Special thanks goes to all the people who allowed me to interview and follow them around for a year—you keep the West wild. Also thanks to Olivia Ngai for her incredible work, Deb, Debi and, of course, Billie. This book was deeply indebted to more than 150 years of strong newspaper and magazine journalism. There are also a host of wonderful historical books for anyone interested in learning further about some of these subjects including: Charles F. Price's Season of Terror: The Espinosas in Central Colorado, James E. Perkins' Tom Tobin: Frontiersman, *and* Candace Fleming's, Presenting Buffalo Bill: The Man Who Invented the Wild West.

Bibliography

"A Battle with Rustlers." *Colorado Daily Chieftain* (Pueblo), February 4, 1898. https://www.coloradohistoricnewspapers.org.

"A Desperate Street Fight." *Arizona Weekly Citizen* (Tucson), October 30, 1881. Library of Congress. http://chroniclingamerica.loc.gov/lccn/sn82015133/1881-10-30/ed-1/seq-3/.

"A Few Scraps — 'Bat' Masterson." *The Salt Lake Tribune*, July 17, 1910. Library of Congress. http://chroniclingamerica.loc.gov/lccn/sn83045396/1910-07-17/ed-1/seq-40.

"A Love Feast." *Herald Democrat* (Leadville), May 25, 1890. https://www.coloradohistoricnewspapers.org.

"A Remarkable Arrest." *The Coffeyville Weekly Journal*, February 9, 1906. http://newspapers.com.

"A Word of Advice." *Rocky Mountain News Weekly* (Denver), January 11, 1860. https://www.coloradohistoricnewspapers.org.

Abbott, Carl, Stephen J. Leonard, and Thomas J. Noel. *Colorado, a History of the Centennial State*. Boulder, CO: Colorado Associated University Press, 2013.

"After Cattle Thieves." *Aspen Evening Chronicle*, October 9, 1890. https://www.coloradohistoricnewspapers.org.

Alderton, Stephanie. "Montezuma Sheriff Reports Increase in Drug, Theft Crimes." *The Journal*, May 19, 2017. https://the-journal.com/articles/48382.

"All Hunting Treasure Trove." *Herald Democrat* (Leadville), April 29, 1906. https://www.coloradohistoricnewspapers.org.

"An Escape from Wolves." *Colorado Daily Chieftain* (Pueblo), March 4, 1892. https://www.coloradohistoricnewspapers.org.

Bibliography

"An Old Shaft at Fairplay Produces." *Park County Bulletin*, May 4, 1906. https://www.coloradohistoricnewspapers.org.

"Attacked by Wolves." *Fort Morgan Times*, February 6, 1891. https://www.coloradohistoricnewspapers.org.

"Attempted Assassination." *Sacramento Daily Record-Union*, December 30, 1881. http://newspapers.com.

"Battle of Burleigh." *The Tombstone Epitaph*, March 27, 1882. Library of Congress. http://chroniclingamerica.loc.gov/lccn/sn84021939/1882-03-27/ed-1/seq-1/.

"Battle of Vicksburg Facts & Summary." American Battlefield Trust. June 25, 2018. Accessed February 17, 2018. https://www.battlefields.org/learn/civil-war/battles/vicksburg.

"Battle with the Cowboys." *The Salt Lake Herald*, October 28, 1881. Library of Congress. http://chroniclingamerica.loc.gov/lccn/sn85058130/1881-10-28/ed-1/seq-3/.

"Ben Thompson." *Kansas Historical Society*. June 2011. Accessed August 05, 2018. https://www.kshs.org/kansapedia/ben-thompson/17141.

Beyer, Beverly, and Ed Rabey. "Denver Blends Old and New Wests." *The Los Angeles Times*, September 20, 1992. http://newspapers.com.

Blumenthal, Ralph. "Man Who Shot Another in Civil War Re-enactment Pleads Guilty." *New York Times*, June 26, 2009. https://www.nytimes.com/2009/06/26/nyregion/26reenact.html.

Bonner, T. D., and Charles Godfrey Leland. *The Life and Adventures of James P. Beckwourth, Mountaineer, Scout, Pioneer, and Chief of the Crow Nation of Indians*. London: T.F. Unwin, 1892. https://archive.org/details/adventures oflife00beckrich/page/n9.

Brown, Robert L. *Ghost Towns of the Colorado Rockies*. Caldwell, ID: Caxton Printers, 1990.

"Buffalo Bill Still Stirs Up the West." *Great Falls Tribune*, August 14, 1948. http://newspapers.com.

Buntline, Ned. *The Hero of a Hundred Fights: Collected Stories from the Dime Novel King, from Buffalo Bill to Wild Bill Hickok*. Edited by Clay Reynolds. New York, NY: Union Square, 2011.

"Capt. James Beckwourth." *Rocky Mountain News Weekly* (Denver), December 1, 1859. https://www.coloradohistoricnewspapers.org.

"Cattle Stealing." *Colorado Daily Chieftain* (Pueblo), February 3, 1884. https://www.coloradohistoricnewspapers.org.

"Cattle Thieves Killed." *Boulder Daily Camera*, November 16, 1892. https://www.coloradohistoricnewspapers.org.

"Cattle Thieves Lynched in Montana." *Silver Standard* (Silver Plume), September 12, 1891. https://www.coloradohistoricnewspapers.org.

"Chased by Timber Wolves." *Cañon City Record*, March 10, 1896. https://www.coloradohistoricnewspapers.org.

"Civil War Casualties." American Battlefield Trust. September 27, 2018. Accessed February 17, 2018. https://www.battlefields.org/learn/articles/civil-war-casualties.

.

"Cody's Wild West." *Arkansas Democrat* (Little Rock), October 1, 1898. http://newspapers.com.

Collins, Jan MacKell. *Brothels, Bordellos, & Bad Girls: Prostitution in Colorado, 1860-1930*. Albuquerque: University of New Mexico Press, 2007.

Constable, George, ed. *The Gunfighters*. Time-Life Books, 1974.

Cook, D. J., and John W. Cook. *Hands Up, Or, Thirty-five Years of Detective Life in the Mountains and on the Plains: A Condensed Criminal History of the Far West; Reminiscences*. Denver: W.F. Robinson, 1897. https://archive.org/details/handsuporthirtyf00cook/page/12

Custer, George A., Gen. *My Life on the Plains.: Or, Personal Experiences with Indians*. New York, NY: Sheldon and Company, 1874.

Dallas, Sandra. *Colorado Ghost Towns and Mining Camps*. Norman, OK: University of Oklahoma Press, 1985.

"Defends 'Wild Bill.'" *The Washington Post*, May 19, 1907. http://newspapers.com.

"Desperate Fight with Thieves." *Colorado Daily Chieftain* (Pueblo), December 21, 1892. https://www.coloradohistoricnewspapers.org.

Devantier, Alecia T., and Carol A. Turkington. *Extraordinary Jobs for Adventurers*. New York, NY: Ferguson an Imprint of Infobase Publishing, 2006.

"Devoured by Wolves." *Avalanche Echo* (Glenwood Springs), November 27, 1891. https://www.coloradohistoricnewspapers.org.

Dimsdale, Thomas Josiah. *Vigilantes of Montana Or, Popular Justice in the Rocky Mountains*. Virginia City, MT: T.E. Castle and C.W. Bank, 1921. https://archive.org/details/vigilantesofmont00indims/page/n3.

"'Doc' Holliday." *Colorado Daily Chieftain* (Pueblo), May 17, 1882. https://www.coloradohistoricnewspapers.org.

"Doc Holliday, Gun Fighter and Some Stirring History." Library of Congress. *Bisbee Daily Review*, July 31, 1910. http://chroniclingamerica.loc.gov/lccn/sn84024827/1910-07-31/ed-1/seq-2/.

"Doc Holliday on Trial for Shooting Billy Allen—some Interesting Testimony." *Carbonate Chronicle* (Leadville), April 4, 1885. http://newspapers.com.

Dunning, Eric, Dominic Malcolm, and Ivan Waddington. *Sport Histories: Figurational Studies in the Development of Modern Sports*. London: Routledge, 2006.

Dusen, Laura Van. *Historic Tales from Park County: Parked in the past*. Charleston, SC: History Press, 2013.

Eschner, Kat. "Civil War Reenactments Were a Thing Even During the Civil War." *Smithsonian Magazine*, December 5, 2017. https://www.smithsonianmag.com/smart-news/civil-war-reenactments-were-thing-even-during-civil-war-180967405/.

"Fearless Negro Deputy Marshal Has Killed Fourteen Desperadoes." *The Washington Post*, March 10, 1907. https://www.newspapers.com/clip/14773605/the_washington_post/.

Fees, Paul. "Wild West Shows: Buffalo Bill's Wild West." Buffalo Bill Center of the West. Accessed June 17, 2018. https://centerofthewest.org/learn/western-essays/wild-west-shows/.

Bibliography

Fleming, Candace. *Presenting Buffalo Bill: The Man Who Invented the Wild West.* New York: Roaring Brook Press, 2016.

Gallagher, Jolie Anderson. *A Wild West History of Frontier Colorado: Pioneers, Gunslingers & Cattle Kings on the Eastern Plains.* Charleston, SC: History Press, 2011.

Gartner, Erin. "The Mystery of Buffalo Bill." *Globe Gazette* (Mason City), January 5, 2003. http://newspapers.com.

Gustkey, Earl. "TOOTH AND NAIL : Era of Bare-Knuckle Boxing Ended With Bloody Title Bout 100 Years Ago." *Los Angeles Times,* July 8, 1989. http://articles.latimes.com/1989-07-08/sports/sp-2705_1_bare-knuckle-boxing

Hartman, Mitchell. "Rodeo on the Rebound." Marketplace. August 24, 2017. Accessed February 22, 2018. https://www.marketplace.org/2017/08/24/life/rodeo-rebound.

Herrero, Stephen, Andrew Higgins, James E. Cardoza, Laura I. Hajduk, and Tom S. Smith. "Fatal Attacks by American Black Bear on People: 1900-2009." *The Journal of Wildlife Management* 75, no. 3 (April 2011): 596-603. doi:10.1002/jwmg.72.

"Holliday Shoots." *Carbonate Chronicle* (Leadville), August 23, 1884. https://www.coloradohistoricnewspapers.org.

"Horrible Murder." *Rocky Mountain News Weekly* (Denver), April 16, 1863. https://www.coloradohistoricnewspapers.org.

"How the New Mexico Outlaw Effected His Escape by Shooting down Two Officers." *Gunnison Democrat,* May 11, 1881. https://www.coloradohistoricnewspapers.org.

"Jas. Crank Relates the Story of Espinoza Brothers." *Cañon City Record,* March 18, 1909. https://www.coloradohistoricnewspapers.org.

Jessen, Kenneth. "Buckskin Joe Was Once a Thriving County Seat." *Reporter-Herald* (Loveland), March 17, 2018. http://www.reporterherald.com/columnists/colorado-history/ci_31738327/buckskin-joe-was-once-thriving-county-seat.

"John Slugs Jake." *St. Paul Daily Globe,* July 9, 1889. Library of Congress. https://chroniclingamerica.loc.gov.

Johnson, John. "Quest for Gold: Treasures: A Tarzana Man Says He's Close to Finding a Lost Spanish Mine That Early Records Call the Continent's Richest." *Los Angeles Times,* February 4, 1991.http://articleslatimescom/1991-02-04local/me-366_1_treasure-hunter.

"Kansas Cattle Thieves." *Las Animas Leader* (Bent County), July 16, 1875. Colorado Historic Newspapers.

Kaplan, Elise. "New Mexico Now Worst in Nation for Property Crime." *Albuquerque Journal,* September 28, 2017. https://www.abqjournal.com/1070482/fbi-data-new-mexico-ranked-no-1-in-nation-in-propertycrime-rates.html.

Ketcham, Christopher. "Dances With Wolves." *5280 Magazine,* June 2015.

"Killed Fourteen Men." *The Muldrow Press,* January 21, 1910. http://newspapers.com.

"Kilrain Is No Kicker." *St. Paul Daily Globe,* December 2, 1888. Library of Congress. https://chroniclingamerica.loc.gov.

Klein, Alec and Lyons, Sheridan. "Re-enactor Heals from Mysterious Shot Suspect Fired Gun Belonging to Stranger." *Baltimore Sun,* July 11, 1998. http://articles.

baltimoresun.com/1998-07-11/news/1998192052_1_war-re-enactor-civil-war-replica-evo.

Langley, Ricky L. "Human Fatalities Resulting From Dog Attacks in the United States, 1979–2005." *Wilderness & Environmental Medicine* 20, no. 1 (March 2009): 19-25. doi:10.1580/08-weme-or-213.1.

"Late Telegrams." *Daily Los Angeles Herald*, March 24, 1882. Library of Congress. http://chroniclingamerica.loc.gov/lccn/sn85042459/1882-03-24/ed-1/seq-1/.

"Lively Days in Dodge with Bat Masterson." *New-York Tribune*, November 6, 1921. Library of Congress. http://chroniclingamerica.loc.gov/lccn/sn83030214/1921-11-06/ed-1/seq-58/.

Lovett, John. "US Marshals Museum Searches for Bass Reeves' Relatives." *AP News,* September 15, 2018. https://www.apnews.com/7215bfb6a96643db86d4831f3 a8664d.

"May Remove Buffalo Bill's Body to Cody, WYO." *The Billings Gazette*, June 26, 1926. http://newspapers.com.

Mazza, Ed. "2 Shot During 'Old West' Gunfight Reenactment In Tombstone." *The Huffington Post.* October 19, 2015. https://www.huffingtonpost.com/entrytombstone-reenactment-shooting_us_562490dee4b0bce347013087.

Mellskog, Pam. "Our Livestock Cop: New Boulder County Brand Inspector Relishes Legacy Job." *Longmont Times-Call*, August 09, 2018. http://www.timescall.com/.

Metz, Leon Claire. *The Shooters.* New York, NY: Berkley Books, 1976.

"Moffat County Man Convicted of Rustling Cattle of Local Ranchers." *The Denver Post*, July 13, 2012. https://www.denverpost.com/2012/07/13/moffat-county-man-convicted-of-rustling-cattle-of-local-ranchers/.

Monaghan, Jay. *The Great Rascal.* New York, NY: Bonanza Books, 1951.

Morgan, Thad. "Was the Real Lone Ranger a Black Man?" History.com. February 01, 2018. Accessed February 14, 2019. https://www.history.com/news/bass-reeves-real-lone-ranger-a-black-man.

"Murder By Cattle Thieves." *Las Animas Leader* (Bent County), August 27, 1875. https://www.coloradohistoricnewspapers.org.

Murphy, Jan Elizabeth. *Outlaw Tales of Colorado: True Stories of the Centennial States Most Infamous Crooks, Culprits, and Cutthroats.* Guilford, CT: TWODOT, 2012.

Nichols, George Ward. "Wild Bill." *Harper's New Monthly Magazine*, February 1867.

[No Title.] *Aspen Evening Chronicle,* July 13, 1889. https://www.colorado historicnewspapers.org.

[No Title.] *Buena Vista Democrat*, August 21, 1884. https://www.coloradohistoricnewspapers.org.

[No Title.] *Casper Star Tribune*, August 8, 1948. http://newspapers.com.

[No Title.] *Colorado Daily Chieftain* (Pueblo), August 8, 1891. https://www.coloradohistoricnewspapers.org.

[No Title.] *Colorado Daily Chieftain* (Pueblo), December 8, 1891. https://www.coloradohistoricnewspapers.org.

[No Title.] *Fort Collins Courier,* July 9, 1885.

Bibliography

https://www.coloradohistoricnewspapers.org.

[No Title.] *Fort Morgan Times*, August 2, 1889. https://www.coloradohistoric
newspapers.org.

[No Title.] *The Republic* (Columbus), March 9, 1985. http://newspapers.com.

[No Title.] *Sacramento Daily Record-Union*, March 23, 1882. Library of Congress.
http://chroniclingamerica.loc.gov/lccn/sn82014381/1882-03-23/ed-1/seq-1.

O'Dea, Janelle. "Colorado Court of Appeals Affirms Cattle Theft Conviction."
Craig Press, February 24, 2015. https://www.craigdailypress.com.
https://www.craigdailypress.com/news/colorado-court-of-appeals-affirms-cattle-
theft-conviction.

"Organized Thieves." *Colorado Daily Chieftain* (Pueblo), July 12, 1895.
https://www.coloradohistoricnewspapers.org.

Otero, Miguel Antonio. *My Life on the Frontier, 1864-1882*. Albuquerque:
University of New Mexico Press, 1987.

Perkins, James E. *Tom Tobin: Frontiersman*. Pueblo, CO: Herodotus Press, 1999.

Phippen, J. Weston. "'Kill Every Buffalo You Can! Every Buffalo Dead Is an Indian
Gone.'" *The Atlantic Magazine*, May 13, 2016. https://www.theatlantic.com/
national/archive/2016/05/the-buffalo-killers/482349/.

"Portrait of First African American Deputy Marshal Bass Reeves Unveiled."
Muskogee Phoenix, March 22, 2016. https://www.muskogeephoenix.com/.

Prevost, Ruffin. "Debate of Buffalo Bill Burial Won't Die." *The Billings Gazette*,
April 9, 2006. http://newspapers.com.

Price, Charles F. *Season of Terror: The Espinosas in Central Colorado, March - October
1863*. Boulder: Universtity Press of Colorado, 2013.

"Recovery of Stolen Cattle." *Colorado Daily Chieftain* (Pueblo), February 4, 1890.
https://www.coloradohistoricnewspapers.org.

Roberts, Gary L. *Doc Holliday: The Life and Legend*. John Wiley & Sons, 2007.

Roberts, Michael. "Jeff Murphy Is 6th to Die Seeking Forrest Fenn's Treasure,
Says Ex-Wife of Victim." *Westword*. February 23, 2018. Accessed April 23, 2019.
https://www.westword.com/news/forrest-fenn-treasure-deaths-victims-ex-wife-
says-six-have-died-10019518.

Roberts, Willie. "Forgotten Bass Reeves Contributed to Old West." *Tallahassee Democrat*,
September 19, 1999.

Romeo, Jonathan. "Bounty Hunters Say Farewell to TV Show, but Not the Chase."
The Durango Herald, January 20, 2016. https://durangoherald.com.

Roth, Ramdolph. "Table and Figures from Criminologists and Historians of Crime:
A Partnership Well Worth Pursuing and Homicide Rates in the American West."
Criminal Justice Research Center. May 30, 2018. Accessed July 12, 2018. https://
cjrc.osu.edu/research/interdisciplinary/hvd/homicide-rates-american-west.

"Running out the Wolves." *Colorado Daily Chieftain* (Pueblo), January 16, 1896.
https://www.coloradohistoricnewspapers.org.

"Rustling for the Rustlers" *Colorado Daily Chieftain* (Pueblo),
April 1, 1892. https://www.coloradohistoricnewspapers.org.

Ruxton, George Frederick Augustus. *Adventures in Mexico and the Rocky Mountains.* New York: Harper, 1855.

Ruxton, George Frederick. *In the Old West.* Place of Publication Not Identified: Outing Publishing Company, 1915.

"Sham Fight at Manassas." *Castle Rock Journal,* June 24, 1904. https://www.coloradohistoricnewspapers.org.

"Scheme to Scare Wolves." *Brush Tribune,* July 19, 1901. https://www.coloradohistoricnewspapers.org.

"Shooting Bears." *Rocky Mountain Sun* (Aspen), February 9, 1889. https://www.coloradohistoricnewspapers.org.

"Six Wolves Captured." *Craig Courier,* June 21, 1902. https://www.coloradohistoricnewspapers.org.

"Slugger Sullivan." *The Salt Lake Herald,* June 30, 1889. Library of Congress. https://chroniclingamerica.loc.gov.

Small, Frank A. "Buffalo Bill." *The Courier Journal* (Louisville), August 20, 1894. http://newspapers.com.

Souter, Gerry, and Janet Souter. *Guns of Outlaws: Weapons of the American Bad Man.* New York, NY: Crestline, 2017.

Staff. "Wolf Reintroduction Changes Ecosystem." My Yellowstone Park. January 15, 2019. Accessed March 20, 2019. https://www.yellowstonepark.com/things-to-do/wolf-reintroduction-changes-ecosystem.

Stanley, Henry M. "Interview With Wild Bill Hickok." *Weekly Missouri Democrat,* April 1867.

Stone, Wilbur Fiske. "From Dornick." *The Weekly Commonwealth* (Denver), May 7, 1863. https://www.coloradohistoricnewspapers.org.

Stone, Wilbur Fiske. "The Mysterious Murders Unraveled at Last." *The Weekly Commonwealth* (Denver), May 21, 1863. https://www.coloradohistoricnewspapers.org.

"Successful Wolf Hunt." *Herald Democrat* (Leadville), March 25, 1892. https://www.coloradohistoricnewspapers.org.

"Sullivan It Is." *Pittsburg Dispatch,* July 9, 1889. Library of Congress. https://chroniclingamerica.loc.gov.

Tefertiller, Casey, and Jeff Morey. "O.K. Corral: A Gunfight Shrouded in Mystery." THA | Interview with Virgil Earp - 2. Accessed September 23, 2018. http://www.tombstonehistoryarchives.com/o.k.-corral-a-gunfight-shrouded-in-mystery.html.

"The Capture of the Espinosas." *The Colorado Magazine.* The State Historical Society of Colorado, 1932.

"The Champion." *Colorado Daily Chieftain* (Pueblo), December 25, 1883. https://www.coloradohistoricnewspapers.org.

"The Deadwood Tragedy." *The Colorado Banner* (Boulder), August 31, 1876. https://www.coloradohistoricnewspapers.org.

"The Death of Billy the Kid." *Fremont County Record* (Canon City), July 23, 1881. https://www.coloradohistoricnewspapers.org.

Bibliography

"The South Park Guerrilla Raid." *Daily Mining Journal* (Black Hawk), August 31, 1864. https://www.coloradohistoricnewspapers.org.

"The South Park Guerrilla Raid." *Daily Mining Journal* (Black Hawk), September 1, 1864. https://www.coloradohistoricnewspapers.org.

"The Wild West." *Fort Wayne Gazette*, June 2, 1885. http://newspapers.com.

"Thousands Pay Last Tribute." *Vermont Union Journal* (Lyndonville), January 17, 1917. http://newspapers.com.

"To Kill off Wolves." *Silver Standard* (Silver Plume), April 22, 1893. https://www.coloradohistoricnewspapers.org.

Trimble, Marshall. "Killin' Jim Miller." *True West*. June 15, 2016. Accessed May 10, 2018. https://truewestmagazine.com/killin-jim-miller-2/.

United States. *Findings Related to the March 2010 Fatal Wolf Attack near Chignik Lake, Alaska*. Alaska Department of Fish and Game. Division of Wildlife Conservation. By Lem Butler, Bruce Dale, Kimberlee Beckmen, and Sean Farley. December 2011. http://www.adfg.alaska.gov/static/home/news/pdfs/wolfattackfatality.pdf.

Walton, W. M. *Life and Adventures of Ben Thompson the Famous Texan.*, book, 1956; Austin, Texas. (texashistory.unt.edu/ark:/67531/metapth38114/: accessed July 11, 2018) University of North Texas Libraries, The Portal to Texas History, texashistory.unt.edu; crediting Austin History Center, Austin Public Library.

"War on Rustlers." *Herald Democrat* (Leadville), December 19, 1891. https://www.coloradohistoricnewspapers.org.

Ward, David. "How Buffalo Bill brought the wild west to Salford." The Guardian, July 26, 2005. https://www.theguardian.com/artanddesign/2005/jul/26/heritage.britishidentity.

Waters, Stephanie. *Colorado Legends and Lore: The Phantom Fiddler, Snow Snakes and Other Tales*. Charleston, SC: History Press, 2014.

Whitley, Carla Jean. "Doc's Gun Is Coming Home." *Post Independent*

Wignall, Trevor. *The Story of Boxing*. New York: Brentanos, 1924.

"'Wild Bill' His Adventurous Life and Tragic Death." *The Colorado Banner* (Boulder), August 31, 1876. https://www.coloradohistoricnewspapers.org. (Glenwood Springs), March 10, 2017.

"Wild West Show." *Buffalo Courier*, August 14, 1895. http://newspapers.com.

"Will Stop Cattle Rustling." *Silver Standard* (Silver Plume), April 22, 1899. https://www.coloradohistoricnewspapers.org.

Wilson, R. L. *Peacemakers: Arms And Adventure In The American West*. Edison, NJ: Chartwell Books, 1992.

Wineke, Andrew. "Mystery Buyer for Buckskin Joe Revealed to Be Billionaire Koch Brother." *The Gazette* (Colorado Springs), August 29, 2011. https://gazette.com/news/mystery-buyer-for-buckskin-joe-revealed-to-be-billionaire-koch/article_291ad215-10e5-5f78-aeb1-9bd786f015a1.html.

"Wolf Chasing." *Herald Democrat* (Leadville), June 5, 1900. https://www.coloradohistoricnewspapers.org.

"Work of District Court." *Greeley Tribune*, May 28, 1896. https://www.coloradohistoricnewspapers.org.

"Wolves Fear Iron." *Herald Democrat* (Leadville), December 13, 1907. https://www.coloradohistoricnewspapers.org.

"WWII Reenactment Too Real for Man Shot in Stomach." *CBS News*, February 12, 2015. www.cbsnews.com.

"Virgil Earp." *Arizona Daily Star* (Tucson), May 30, 1882. http://newspapers.com.

Zubeck, Pam. "Police Bust 156 Violent Offenders in Recent Sweeps." *Colorado Springs Independent*, August 22, 2018. https://www.csindy.com/.